# MORAL
## UNCERTAINTY
Inside the Rodney King Juries

**Never-published details
from the two jury rooms**

Dorothy Bailey, Simi Valley foreman,
and Bob Almond, federal foreman,
with Kathleen Neumeyer

Published in the United States by Andalou Books.

Almond, Bob; Bailey, Dorothy; Neumeyer, Kathleen
    Moral Uncertainty: Inside the Rodney King Juries
    Never-published details from the two jury rooms
    ISBN 978-0-9904664-3-7
    Library of Congress Control Number: 2017936372
    1. King, Rodney. 2. Trials (Police misconduct)—California—Los
    Angeles. 3. Los Angeles (Calif.)—Race relations. 4. Riots—
    California—Los Angeles—History—20th Century. 5. Los
    Angeles (Calif.) Police Department. 6. Civil rights—California—
    Los Angeles—History—20th century. 7. Police brutality—
    California—Los Angeles—History—20th century.

Cover photo by Kirk McKoy: Rioters set fires to Los Angeles businesses
following the first Rodney King verdict. Originally printed on A1 of the
*Los Angeles Times,* April 29, 1992. Copyright © 1992 Los Angeles Times.
Reprinted with Permission.

# INTRODUCTION

*Moral Uncertainty: Inside the Rodney King Juries* is the first-person account of the foreman who led the six-man, six-woman jury that rendered a verdict that triggered the worst rioting in the history of the United States of America.

It is also the first-person account of the foreman of a second jury sequestered for fifty-two days to hear the same four officers tried a year later for violating Rodney King's civil rights, a jury which heard essentially the same facts but was asked to consider somewhat different legal charges against the officers, and reached a verdict with radically different consequences, not only for the officers, but also for themselves and for the rest of America.

Dorothy Bailey, a wife, mother and grandmother, on the verge of retiring from a career managing multi-million-dollar government contracts, so abhorred violence that she left the room when scenes were shown on television of police beating Rodney King. When she was called to jury duty, she thought it was her civic responsibility to serve. She took careful shorthand notes throughout the proceedings, and took seriously the judge's admonition to set aside preconceived notions, but she never lost the nagging gut feeling that at least two of the officers had used excessive force.

In the end, however, Dorothy Bailey and her fellow jurors could not overcome what they thought were reasonable doubts. They were not convinced that any reasonable officer would have behaved differently when faced with such an uncooperative suspect.

Just one year later, a federal jury grappled with most of the same issues as the state jury, and shared much of the first jury's concern that there was reasonable doubt about whether or not the officers intended to hurt King, or if they were just doing their duty as law enforcement officers. However, the federal jury's decision to acquit two of the officers of all charges and to find two guilty seemed to support public opinion that the first jury got it wrong.

There was no rioting following the federal jury decision, and no vilification of that second jury, whose members' identities were kept secret, in accordance with a federal court order.

Bob Almond, a right-of-way engineer for the Port of Los Angeles, was driving on the freeway when riots broke out after the first trial. He too had watched the television pictures of the beating and been sickened by it. He remembers wondering what Rodney King possibly could have done for officers to beat him like that.

When Bob Almond received a summons for federal jury duty in the fall of 1992, he felt certain that he would be chosen for the second Rodney King trial. During testimony, he shared the same nagging feeling that Dorothy Bailey had during the first trial, that the four were guilty, but he thought that the prosecutors had failed to prove the guilt of two of the four officers. After he was elected foreman, he struggled to maintain order among emotional jurors who screamed, cried, revealed intimate personal secrets and called each other names.

From the jury selection to the testimony of the witnesses and the behind-the-scenes reactions and quarrels of the jurors, this book takes the reader into the privacy of both jury rooms for the tearful and anguished deliberations.

Following the first verdict, one of the defense attorneys said that those who criticized the jury "just don't get it." The American system of law is based on the concept that twelve randomly selected citizens can weigh evidence and make decisions on behalf of the rest of society, that they can be trusted to be our surrogates and to reach the right conclusion after hearing both sides of a story.

And yet, in many widely publicized cases, the public has second-guessed juries that have acquitted defendants that most people presumed guilty. In the U.S. judicial system, defendants have a right to be presumed innocent; the prosecution must prove that they are guilty beyond a reasonable doubt. Ironically, that very system creates the presumption of guilt. Often, after an arrest, it is the police version that is made available to the news media. Rarely does the suspect tell his side at this point. At trial, months or even years after the crime, the prosecution presents its case first. By the time the defense tells its story, the public often already has been convinced of guilt, or has lost interest. The public reaches its conclusions from what it sees in the media, but jurors are required to ignore what they already knew and confine themselves to what they learned in the courtroom, and what the judge instructed them was the law.

*Moral Uncertainty: Inside the Rodney King Juries* explores these and other perplexing issues that Bob Almond, Dorothy Bailey and their colleagues had to face. This is not the comprehensive analysis of legal scholars, politicians or law enforcement officers about what happened or should not have happened near midnight on March 3, 1991 when a husband-and-wife team of California Highway Patrol officers pursued a speeding Hyundai off a freeway north of downtown Los Angeles. Moments later, an amateur cameraman captured an eighty-one-second videotape showing four white Los Angeles Police Department officers beating Rodney Glen King into submission on a dark cul-de-sac as twenty other law enforcement officers looked on. This book is an inside look, never told before, into two of the most publicized trials of the twentieth century, and takes the reader inside two jury rooms as twenty-four citizens grappled with the facts, the law and their emotions. It will surprise many readers and reassure others. In the end, it is a story of two citizens who took their oath seriously and did their duty, regardless of the consequences.

*Moral Uncertainty*

# PART ONE

## Chapter One: Dorothy Bailey's Story

A year after four police officers were acquitted of criminal charges in the Rodney King beating, I was interviewed by NBC newswoman Katie Couric. The same police officers were being tried in federal court on charges that they violated Rodney King's civil rights.

I had been the jury foreman in the criminal trial, so I appeared on NBC's *Today* show via a remote hookup from a studio near my home in Utah. Ms. Couric asked me three separate times if I thought Rodney King's civil rights had been violated. I felt that she was becoming very annoyed with me because she couldn't get me to answer the question the way she seemed to want me to.

I was getting annoyed with her too.

It seemed to me that one thing everybody should have learned from the first Rodney King trial is that you shouldn't try to second-guess a jury.

I wouldn't dream of hazarding an opinion as to whether Rodney King's civil rights were violated. Unless I sat in that courtroom every single day and listened to all of the testimony and evidence for both the prosecution and the defense, and listened to the attorneys' arguments, and read the instructions from the judge to the jury, I couldn't possibly make any fair assessment of what that jury would decide, nor would I presume to criticize them for the decision they reached.

The federal jury found two of the officers, Sergeant Stacey Koon and Officer Laurence M. Powell, guilty of depriving Rodney King of his civil rights when they arrested him. The jury acquitted the other two officers, Timothy Wind and Theodore Briseno. Although the cases were different, because in the federal case the prosecution had to prove intent and in the state's case they didn't, the results were not really very different from the decision our jury reached. We also found Officers Wind and Briseno not guilty, although most of us felt in our hearts that Officer Powell was guilty. If we had been able to overcome our reasonable doubts and had convicted Officer Powell, then we also would have convicted Sergeant Koon.

But we had doubts that we could not overcome.

I guess most people who saw the tape on television thought that the officers were guilty of using excessive force. After all, the videotape very clearly showed a human being savagely beaten by what seemed to be a gang of uniformed thugs. Because they watched that beating, they saw it with their very own eyes, and they were certain that those police officers were guilty.

The trouble is, the jury saw and heard far more than the videotape that was shown on television. The jury knew things the public didn't know. We saw the whole tape, which showed Rodney King lunging toward the police officers. We heard testimony about his shaking his buttocks at them, flaunting his lack of respect for their authority, and behaving in a bizarre manner that suggested that he was under the influence of alcohol or drugs. We heard from eyewitnesses who had contradictory accounts that did not always square with the videotape. We hefted the boots the officers wore when they kicked him to assess how heavy they were, and lifted the twenty-four-inch steel batons used to bludgeon him.

The public also knew some things the jury didn't know. Forbidden to read newspapers or follow television accounts, the jury was unaware of the comments that were being made by public figures about the case. The public heard Los Angeles Police Chief Daryl Gates say, on the eve of the trial, that the beating shocked him. The jury didn't hear about that.

The jury didn't hear news commentators' analyses, or what listeners were saying when they called in to radio talk shows. They didn't see the political cartoons or read the editorials.

The reason the jury didn't know these things is that we as a society have decided that it is better for juries not to know things like that. And so the judge forbade us to read the news accounts or to watch them on television.

The American judicial system is based on the premise that we can select twelve citizens almost at random, and let them listen to the evidence impartially, and that they will be able to decide, on behalf of the rest of us, whether or not laws have been broken. We trust these strangers to be our surrogates and to reach a fair conclusion after hearing both sides of the story.

When I as a parent served as both the judge and jury when my children transgressed, I didn't follow any courtroom rules. If one of my children had a habit of crayoning on the walls, I took that into consideration when I found new marks, and I found him guilty. Just as I am sure many other parents do, I sometimes judged guilt or innocence on the basis of prior history. Sometimes I even punished more than one child when they couldn't get their stories straight, on the theory that somebody was guilty and that it would serve as a deterrent to everyone if they all spent a little time in their rooms cooling down.

The courts don't work that way. In order to safeguard the rights of the defendants as well as to see that the public good is served, we have a whole system of rules about how evidence can be presented, and what is fair for the jury to hear and what isn't. What happens in a courtroom is like a game with a set of strict rules. Over the course of our nation's history, Congress and state legislatures and the courts have devised this system to try to make a courtroom a fair place for a defendant, a place where a jury can listen impartially to evidence, following rules intended to create a level playing field for both sides.

There are bits of information that juries are never told, to protect the rights of the defendants. Juries usually don't know about the prior criminal records of defendants, on the theory that just because someone made a mistake once doesn't necessarily mean that they are guilty this time.

The public knew that on a prior occasion, one of the defendants, Theodore J. Briseno, had been suspended from the police force for sixty-six days for using excessive force. The jury didn't know that. The public knew that one of the other defendants, Timothy Wind, had been fired by the Los Angeles Police Department after the incident. The jury didn't know that.

We did know that Rodney King was on parole, and that he had been convicted of armed robbery, but we were not given any details of his criminal past. He could have been a murderer, for all we knew. We certainly never thought of him as an innocent citizen who was beaten up by the police after being stopped for speeding on the freeway. We thought of him as a parolee resisting arrest.

So the jury knew both more and less than the public knew.

Other Americans watched that videotape and thought to themselves that it just wasn't right for the police to beat up a suspect the way Rodney King was beaten. They thought that the police should be punished for doing that.

But it wasn't the jury's job to decide whether or not the beating of Rodney King was right, or moral, or just. Our job was to determine whether the specific actions of four citizens were in violation of certain California state laws.

It isn't even a jury's job to find someone guilty or innocent. What juries decide is whether or not someone is guilty or not guilty. There is a big difference between being innocent and being not guilty. If a person is innocent, he did nothing wrong. He is pure. When a person is found not guilty, it means that there was not enough evidence to prove that he committed a crime. Not being guilty is not the same as being innocent. Nobody who saw the beating of Rodney King thought that it was a good thing that a man was beaten. Nobody liked seeing it.

The members of the jury on which I served were shocked by what happened to Rodney King. I was horrified to learn during testimony that police training teaches officers how to use their nightsticks to deliberately break bones. I couldn't believe how inhumane the use of the baton was. But that didn't mean that the officers broke the law when they used their sticks to beat Rodney King, because the law permits—even requires—police officers to subdue fleeing suspects and to arrest them.

Before I served on the Rodney King jury, I had never been in a courtroom except to get a divorce ending my first marriage more than thirty years earlier. I was not a legal scholar and I was no expert on the judicial system. But I had a lot of time to think about it as a result of my jury experience and the events that unfolded afterward. The American jury system may be imperfect, but I still think that it is the fairest system that has yet been devised. I am proud that I did my duty as a citizen and served on the first Rodney King jury.

I will be haunted for the rest of my life by the images of the rioting and burning that followed. The repercussions changed my life forever. I woke from nightmares of a city on fire, asking myself, "Did I cause all of this?" I concluded that neither the verdict nor my fellow jurors and I caused the Los Angeles riots, but there was no escaping the fact that it was our verdict that triggered them. I will have to live with that all of my life.

I served on one of the most controversial juries of all time, and I did it to the best of my ability. I have a clear conscience that I did the best job that I could do, in following the evidence and the instructions. A few weeks after the verdict, I sat down at the computer and began to write. I wanted to explain, as much for the sake of my children and grandchildren as anything else, how we reached our decision. I know most people who have decided it was the wrong verdict aren't going to change their mind. Even after they read this, they may still disagree, but I don't want to die without trying to explain to the people I care about exactly what happened.

# Chapter Two: Jury Selection

In January 1992, I received a summons to appear at the Ventura County Courthouse for jury duty, so I filled out the form and mailed it to the listed address. Then, as instructed, on Sunday evening, February 2, I telephoned, and heard a recorded message. The instructions were given by group numbers. My group was directed to appear the next morning.

Before I left the house, my husband Dick remarked, "You know, you might get to be on the Rodney King jury."

That seemed unlikely to me.

The trial of the four police officers had been moved to where we lived, in Ventura County, which is just adjacent to Los Angeles County, to the northwest along the Pacific coast. The incident had occurred in Los Angeles, but there had been such an uproar after the videotapes were repeatedly shown on television that a California state appellate court panel ruled that political fallout and community divisiveness made it impossible for a Los Angeles County jury to impartially decide the case. There had been a lot of publicity in our area too, because we watch the Los Angeles television stations, so I knew that jury selection was about to begin in that case, but I thought the odds of being chosen were slim. Most people I knew who went for jury duty wound up just sitting around reading and playing cards in the jury room and were never called to serve on any case.

At the courthouse, they gave an orientation and showed a video before asking for volunteers to appear at the East County Courthouse in Simi Valley on Thursday, February 6. The Simi Valley courthouse, which was brand new, was where the Rodney King trial was scheduled to be heard.

I volunteered.

As it turned out, it would have made no difference whether I volunteered or not. I learned later that everyone in the jury pool who wasn't selected for jury duty that day at the Ventura Courthouse was directed to report to Simi Valley on Thursday. If I had not volunteered, I would have been drafted.

THURSDAY, FEBRUARY 6, 1992

It was raining. A sign at the North Simi Courthouse directed potential jurors upstairs. At the top of the stairs was a security arch, much like airport security. We had to deposit umbrellas, purses, etc., on a table and walk through the arch. We were accompanied by a deputy to a very large auditorium with folding chairs, where we were given name badges. About 250 people were there.

Jury Services manager Betty King told us the King jury would be the first jury sworn in at the new courthouse. "I guess that's an honor."

Some people laughed.

"Why don't you turn to the people next to you and introduce yourself," she said. "You're going to be here most of the day, and you might as well be friendly."

An events calendar was distributed to each person, indicating that another group of potential jurors had been brought in the previous day. They were going through the selection process with two different groups, ostensibly to make the group size more manageable. We were informed that when the judge appeared in about an hour, the auditorium would become a courtroom. If anyone had a reason to be excused because of hardship, they would be given the opportunity. Financial hardship was an acceptable excuse, since the trial might last as long as four months, and jurors would be paid only five dollars a day plus fifteen cents a mile, one-way, for driving to court. My employer would continue to pay my salary during jury duty, so that was not a factor for me.

Then we sat and waited, or stood and waited, or walked and waited. There was a lot of talk among the potential jurors, getting acquainted. Some chose to read or look out one of several large windows that overlooked a vacant field, full of trailers and a great deal of television equipment. After we had waited for about two hours, the deputies brought the United States flag and the State of California flag in and stood them in the front of the auditorium, flanking the lectern. In front of the lectern were two long tables. Several gentlemen wearing suits and ties took seats at the tables in the front.

When Judge Stanley M. Weisberg arrived, court was in session. We were collectively sworn in, promising to be truthful in all our answers. The judge said the trial would most likely last two months, possibly longer. He asked for a show of hands of those wishing to apply for hardship excuses. Probably twenty or thirty. Application forms were distributed to be turned in to the clerks or deputies before leaving that day.

Judge Weisberg was a Los Angeles County Superior Court judge who was hearing the case in Ventura County because the change of venue had been ordered. A balding man with round, wire-rimmed glasses that gave him an owlish appearance, Judge Weisberg had been, I learned later, a prosecuting attorney for seventeen years before he became a judge. He had a reputation for being stern and no-nonsense, and for running a very tight ship.

He introduced the men at the tables as the four Los Angeles police officers and their attorneys, as well as the two prosecuting attorneys in *The People vs. Powell*. For the first of many times, he admonished us not to watch television news accounts about the Rodney King case, read newspaper articles about the trial, or to discuss it among ourselves or with other people.

A forty-page questionnaire was given to each person. We were told to take it home, answer the questions, and return it the following day. The answers we gave turned out to be the single criterion by which we were chosen, or more accurately, by which we were not excused. The questions all seemed to be concerned with creating a psychological profile. Questions like "Do you watch television cop shows such as *Top Cops*?" and "Who are your favorite authors?" seemed to be trying to reveal personality traits. Some of the questions, however, were direct inquiries, such as "Do you have any relatives who are or have been policemen?" There were questions about policemen and their role, such as "Do you think it is the responsibility of policemen to punish criminals?"

I answered that it is the job of the courts to mete out punishment.

That night, I worked on the questionnaire. I answered each question as honestly and as candidly as I could. Dick said he thought it would be interesting if I were picked for the King jury. I was really curious to see what was involved, but I had mixed feelings about being picked. I would have to be away from work for a lot longer than I had anticipated.

We reconvened in the large auditorium and gave our completed questionnaires to the clerks. After another long waiting period, the judge arrived and gave us Part Two of his orientation lecture. Today, he talked about the specifics of being a juror. I took notes in shorthand. He explained that the lawyers could exercise peremptory challenges allowing them to excuse potential jurors without telling the reason. He also explained some of the differences between a criminal and a civil trial. In a civil trial, three-fourths of the jurors must agree on a verdict. In a criminal trial, all twelve jurors must agree.

He explained that in a criminal trial, the burden of proof beyond a reasonable doubt lies with the prosecution. He said that it cannot be a possible or imaginary doubt, but a reasonable doubt. He also said that a defendant must be presumed to be innocent until proven guilty. The defendant is not required to do anything or say anything, and the defendant does not have to testify. He said that there would be physical evidence, which are called exhibits.

He said that the jury judges the facts and evaluates witnesses. The same standard of evaluation must apply to all witnesses. He said the factors that a juror must watch for are inconsistencies, whether the witness seems to have a good memory, whether the witness seems biased, in addition to the information they give.

He also talked about direct and circumstantial evidence. Direct evidence is something that directly proves something. Circumstantial evidence is one step removed; a fact from which the inference of another fact may be drawn. They both are equally admissible.

He said it was probable that the jury would be sequestered in hotels at night during deliberations. Until deliberations the jury would not be allowed to discuss the case with each other in the jury room, on breaks, or at any other time. He emphasized very strongly the requirement that jurors talk and listen to the other jurors during deliberations. They should each express their own views.

Judge Weisberg also emphasized that the decision must be based on the evidence heard in the courtroom and the rules must be applied. Sympathy and bias cannot be considered. Finally, he informed the potential jurors that there would be four trials going on simultaneously, for the four separate defendants, and that the jurors must make their decisions separately for each defendant and each charge.

So far, I was finding this process fascinating. I was enjoying the lectures on the law, and I was enjoying the courtroom atmosphere. I have never paid much attention to lawyer shows on television, preferring situation comedies and news programs, but the real thing was fun to observe. During this part of the process, when we were not in the courtroom, I mostly kept to myself and didn't get acquainted with anyone. There were some interesting-looking people there, but I was reading a very good book and was enjoying the unaccustomed freedom of having so much time to read. One drawback was that the folding chairs became quite uncomfortable, so I spent a lot of time standing and reading, or walking around the room.

One prospective female juror was irate because of the parking situation. We had been told there would be special parking areas, but I guess they ran out of room and some people had to park in an unpaved area. It was raining and the area became very muddy. When we were asked if we had any questions, this woman expressed her displeasure at being treated as a second-class citizen and wanted to know if she was going to be reimbursed by the county for the expensive shoes she had ruined walking through the muddy parking lot.

We had been told that there was no place to buy lunch in the immediate vicinity of the courthouse. After the first day, I brought a Thermos of coffee and a sandwich. It helped, since we were not allowed to leave the auditorium except for organized, allotted breaks and lunch.

After the judge's orientation, we were directed to form a line in front of the two tables manned by jury services personnel and return our questionnaires and be assigned a day to report back to the courthouse. In the interim, the attorneys for both sides would review the questionnaires.

I left the courthouse with almost two weeks ahead of me, including one holiday, Presidents Day. I returned to work and got back into the routine of my normal schedule, trying to accomplish tasks that would assist my coworkers in taking care of things in my absence, just in case I should be chosen as a juror, which I still considered unlikely. With all the people they had to choose from, and because of the candid manner in which I answered the questions, I was sure they would not select me.

THURSDAY, FEBRUARY 20, 1992

I arrived at the courthouse at 8:30 a.m., and went up the stairs to the large auditorium. According to the judge's calendar, each day there would be forty prospective jurors questioned. This was to have started on the nineteenth. The clerk read off several names including mine, and told us to go to the smaller jury services room. And there we waited.

I still was not talking to very many people. Around mid-morning, I walked out into the hall and spoke to a gentleman who had found a door marked EMPLOYEES LUNCH ROOM. He had gone in and found two vending machines, one with snacks and another with soft drinks. I immediately got out my wallet, only to discover that I had nothing smaller than a five-dollar bill. He put one of his own dollars in the snack machine for me. I never saw him again, and was unable to repay him.

Shortly after noon, we were taken down to the law library and told to wait for our individual interview with the judge and attorneys. Toward late afternoon, I was called into the courtroom and escorted by the bailiff around a thirty-inch-high partition that ran the length of the jury box. I was told to take a seat directly in front of the microphone that had been placed on the partition. The judge was seated on his raised bench, the court reporter was in her position in front of and slightly to the right of the witness stand, and the attorneys were sitting at the counsel tables in the front of the room. It was more than a little intimidating sitting up there all alone, being interrogated.

I was surprised that the judge was the only one asking the questions. I had expected to be questioned by the prosecution and defense attorneys. Only a few questions were asked of me. The judge asked if I believed I could judge the case fairly and I said that I felt I could. I said that I had not followed the case closely enough to have formed any firm opinions one way or the other. The judge excused me and told me to report back the following Thursday.

I left the courthouse and went directly to work. Normalcy set in again, and my life was back to its usual routine. The only difference was all the questions I got from my fellow workers. I told them about the process, but explained that we had been ordered not to discuss the case itself. On Wednesday evening, I dialed the number we had been given to call to receive any last-minute instructions. I listened for a long time and heard nothing about *People vs. Powell.* I should have listened longer, because when I reported the next day, Thursday, there were no jurors at the courthouse. They had been told to report on Friday, February 28. I saw the court clerk in the hall and he gave me the message. So I went back to work.

FRIDAY, FEBRUARY 28, 1992

When we reported to the courthouse this morning, we were directed to the two smaller jury services rooms. Both rooms were full. The jury services clerk had set up a table where two clerks sat. We were told to line up and go to the table to draw a number and to place it in the right-hand corner of our badge. I drew Number 141.

We were escorted back into the large auditorium and waited. The female jury services clerk came into the large room and explained that we would be called by groups into the courtroom for the peremptory challenges. I was in the first group called, Numbers 101 through 149. We were escorted downstairs and into the courtroom and occupied the audience seats. There were about three seats in each row cordoned off for the press, with one seat in each row left vacant between the jury pool and the press.

Judge Weisberg explained that we would be called by our number to protect our anonymity. "We will refer to you by number rather than by name. I realize that this is very impersonal. The reason is to give you a degree of privacy while you are jurors in this trial."

After the trial, he said, the names of the jurors would become public. "The public has a right to know the names of the jurors who decide this case," he said.

"What you see in a courtroom is not *L.A. Law* or any of those TV shows. Those shows are designed to sell commercials and they tend to be very melodramatic. Lawyers won't be making long speeches to witnesses. And they won't be leaning over the jury box to talk to you. Those kinds of things don't happen."

The general voir dire started. The clerk called Number 101 and directed that person to take seat Number 1 in the jury box. The next number was called in order and the person directed to take seat Number 2 in the jury box. This continued until the jury box was filled through seat Number 12. Six folding chairs had been placed in front of the jury box partition for the alternate jurors. The next number in order was called and that person was directed to take the first folding chair. This continued until all six seats were occupied.

The judge asked questions apparently prepared in advance by the attorneys. One male potential juror was asked for details about an arrest in the past, which he said had been a case of mistaken identity.

Judge Weisberg had told us that the news media would have access to the questionnaires, but said if there was anything we wanted to keep confidential, we should tell him and he would decide if there was a legitimate reason to keep anything private. Some of the prospective jurors had asked that certain items on their questionnaire not be revealed to the public, and some of them were called over to the judge's desk to discuss it privately.

When all of the questions had been asked and answered, the judge asked the prosecution and the defense attorneys, in order, for their challenges. The attorneys would say, "The defense thanks and excuses Juror Number (blank)," or "The prosecution thanks and excuses Juror Number (blank)." That person would be escorted by the bailiff from the courtroom. Then the person occupying the next-in-order alternate seat would enter the jury box and assume the vacant seat. When all six of the alternate seats were vacant, the judge asked the clerk to call six more potential jurors by number. They came forward and were escorted into the vacant alternate seats. This procedure continued all day long until the last number called was Number 139, two numbers away from mine. We were excused and court was adjourned until Monday morning.

MONDAY, MARCH 2, 1992

I was one of the first prospective jurors called this morning, occupying one of the alternate jury seats, and eventually filling one of the vacant seats in the jury box.

A black woman who called the incident a "dog beating" was excused. A woman who said she was a newspaper reporter, but insisted she had no plans to write a book about the trial, was also excused.

The judge asked me only one question: "When your husband was in the military service, was he ever in the military police?" I answered, "No." I really wanted to tell the judge that when my husband was in the service, he played the saxophone in a band in Germany, but I felt the judge might think it flippant, though true. A large number of people were being thanked and excused, and I figured that at any moment, they would excuse the juror in seat number 11, which was me. To my complete surprise and shock, suddenly there were no more jurors excused.

"The prosecution accepts the jury."

"The defense accepts the jury."

Those words came as such a complete surprise that I experienced a physical reaction. My heart started beating very rapidly and my stomach lurched violently. I was so absolutely certain that I would not be chosen that I was having a problem grasping the reality of it. After all, I was among the first jurors questioned. There were probably another hundred jurors upstairs waiting to be questioned. It seemed logical to me that a large percentage of the first group of jurors would be excused, particularly in light of the controversial nature of the trial. It had all happened so quickly. Altogether, 260 prospective jurors had been questioned. And I had not been excused.

"You are the jury," Judge Weisberg said.

Immediately, the bailiff told us to raise our right hands and we were sworn in as jurors.

I was a juror! The judge told us to report back on Thursday, March 5.

I had varied reactions from friends and fellow workers. One friend said, "Why on earth did you allow yourself to get involved in this? You could have found many reasons to get out of it." He was right. I could have. But I went into the process determined to be as honest as I could possibly be. If I had looked for a way out, I would have had to be less than honest. There simply was no justifiable reason for my not being a juror on this trial.

# Chapter Three: The Trial Begins

The defendants certainly looked innocent, not at all like criminals.

During jury selection, although the four police officers and their attorneys were always present, I had not paid much attention to them. All of my attention was riveted on the judge. The attorneys and defendants had sat at two tables, but we couldn't really see them very well.

In the actual courtroom, the judge was sitting up on the bench, of course, and the lawyers and the four police officers sat at the counsel tables. The defendants were all very well-groomed and looked comfortable in their business suits. Sergeant Stacey C. Koon, at 41, was the oldest. He had close-cropped blond hair and a kind of a swagger. Officer Theodore J. Briseno, 39, had a thin, narrow face, black hair and a neat mustache. Officer Timothy E. Wind, 31, and Officer Laurence M. Powell, 29, were sturdily built younger men. Although all four officers were younger than I was, and in fact two of them were about the age of some of my children, they seemed like mature men. Officer Powell, particularly, did not look like he was only 29. They were none of them babies, and I had no particular sympathetic feelings for them.

A lot of thoughts went through my head as I looked at them. I wondered how police officers could get themselves into the situation that they were in. I knew that sometimes people go into law enforcement as a career because they enjoy exercising authority and power over others. I wondered if that was true of these four and if that was what had happened that night a year ago. I couldn't tell much from their faces. They were all quite stone-faced.

Beginning that morning and throughout the trial, I made a point of not looking directly at either the defendants or their lawyers. It was my job to be impartial and to listen intently to the testimony. I wasn't supposed to communicate with the lawyers or defendants, and I felt that making eye contact was a form of communication I should not engage in.

That morning when we arrived in the courtroom, there was a stenographer's notebook on each of the upturned seats in the jury box. During the selection process, I had been identified as Number 141. Now that I was actually a member of the jury, from this point on, I would be known as Number 11, my position in the jury box. I was expected to sit in the same seat every day. Written on the cover of each notebook was the juror's number and the words DO NOT REMOVE FROM COURTROOM. The judge advised us that we could take notes, but not to attempt to record any of the testimony verbatim. He said that we would have the testimony available to us during our deliberations and that he wanted us to concentrate on listening to the witnesses. He was concerned that if we were too intent on taking notes, we might miss some important testimony. I take shorthand and am accustomed to taking notes, so I scribbled away throughout the proceedings.

Judge Weisberg explained that we would begin with opening statements from both sides, which he described as "basically a road map" of what the evidence would be.

First we were to hear from the prosecution, and then, in turn, from each of the four defense lawyers. A year and two days after Rodney King led the California Highway Patrol on a high-speed chase along Los Angeles freeways and was beaten by the officers who arrested him, attorneys for both sides presented their versions of the facts.

I got two major surprises during the opening statements. The first was the video. It was impossible to have lived in California and not have seen the videotape of the four officers beating Rodney King. Perhaps it was impossible to live in America and not see it. If you had a television set on in your house during March 1991, you saw that tape. But before the trial began, I had watched it on television only a couple of times. After that, because of the aversion I have to violence, I deliberately left the room or changed the station if it was on.

I had not paid any particular attention to news accounts about the incident, either, but my general impression was that the police had treated a suspect in a brutal fashion. Although I had not had any personal experience with police brutality, I was not so naive as to think that it didn't happen. Maybe not in Camarillo, the Southern California seaside community where my husband and I had lived for the past eight years, but I had no doubts that the reports I had heard about police brutality against minorities in big cities were true. I was aware of the Los Angeles Police Department being accused of police brutality against minorities. It was horrible, certainly not anything I condoned, but I was not so naive as to be unaware of the phenomenon.

I knew that part of the reason this case had attracted nationwide attention was that the beating had been captured on videotape by an amateur cameraman in a nearby apartment, so the police could not deny that it had happened. Minorities had complained for years that this sort of thing went on, but it was always the word of a suspected criminal against a police officer, so it was difficult to prove. In this case, there was video that made it obvious that a man had gotten beaten, and that there were a whole lot of officers there when it happened. It certainly looked like there had been excessive force used.

I know that there are two sides to every story, so I expected that the defense would have a case to put on. But I assumed that the videotape showed everything that had happened. I was amazed to discover, when the jury saw the whole tape for the first time, how much more of it existed than had been shown on television. The whole tape was only eighty-one seconds, but even so, only a small portion of that eighty-one seconds had been shown on television. The whole tape, seen in context, presented a far different scenario than what the public had seen.

We saw the whole tape for the first time during the prosecution's opening statement. They put a big screen television right next to the jury box and showed us the whole tape, the blurry portions having been enhanced in the FBI laboratory. During the course of the trial, we saw it over and over, at regular speed, in slow motion, and frame by frame. It was brutal and hard to watch. I wanted to avert my eyes, but I had answered in the affirmative the judge's query about my ability to observe the video, so I forced myself to concentrate on it, in spite of the violence.

In his opening statement, Prosecutor Terry White made it clear that he felt that the video alone would be enough to convince us that excessive and unreasonable force was used. Right from the start, I was not particularly impressed with Mr. White. A professorial-looking black man, short and slight, with glasses and a receding hairline,

Mr. White tended to be overly dramatic and very emotional in his presentation. It seemed like an act to me, like he was putting on a show for us.

Mr. White said that the video clearly showed Mr. King on the ground, not resisting, yet the beating continued. He conceded that Mr. King had been drinking and had led the California Highway Patrol officers on a high-speed chase, which was why they had stopped him in the first place. But "whatever King was or what he did, it did not justify what you saw in that videotape," he told us.

He said that the evidence would show that Officer Powell had struck Mr. King repeatedly in the head "much as a batter would swing at a pitch." He said the blows split the skin on King's cheek, causing blood to "spurt out."

Mr. White told us that we would be seeing the videotape several times during the course of the trial.

"You will see a man who was down, a man who was not aggressive, who was not resisting. And those blows continued and continued for no just reason." Mr. White said that at one point Officer Briseno seemed to step forward and try to restrain Officer Powell from using his baton. Moments later, Mr. White said, Officer Briseno walked over to Rodney King and stomped on his head and neck.

Mr. White said that the evidence would show that when they got back to the police station, Sergeant Koon and Mr. Powell had prepared false reports "because they knew they could not justify the beating."

After Mr. White had finished his opening statement, it was the defense's turn. Of course, I expected that their point of view would be different. Darryl Mounger spoke first, on behalf of Sergeant Koon, saying, "This is the first opportunity to tell you what really happened."

Mr. Mounger said there was no evidence that Sergeant Koon had struck Mr. King, or anyone else. He said that as superior officer at the scene, Sergeant Koon, who had fourteen years experience in law enforcement, was in charge of the other officers. But he said the person who was in control that night was Rodney King himself. If Mr. King had not behaved in the way he did, then the officers would not have had to act the way they did, Mr. Mounger contended.

He implied that only someone running from the law would

fail to stop when a highway patrol officer was chasing them "with flashing lights and blaring sirens."

He said that Sergeant Koon observed that "King appeared to be under the influence of something, with perspiration, a blank stare and watery eyes."

Mr. Mounger said that Sergeant Koon stopped CHP Officer Melanie Singer, who was approaching Mr. King with her gun drawn, and said his officers would "handle it" because he didn't think there was any need for deadly force. He said that Sergeant Koon fired two shots from a legal Taser stun gun to try to subdue Mr. King.

"Sergeant Koon was out there doing his job, and so were his officers," Mr. Mounger said.

Speaking for Officer Powell, attorney Michael Stone replayed parts of the video. He said that the FBI enhancement of some blurry parts of the tape made it easier to see that Mr. King was defying the officers who were trying to arrest him. "You will realize that there's a lot of things you don't see at first when you look at the tape."

Playing the videotape and holding up blown-up still photos, Mr. Stone said, "See that? You can see Mr. King coming up off the ground. He starts up and lunges at Powell. Then he gets knocked back down to the ground again."

He said that officers are trained in the use of force to restrain suspects, and that in the case of Mr. King, they had to use "every level of force except deadly force."

He said that Mr. King displayed all the symptoms of someone on the hallucinogenic drug PCP, and that the officers believed he was on PCP. He said that Mr. King continued to ignore the commands of the policemen, even with guns drawn. He made the point that Officer Powell did not use the baton until Mr. King had advanced toward him in a threatening manner. Mr. Stone said that Officer Powell never actually struck Mr. King in the head and that close scrutiny of the video would prove that fact. He contended that Officer Briseno raised his arm to restrain the baton of Officer Powell to keep Powell from being shocked by the Taser gun that Sergeant Koon was about to fire. This seemed to directly conflict with Mr. Barnett's statement that Officer Briseno was trying to keep Officer Powell from beating Mr. King.

In his opening statement for Officer Wind, attorney Paul

DePasquale said that his client, who graduated from the police academy only four months before the incident occurred, stayed well within department policy for use of force. He said that Officer Wind applied proper textbook, classic form in his use of the baton, backing off and assessing the situation, and using the baton only when Mr. King started to rise.

Mr. DePasquale said that when Officer Wind first arrived at the scene, he heard someone say that Mr. King was on PCP. Officer Wind had never dealt with a suspect on PCP, but he had been taught in his training that officers had been killed dealing with such suspects. Because of that, Officer Wind felt that the lives of the policemen were in danger, Mr. DePasquale said.

"The potential for a life-threatening confrontation. That's the state of mind, the evidence will show, of Tim Wind."

He said that Wind had only used his baton when Mr. King started to get up, and he used it in accordance with his training, because it was "his responsibility to participate and to keep Mr. King from getting up."

Mr. DePasquale said that Mr. King failed to react to the Taser darts, which added to Officer Wind's belief that he was on PCP. "That should have ended it. Those things hurt. It should have been the end of it, but it wasn't."

The second big surprise of the day for me came when defense attorney John Barnett separated his client, Officer Briseno, from the other defendants. He contended that his client tried to protect Rodney King from the baton blows of the other officers.

We had been told by the judge that even though the four defendants were being tried at the same time, it was our job to consider each one separately. However, I had envisioned a unified position on the part of the four officers, and that they would all tell the same story. I did not expect that Mr. Barnett would accuse the other officers of excessive force. But it was quite obvious from Mr. Barnett's opening statement that Officer Briseno thought that the other three were guilty.

Mr. Barnett was very dramatic, using the term "senseless beatings." He said that Officer Briseno was trying to stop the other officers because he believed they were "out of control and he had to be mindful of his own safety." He said that when Briseno kicked or stomped on Mr. King he was not trying to inflict injury, but rather to hold Mr. King down to prevent any further baton blows.

Wielding Officer Powell's baton like a baseball bat and standing facing the jury box, Mr. Barnett said, "Mr. Powell was using power strokes, hitting backward and forward like the Louisville Slugger." He said his client pushed Mr. Powell back "because he was afraid Mr. King was going to be further beaten."

Mr. Barnett almost sounded as if he were part of the prosecution. His position that Officer Briseno thought that the others were guilty came as a shock to me.

# Chapter Four: The Case for the Prosecution

After all five attorneys had given their opening statements, the first witness was called. The witness box was a very short distance from the jury box, so we had a very good view.

The first prosecution witness was George W. Holliday, the man who had recorded the videotape we had seen twice already today. The prosecution entered the original tape into evidence officially as People's Exhibit Number 1.

I was surprised that the beginning of the tape showed two of Mr. Holliday's female relatives sitting on a couch with what appeared to be joysticks in their hands, playing a video game. Apparently, this really was the original tape, not edited in any way.

Mr. Holliday testified that he had been awakened by the sound of sirens and a helicopter overhead. He looked out the window just as Mr. King was being stopped by the police officers. He rushed to get his new video camera and started recording. He said he was amazed by Mr. King's failure to react as the officers clubbed him. He remembered thinking that Mr. King must have been "drunk or something." The next day he took his video to Channel 5 television station and sold it to them for $500.

The next witness was Mr. Bryant Allen, an old friend of Rodney King, who testified that he was sitting in the backseat during the high-speed chase. He looked uncomfortable in his suit and tie, as though he didn't usually get that dressed up.

He said that on March 2, 1991, Rodney King had picked him up at his mother's house in Altadena between 5 and 6 p.m. The two of them picked up another friend, Freddie Helms, who had since died, and the three men went to a liquor store, where they each bought a forty-ounce bottle of Olde English malt liquor. For the next two hours the three of them sat drinking in a park, Mr. Allen said. He said that as far as he knew, that was the only alcohol that Mr. King had consumed. He was not drunk, he said. When asked if Mr. King had been under the influence of PCP, he answered, "No."

Around 10 p.m. the three returned to Mr. Allen's mother's house, and sat in the car listening to music and singing, until Mr. King "just pulled off" and headed for the Foothill Freeway.

"We were just rapping—singing." He said he figured that Mr.

King was intending to "look for girls" and that he was going no more than eighty miles per hour when he saw the police lights flashing. Mr. Allen said that when he saw the red lights from the California Highway Patrol vehicle, he repeatedly urged Mr. King to pull over, but got no response from Mr. King.

"I said, 'Rodney, why don't you pull over?' a couple of times. He wasn't saying nothing. He just kept driving. At one time, I wanted to just jump out of the car. He was acting strange."

He said that although Mr. King seemed to be "in a trance," he was obeying all traffic lights and stop signs. "It seemed like he was going slower and slower. He wasn't driving crazy or nothing, he was just driving."

When they finally stopped, he said that Mr. King got out of the car and immediately got down on the ground. He also got out of the car and immediately went down on the ground, as directed by the CHP officers, and he could hear the baton blows to Mr. King and could hear Mr. King yelling.

The prosecutor, Mr. White, asked him to point out on a map where the incident occurred, but he couldn't show it on the map. During Mr. Barnett's cross-examination, he relentlessly pursued the point that Mr. Allen was not able to understand map directions and did not recognize locations on the map.

"You thought King was acting crazy, so crazy that you at least considered jumping out of the car?" Mr. Barnett asked.

"Yes," Mr. Allen replied.

In response to Mr. Barnett's questions, he said that when Mr. King finally stopped, he started to get out of the car, but was held back by the seatbelt. He got back in and removed the seatbelt and then got out of the car. He heard Mr. King "howling" and "screaming," and "the sounds of batons . . . like bones being cracked."

Mr. Allen seemed to have some trouble understanding the questions. Several times, Mr. Barnett pointed out that there were inconsistencies between what Mr. Allen was testifying now and what he had told the prosecutors in earlier interviews. It was obvious that the defense lawyers were trying to show that Mr. Allen was practically illiterate. They really badgered him, but he seemed like a fairly strong person. I did not feel sorry for him. He seemed able to take care of himself.

During Mr. Stone's examination, Mr. Allen was not able to identify streets that were traveled during the pursuit. He said that they had not smoked any marijuana that night.

Again, during Mr. Mounger's and Mr. DePasquale's cross-examinations, Mr. Allen was unable to identify periods of time or measurements of distance.

One of the attorneys asked that it be stipulated that Mr. Allen had two previous convictions as a felon. When something was stipulated, one side would state the information, and if the other side offered no argument, we were allowed to accept it as fact.

It was obvious that Mr. Allen was not well-educated or particularly bright. My impression was that he was a criminal, unemployed, not exactly an upstanding citizen. The fact that he complied with the police when they were stopped, and he was not beaten, verified in my mind that Mr. King must have been doing something to cause the police to react the way they did. I believed that Mr. King must have been drunk or on something. He apparently had been deliberately trying to elude the police. If he had been as cooperative as Mr. Allen, the police wouldn't have hit him either, I thought.

The next witness for the prosecution was Sergeant Robert Ontiveros, who was questioned briefly by Mr. Alan Yochelson, the other deputy district attorney besides Mr. White. He was assigned as Assistant Day Watch Commander at Foothill Division on March 3, 1991 and said that he worked with the four defendants. Mr. Yochelson played the videotape and asked if Sergeant Ontiveros recognized any of the individuals on the tape. He pointed to Officer Powell, Officer Briseno, Officer Wind and Sergeant Koon, and identified them.

He identified the master work sheet dated March 3, 1991 for Foothill Division, which listed the unit numbers of the officers. He identified Officers Powell and Wind as Unit 16A23. This all appeared to be very routine information.

The very eventful first day of the trial ended. When the judge excused the jury, he admonished us not to discuss the case or watch news broadcasts or read newspaper articles about the trial.

As we stood up to leave, Jerry, the court bailiff, stepped forward and stood between us and the audience in an almost protective stance, as if to prevent any contact, visually or physically, between the jury and anyone else in the courtroom. Jerry was a very powerful-looking man whose shirts were tailored to fit very snugly, particularly over the biceps. Standing there with his hands behind his back, legs slightly spread, he was a very commanding presence.

The judge had told us earlier that we were a "very precious commodity" and Jerry's protective stance seemed to verify it. I am sure that a compelling reason for it was to avoid any semblance of appearance of jury tampering, which could have caused a mistrial.

The jury filed out of the courtroom, assembled in the law library, went upstairs to the jury services room, gathered personal belongings and proceeded down the stairs. All the while we were accompanied by two sheriff's deputies, Rhett and Mary. When we arrived at the north entry door, we were accompanied out to the parking lot perimeter, where Pinkerton rent-a-cops escorted us to our cars.

That first night, and each night thereafter, after we were excused from court, I went to my office where I worked as a program manager for a small, minority-owned business that was engaged primarily in government contracts. Geoff, the young man sitting in for me, would leave notes informing me of what had happened, and asking questions about problems that had arisen. I would look at the in-basket and take care of any matters that I felt I should handle. Gene, my boss, would leave me notes about corporate matters that needed my attention and I would take care of them. I generally did not spend more than an hour or two.

When I arrived home, I would call Geoff and we would talk about problems or strategies. On several occasions, I got to the office in time to attend Program Manager meetings that ran late. Sometimes, I was able to talk with employees who were working overtime. I also telephoned customers from time to time to be sure their needs were being met. So I did not lose complete contact with my job. However, I was so comfortable with how the job was being handled that I had no need to let it interfere with my thoughts while in court.

It had been the first day of a set routine. Each day when we arrived, the first order of business was to look at the menu from the restaurant du jour and write our choice on a separate sheet of paper by our number. Our lunch was brought in from a different place every day, limited by the number of restaurants with which the county of Los Angeles had made prior arrangements.

After we ordered our lunch, we waited to be called into the courtroom, sometimes for only a few minutes, but more often for one or two hours. Each day we had a morning break, a ninety-minute lunch break and an afternoon break.

At every break, the same routine occurred. We filed out of the courtroom, assembled at the law library, and proceeded upstairs to the jury services room. Usually, there was a restroom stop along the way. Sometimes, we stayed downstairs for the break if it was going to be a short one.

In the jury services room, there was a refrigerator, a table for coffee, and a lot of tables and chairs. The coffee was prepared for us and ready when we arrived each day. Mary, the female deputy, took care of the coffee preparation. Twice we all pitched in a dollar to cover the cost of the coffee, sugar and cream. I don't know who paid for the rest of it, but I'm sure the jurors did not furnish enough money to cover the entire cost.

Someone had left jigsaw puzzles, cards, and various old, old magazines.

Sometimes we would be in a light mood in the jury room, laughing and talking, and when we were called into the courtroom, we would still be laughing and smiling as we went in. I felt that if I were a defendant, with my future on the line in that courtroom, I would expect the jurors to have a more solemn demeanor. So I tried to turn off the frivolity when I went into the courtroom, and appear serious-minded and businesslike.

Smoking was not allowed in the building. Fortunately for the jurors who smoked, one of the deputies also smoked, and was highly motivated to find time and places for the jurors to smoke.

We were very carefully guarded. Most of the restroom visits or PRs (potty runs) as they would come to be called, were done in groups. One deputy would sit and guard those who chose not to go, and another would accompany us to the restroom. Before we were allowed to enter, the deputy would stick his or her head in and call out to be sure the restrooms were empty. If they were occupied, we waited in the hall until they were empty and then we were allowed to go in. I was very impressed with how much care was taken to allow us absolutely no contact with anyone in the building. Just down the

*Moral Uncertainty*

hall and around the corner from the jury services room was a room occupied by the defense lawyers. On occasion, we would see one of the defense attorneys in the hall. When that happened, we were stopped by the deputies until the attorneys were out of sight and then we were allowed to proceed.

We were a cross-section of the community and all very different. But we had a lot of time to get acquainted. We were excused from the courtroom a lot of times in addition to the breaks and lunch.

The waiting was the hardest thing for me. I was accustomed to being busy every minute of the day, and it was hard to adjust to idle time. It would have been easier if we could have discussed the trial with our fellow jurors. I understand the reasoning behind it, but it was difficult. Eighteen separate personalities, with only one strong thing in common and we couldn't discuss it.

So instead of talking about what was really on our minds, which was what was going on in the courtroom, we talked about each other's lives. One woman had a son in medical school and was very proud of him. One of the men was a retired teacher and Navy pilot and sometimes he talked about that. Three of the men talked about computers.

To start with, there were seven men and five women on the jury, and six alternates, so there were a total of eighteen of us in the jury room. Two of the female alternate jurors always sat down near the door, and I never did know what they talked about down at that end of the room. One of the female alternates was in her early thirties, and a man and a woman were already 65, and I turned 65 during the trial, so we three were the oldest. There was a retired real estate broker who lived in Ojai, a park ranger, and a woman who worked for a bank as a printer. Two jurors were divorced and all the rest of us were married.

For all the talk after the trial about it being a "Simi Valley" jury, the fact was that only three of the jurors lived in Simi Valley. Three of us lived in Camarillo, and the others in the nearby Ventura County communities of Santa Paula, Ventura, Thousand Oaks, Saticoy and Piru.

# Chapter Five: The State's Star Witness

On the second day of the trial, we arrived at the courthouse very close to 8:30 a.m. and were escorted individually or in groups by the Pinkerton guards to the perimeter of the parking lot and then a deputy came out to accompany us into the building. We proceeded to the door just in back of the lobby, which had to be opened with a key card by the deputy. We were then turned over to another deputy who escorted us to Courtroom Number 2, where we assembled until all the jurors were present, then we were taken upstairs to the jury services room.

The lunch menu was from a coffee shop called Marie Callender's that specialized in pie. Someone said that it would not be appropriate to order from Marie Callender's without getting pie, so almost all of us ordered dessert. This set a very bad precedent, as each day thereafter, we ordered desserts.

California Highway Patrol Officer Melanie G. Singer was the only witness of the day. She described her experience and training with the CHP, identifying People's Exhibit Number 5, a PR-24 side handle baton, which she had been trained to use. We were to learn that these Monadnock batons were the "nightsticks" or "billy clubs" used by the Los Angeles Police Department and California Highway Patrol to control suspects.

Officer Singer said she was patrolling the 210 freeway in the northern part of Los Angeles County, with her husband, Officer Tim Singer, who was her CHP partner, in the passenger seat. She said they began chasing a white Hyundai traveling at an excessive speed.

At one time the CHP vehicle speedometer read 115 miles per hour and they were still not catching the vehicle, which was pulling away from them, she said. She turned on the red overhead lights when she was about seventy-five to eighty feet behind the vehicle. She also activated the siren and the spot lamps so they could see inside the vehicle. She said the occupants were not wearing seatbelts.

She said that the Hyundai got off the freeway on Paxton Street, and they followed. She described the entire exact route of the

7.8-mile chase, including the running of a red light. She said she radioed for help because she and her husband/partner considered the behavior of the driver made it a high-risk stop. During the chase, another official vehicle joined them, which she later learned was a Los Angeles Unified School District police vehicle.

She said her husband used the loudspeaker to tell the driver to pull over, reassuring him that, "You won't get hurt."

The car stopped, and the driver started to get out, then got back in, finally getting out and putting his hands on the roof of the car, with his elbows extended. She said the driver waved at the police helicopter overhead. She had her gun drawn and when she told Mr. King to get down on the ground, he put his hands on his buttocks and shook them at her.

"I told him to get his hands up and he grabbed his right buttock and shook it at me," she said. "I yelled at him to get on the ground and the other officers were yelling at him, shouting commands. He was dancing, like a pitter-patter."

By this time, other LAPD vehicles had arrived, and Sergeant Koon was on the scene. The officers surrounded Mr. King, who was now partially on the ground, and Officer Powell tried to handcuff him. Mr. King pushed them away and began flailing his arms wildly. Sergeant Koon ordered his officers to back away. He told Mr. King to get back down on the ground or he would use the Taser. Mr. King did not comply, and Sergeant Koon shot the stun gun, hitting Mr. King in the back with fifty thousand volts of electricity. Mr. King screamed and uttered a kind of a moaning sound, but he was still standing and was still swinging his arms wildly. Officer Singer said Mr. King moved toward Sergeant Koon. Sergeant Koon fired the Taser at Mr. King again, hitting him in his front torso area.

"He began to stagger like a monster, he staggered this way and then he staggered the other way. And he staggered one more time and he fell with all his body weight. He caught himself on one knee and he was balancing himself with his hands."

Officer Singer said that Officer Powell struck Mr. King's left cheekbone with his baton and split Mr. King's cheek from his ear to his jawbone. She said that Officer Powell also struck Mr. King's knuckles in a "power stroke."

"He dropped to his knees and Officer Powell continued to strike his head area about four more times." Sergeant Koon said, "Stop, that's enough." She remembered Officer Briseno grabbing the baton, and pushing it away.

During cross-examination, Officer Singer told Mr. Stone that it was CHP policy to approach a suspect with gun drawn. Mr. Stone had her place stickers on a blown-up photograph of Mr. King's head, showing where she thought the blows had landed and the injuries had occurred. Mr. Stone said that there were no major injuries visible where she said the blows had hit Mr. King, and asked her if she had any explanation for this.

"I saw what I saw," she said.

At Mr. Stone's direction, Officer Singer got up and demonstrated the blows to Mr. King, re-enacting them with the side handle baton on Mr. Mounger, one of the other defense lawyers. He had her describe Mr. King's position when the blows were being delivered by Officer Powell. Mr. DePasquale narrated the demonstration.

An objection was voiced by the prosecution, and the attorneys went up to the sidebar for a lengthy consultation with the judge, who then told the jury this was not to be perceived as a "re-creation" but simply a "demonstration." The "demonstration" continued.

When Officer Singer demonstrated a power swing, the baton came very close to the jurors in the front row. They recoiled, and the judge instructed her not to do it again.

Mr. Stone asked the witness if she had seen Officer Powell use the power stroke the night of the incident and she said she had not. The judge interrupted Mr. Stone's examination of the witness until they could have a conference on some point of law outside the presence of the jury.

Mr. Mounger cross-examined Officer Singer very briefly, asking her general questions about her experience with pursuits and her reaction to the potential dangers. He then had her compare this pursuit with others. She said she was concerned during this pursuit, but not afraid. She had considered the possibility that the suspects were going to run because of where they stopped by a park, and said she had never seen such strange behavior by a suspect.

She said officers want a high-risk suspect to assume a fully prone position and that Mr. King was down but not in a fully prone position when she approached him with her gun drawn. He was on all fours, "almost like a dog. He wouldn't get all the way down." That was when Sergeant Koon ordered her to back away, which she did.

The judge interrupted Mr. Mounger's examination and the jury was excused for the day and for the week. We were dismissed by the judge with his usual admonishment, "Do not discuss this case with anyone, including your fellow jurors. Do not read newspaper accounts or watch television reports concerning the trial." We all felt relieved that the week was over. It had been very stressful. The jury members were just getting acquainted with each other and with the routine, and there had been a lot of surprises in the opening statements and in the testimony. I was still trying to oversee my job, so I was very tired when I got home each night. When I arrived home on the Friday evening, I found it difficult not to discuss the case with my husband. We had been married for a long time, and I was accustomed to being able to talk to him about what I was thinking. It was strange to have my attention so consumed by something I was not allowed to discuss with him.

However, rather than being curious, he was extremely helpful in assisting me to honor the judge's instructions. If we were with friends socially, and someone wanted to bring up the subject, he would say, "She can't discuss the case," before I had a chance to say anything. If we were watching television and the remote control was close to him, he would immediately turn off the television when the case was mentioned. I would leave the room until he told me it was okay to return.

I did read the newspapers, but if I saw an article about the case, I simply ignored it. Also, my husband quite frequently would cut the article out of the paper. I tried to be very careful to strictly adhere to the judge's admonition. All during the trial, I was essentially in a vacuum about the case, and literally knew nothing except what I heard and saw in court. I had taken an oath that I would deliberate and judge the defendants based strictly on court testimony and nothing else. I was intent upon honoring that oath. After the trial was over, I read articles and saw some television broadcasts that indicated that they did not really expect jurors to abide by those restrictions, but I did. Furthermore, all the other jurors that I talked to did the same.

I worked most of Saturday at my office, but spent Sunday at

home. I had an advantage over most wives, in that my husband was retired and kept the housework done, so that I did not have to spend hours on household chores.

MONDAY, MARCH 9, 1992

The jurors arrived a little before 8:30 a.m., and the wait to get started was shorter than usual. The jurors were called into court at 9:15. Cross-examination of Officer Melanie Singer by Mr. Stone continued.

He offered as Exhibit 303 the FBI-enhanced version of the videotape, and played the video in slow motion, asking her to point out where Mr. King was moving toward Officer Powell. When asked if she saw Mr. King get up and charge Officer Powell, she said that she had not seen it the night of the incident, but that she could see it now in the fuzzy part of the video. She was shown a photo of Mr. King and asked if she could see any marks on Mr. King's knuckles and she said she could not.

Mr. Stone asked the witness to look at the report her husband, Officer Timothy Singer, had filed and she pointed out some inconsistencies about the speed of the vehicle and lane changes. Mr. Stone introduced four photographs of the Paxton off-ramp from the 210 freeway, taken from different directions. He asked Officer Singer to identify the intersection. He asked her to look at the arrest report where it referred to the pursuit at that point. He seemed to be trying to point out inconsistencies between her testimony and her husband's official report. He also cited the grand jury transcript, where she had testified that at one point traffic was endangered by Mr. King's vehicle. She verified that fact. Mr. Stone read the entire arrest report, asking her questions about its accuracy.

Mr. DePasquale cross-examined her next. She said that she had smelled alcohol on Mr. King's breath at the scene and had determined he was under the influence of alcohol, but did not order any blood or urine tests at the hospital. She testified that her report indicated that Mr. King took swings at the officers and appeared to be punching them. She said that the word "punch" was a mistake. She said she never saw Mr. DePasquale's client, Office Briseno, at the scene. Mr. Mounger asked Officer Singer about the amount of elapsed time from the time of the stop to a Code 4, which means the situation is stabilized. She replied it could have taken ten minutes or more.

The judge declared a longer than usual afternoon recess to discuss a matter with the attorneys. We spent the time getting acquainted with each other and with the deputies who would be our caretakers throughout the trial. There were some card games being played, a jigsaw puzzle being worked on, but mostly we just milled around and talked to each other. A couple of us looked out the window through the slats of the metal blinds. Rhett, the deputy, came over and gave us a very serious talk about the fact that there were high-powered cameras down there that could photograph us. From that point on, we were watched very carefully when we were close to the windows.

Rhett was quite handsome. Those who watched the trial on television saw Rhett in the courtroom occasionally, standing against the wall and performing a variety of duties, such as escorting the witnesses into the courtroom, helping set up exhibits, etc. He took his job very seriously, but had a very loud, infectious laugh. Even if I was in another part of the room when he started laughing, and was totally unaware of what caused the laughter, I laughed also. Along with the other deputies, he was also in charge of being sure our lunches were ordered, delivered and sent in to us. Rhett seemed to enjoy calling us all together, asking for our attention, and giving us information concerning a variety of matters. I guess, at a minimum, you could say Rhett was gregarious. This was in comparison to Mary, our other constant deputy companion, who certainly did not lack self-confidence, but was not as vocal. We would grow quite fond of both of them.

After the break, Prosecutor Terry White re-examined Officer Singer, asking her questions about Officer Powell's report. He asked her about the statement in the report of traffic having to yield and she said there was none. She also said that she did not see any vehicle slamming on its brakes to avoid a traffic accident.

She was finally excused, with the possibility of being recalled later. My impression of her was that she was rather unemotional. She claimed that she saw blows to the head, but apparently, according to the questions asked her, the physical injuries didn't confirm that the blows were where she said they were.

The next witness for the prosecution, questioned by Mr. Yochelson, was Melanie Singer's husband, CHP traffic Officer Timothy J. Singer. He said that Mr. King was speeding and failed to yield. When Mr. King's vehicle stopped, Tim Singer said there was loud feedback from the public address system of the patrol car and from the Unified School District's siren. He yelled to the driver to exit the car. After a brief time, the driver got out of the car, and slowly put his hands on the roof of the car. He said Mr. King pointed to the helicopter and waved at it and finally got down on the ground.

He said that he heard popping sounds, apparently from the Taser gun, and saw Mr. King rising off the ground and turning toward him. He heard more popping sounds and Mr. King stood up all the way. He said that Mr. King was staggering and that his face was convulsing from the Taser shots. He testified that Officer Powell struck Mr. King on the right side of his face with his baton. He said Mr. King continued toward him and that Officer Powell struck him again, along the right side of his face. He said he saw six blows and he thought that all but one had hit Mr. King in the head. Tim Singer said he had turned his attention to the two passengers and thought the incident was over. The next time he saw Mr. King, he was being loaded into the ambulance.

He said that although the CHP car was the primary unit chasing Mr. King's car, Sergeant Koon requested that the LAPD take over. Officer Singer asked his supervisor by telephone whether to turn it over to LAPD, and was instructed to let the LAPD handle the case. At the hospital, he said that Sergeant Koon said to him, "Just tell this officer what happened." He told Sergeant Koon that he would rather write a report himself, which he did, giving the report to Officer Powell.

Tim Singer said that he heard nothing mentioned the night of the incident about PCP. Mr. Yochelson asked him several questions about statements in the arrest report, with which Officer Singer did not agree.

At the end of Officer Singer's testimony for the day, the jury was excused, with the usual admonition to refrain from discussing the trial or watching any media reports. We went down the hall to the law library, made the obligatory PRs, headed upstairs to the jury services room to collect our belongings, and went down the stairs and out to the parking lot.

# Chapter Six: A Change in the Jury

As soon as the judge bid us a good morning, he asked jurors wearing sunglasses to remove them. The only juror wearing sunglasses was Number 10, sitting next to me. The judge's request unnerved several of the other jurors. A middle-aged Hispanic woman who wore tinted glasses asked me later if I thought the judge was talking about her. But it was clear that he meant Number 10, who usually dressed in tank tops and other clothing that seemed overly casual. He told some of the jurors that when Elvis Presley died, he had left him his voice.

Mr. Yochelson's direct examination of Officer Timothy Singer continued. Officer Singer repeated that he heard no talk about PCP at the field or at the hospital. He said he had made eighty to one hundred PCP arrests during his thirteen years as a CHP officer and that the thought that Mr. King might be under the influence of PCP never crossed his mind.

During cross-examination by Mr. Stone, Officer Singer identified photos of intersections involved in the high-speed chase. He said that Mr. King was driving about forty-five to fifty miles per hour through the intersection of Paxton and Glenoaks and that he ran a red light. At times Mr. King was driving eighty miles per hour, he said.

Putting a big piece of paper up on an easel, Officer Singer made a simple drawing with a marker of the position of Mr. King at the scene as it related to the cars. He again told of the two popping sounds and described Mr. King's convulsing face and said Mr. King had staggered toward him. He stated that Officer Powell struck Mr. King above the right ear with a powerful blow but it had absolutely no effect on Mr. King who remained on his feet. Officer Singer said that the second blow was delivered on the right side of Mr. King's jaw. He said this knocked Mr. King backward and he began to go down. He fell with his hands outstretched. He said Officer Powell continued with three or four baton strokes while Mr. King was on the ground. He said they were powerful blows with nothing held back. He said that he then refocused his attention on the passengers.

He said he did not see Mr. King with his hands over his face. Mr. Stone showed Officer Singer photographs of Mr. King, asking him if he could see signs of injuries on his face, and he could not.

Under cross-examination, Officer Singer said that he did not see Officer Briseno push Officer Powell away until he saw it on the videotape. He again said that Mr. King was a very large man, weighing in excess of two hundred pounds and that he appeared to be like a monster out of the movies, that after the monster gets shot, he just keeps on coming.

"One of the several thoughts that flashed through my mind was it appeared like a scene from a monster movie," he said. "I'd seen this man shot with a Taser, hit with a baton, a powerful blow on the head, and he was still on his feet."

"And you were scared, weren't you?" Mr. Stone asked.

"Yes, because he still appeared to be advancing on me," Officer Singer said.

I thought to myself, *If I were a police officer, this would frighten me.*

Officer Singer also stated that he had formed the opinion that Mr. King was under the influence of alcohol; he guessed .08 or higher. He said that if Mr. King was a heavy drinker he might be able to disguise it. He said that .19 alcohol blood level would make anyone a dangerous driver. He also said that the video showed a lot more than he knew was happening that night. He told Mr. Barnett that after looking at the video, he felt that he had testified honestly earlier, but inaccurately.

Mr. Yochelson asked Officer Singer during his redirect examination if he was aware that there was a chemical odor associated with PCP. Officer Singer said he was, but that he did not detect that odor on Mr. King in the field or at the hospital.

He told Mr. Yochelson that his recollection was that after the first blow by Officer Powell, Mr. King remained standing. The second blow was the one that caused Mr. King to fall. He remembered thinking, How can he be doing this?

"I knew it was against CHP policy to strike someone in the head because it was deadly. I knew it was wrong," he said.

Officer Singer was dismissed after a brief re-cross examination by Mr. Stone.

He struck me as a terse-talking, very professional officer. For the most part, his testimony seemed the same as his wife's, but there were many discrepancies in the details. Both of them said Officer Powell hit Mr. King in the head. But Melanie Singer said that Mr. King was on all fours when the first blow was struck, and her husband said he was standing. The videotape confirmed that he was on his feet.

Tim Singer admitted that his recollection of what happened did not square with what he saw on the tape. He said he could not account for the difference in his perception and what the film showed.

The next witness was Officer Frank Michael Schulz of the California Highway Patrol. He testified very briefly that he had gone to the termination of the pursuit and witnessed a black male handcuffed. In a later conversation with Officer Melanie Singer, she told him that Mr. King was hit in the head with a baton.

The next witness was William Tom Rhiel, a communications technician for the city of Los Angeles, whose job was to repair and maintain the communications dispatch system between the squad cars and headquarters. He said that the time-keeping system was accurate to one millionth of a second. He explained the mobile digital terminal (MDT) system and said that on March 3, 1991, the MDT was approximately five seconds behind the voice radio.

After Mr. Rhiel's testimony, the jury was excused for the day. While we were in court this day, the deputies had arranged to have a refrigerator put in the law library. Because of the close proximity of the library to the courtroom, we had requested to convene and wait there for our courtroom calls. It seemed pointless to trudge up the stairs to the jury services room two or three times a day. I believe it caused the deputies some concern also, trying to herd us up and down the stairs without encountering any other people that might contaminate our decision process.

I am sure that the law library had not ever encountered such heavy usage, nor is it likely to again. The bookcases were loaded each day with our personal belongings, but that didn't cause much wear and tear. My concern was for the huge table, around which the jurors assembled each day thereafter, reading books, playing cards or eating. It was obviously made of very good wood, mahogany I think, and had a very fine hand-rubbed finish. Each night when we left, it showed the evidence of the day's use. When we arrived the next day, it had been oiled and polished, and looked beautiful again. I don't believe we did any permanent damage. Most of us tried to put down paper towels to act as coasters for our drinks and food, but it was still painful to watch the abuse.

Each juror chose a seat at the large table or in the chairs against the walls, and with few exceptions, kept those spots the whole trial. The law library was much more comfortable than where we had been kept before. We could walk out to the atrium or courtyard adjoining the library. It was in a very attractive setting with flowering shrubs and concrete benches to sit on, giving us a chance to get outside. Later, we would be allowed to eat our lunch in the courtyard on folding tables, if we wished. It was especially good for the smokers, because now they had a place to smoke at will.

The library had a small kitchenette area with cupboards and a boiling water tap for tea. In addition to the refrigerator, the deputies brought in a small table and coffee urn. Each day, the jurors brought in a variety of goodies, mostly sweet rolls or doughnuts. Coffee was prepared and ready for us each day when we arrived. It wasn't home, but it was comfortable.


WEDNESDAY, MARCH 11, 1992

The next prosecution witness was Officer Edward Jordan, Custodian of Records for the LAPD, who identified some exhibits. During this day, there were six sidebars. It was a little disconcerting for the jurors to sit and watch and not know what was taking place. Usually, the question and subsequent objection immediately prior to the sidebar gave us a clue, but sometimes we simply did not know why the objections and sidebar conferences were occurring.

When the attorneys and the judge needed to confer outside the presence of the jury, Judge Weisberg would come down off the bench and join the six attorneys over against the wall on the opposite side of the courtroom, as far away from the jury as they could possibly get. The court reporter would pick up her transcribing machine and walk over and stand there with the seven men as they murmured to one another. We could never hear a word they said. We would just sit there and wait. Some of the other jurors whispered to each other.

I tried not to do that. To amuse myself, I began timing how long the sidebars lasted. They ranged from about three to ten minutes most of the time.

Sometimes I studied the audience. There were always at least fifty spectators in the room, I'd guess. There were the same members of the news media every day, and there were other spectators, who seemed to lose their seats if they got up and went out. Someone else always immediately came in to fill the seat.

Next on the stand was Leshon Frierson, a Police Service Representative for the LAPD. A radio communication was played from someone who seemed to be Officer Powell. The voice requested a rescue ambulance for a victim of a (pause) and a voice in the background says "beating." The voice says "yeah" and then there is laughter, and the voice says, "numerous head wounds." Officer Frierson said the voice appeared to "laugh or giggle," and he thought the transmission was odd because officers don't ordinarily use words like "beating."

The implication seemed to be that here we had a serious beating, and Powell was laughing about it. I thought it was more likely nervous laughter than amusement. I don't think it is unusual for someone to laugh when they are merely tense. I doubted that the laughter was because he was callous or unfeeling.

In cross-examination by Mr. Stone, Mr. Frierson said that at the time he did not get the impression from the transmission that there was any wrongdoing. He conceded that the transmission was hard to understand.

In redirect examination by Mr. Yochelson, Mr. Frierson said that it appeared that Officer Powell paused because he did not know how to describe what had happened.

The prosecution then called Dr. Antonio Mancia, an intensive care specialist who was moonlighting the night of the incident at Pacifica Hospital and who examined Mr. King when he was brought in. The examination revealed five or six facial lacerations.

Mr. King's medical chart with notes was introduced as People's Exhibit Number 13. Dr. Mancia testified that there were two lacerations in Mr. King's hairline that required two stitches, one about three centimeters in his cheek, one about five centimeters on the right side of his chin that required five stitches, and one on his upper lip that required two stitches. He said there were two lacerations inside Mr. King's mouth. He said a total of about twenty stitches was required.

Dr. Mancia had a very thick accent that made it a little hard to understand him.

He said there were bruises on Mr. King's scalp and chest, and on his back and legs. He made sure that Mr. King was stable and asked that he be transferred to the University of Southern California Los Angeles County General Medical Center. He concluded that Mr. King had been hit with some object, and recommended X-rays and a CAT scan. He said Mr. King was quiet and cooperative and he didn't think he was under the influence of any drug.

In his cross-examination by Mr. Stone, Dr. Mancia said that he was trained in the emergency area of pediatrics, but had replaced a friend on duty that night. He was not prepared to say the cause of Mr. King's injuries.

"It could be the result of slamming his head into the asphalt?" Mr. Stone asked.

"Yes," the doctor answered.

He said that Mr. King was handcuffed to the gurney and was non-communicative. He detected no odor of alcohol on his breath.

When Mr. DePasquale cross-examined Dr. Mancia, he said that Mr. King was not in shock and that he had not lost consciousness. He wrote "PCP ingestion" and "PCP overdose" on the report because he had heard it from the nurse in charge. He indicated that it was his diagnosis that Mr. King was not in critical condition.

Under cross-examination from Mr. Barnett, Dr. Mancia said someone under the influence of PCP would have superhuman strength, be oblivious to pain, would not respond to normal commands, and would appear to be in a trance.

I was having a hard time making up my mind whether or not Mr. King was on PCP or just intoxicated, but I wasn't sure that it made any difference what substance he was on. His behavior seemed to make it obvious that he was "on" something.

On re-cross examination by Mr. Stone, the doctor said that he had not concluded there were serious head injuries. At the end of Mr. Stone's examination, the jury was dismissed for the day and told not to report to the court until 1:30 p.m. on Thursday.

We had been told by the deputies for several days that they would be taking us out to a restaurant for lunch. Today was the day. When we were dismissed at noon, we were escorted to a large bus with VENTURA COUNTY SHERIFF'S DEPARTMENT painted on the side. Ordinarily, it was used to transport suspects from jail to court and back. The right side of the bus was outfitted with normal bus seats, but the left front portion was partitioned into locked steel cages containing one seat each. All the windows had steel bars on them. There were more locked steel cages in the rear of the bus. There was an obscenity carved on one of the windows. It was quite an experience to ride down the streets and the highway and have everyone stare. It was very conspicuous. I'll never forget the feeling of being transported in a portable jail.

The driver parked the bus in front of a restaurant called Tony Roma's, and one of the deputies stayed in the bus while the other went in and cleared the way. We were escorted as quickly and inconspicuously as possible in the front door, up the stairs, and into a room reserved for us exclusively. We had ordered our meals before arriving and they served us promptly.

The problem occurred when the waitresses brought in dessert trays and most of us chose desserts. That was not in the county's budget. I guess that meal became very expensive, because the next day we got the word that we now had a ten dollar ceiling on our individual lunches. This was not a problem, because most of us were always well under the ten dollar limit, but it became a subject for much discussion and joking. It was also our last lunch off the courthouse premises.

THURSDAY, MARCH 12, 1992

Any time we were excused for an entire or partial day, I went to work. I was still very concerned about what was happening there and could not just turn it off at will. When I reported for work on Thursday morning, I took care of several pending matters, and contacted our government customers for a status report on how things were going. For the most part, I was beginning to feel that if I tried to get involved in too many activities, I would simply be interfering. I managed to accomplish some tasks that kept me busy until noon when I left for the courthouse.

When the jury was called in at 1:30 p.m., the first witness was Dr. David Giannetto, an emergency room physician who was on duty at the USC Medical Center and examined Mr. King at about 6:15 a.m. in the jail ward on the thirteenth floor. He said Mr. King was alert and that his vital signs were slightly high, and that he had two fractures on the side of his face and a broken leg. He said Mr. King was still mildly intoxicated.

Under cross-examination by Mr. Stone, Dr. Giannetto pointed to the place on a human skull where the injuries occurred. He said the bone was very thin and would easily break. When asked by Mr. Stone if he could tell the amount of force required to cause the injuries to the right side of Mr. King's face, the doctor replied that he had no formal bio-physics training and could not tell. Dr. Giannetto identified the X-rays labeled as Exhibits 315 (A through F) as those of Mr. King's injuries.

This witness created some doubt in my mind about whether or not the baton blows were what caused Rodney King's facial injuries. He seemed to be saying that the cheekbones are so fragile that if he had really been smashed right in the face with the baton, the bones would have been shattered instead of just broken.

Dr. Giannetto said that Mr. King's blood was tested for alcohol and drugs. He said that PCP is not always present in urine and that there was no physical ability test made for intoxication. His alcohol blood level was .19 five hours later.

Dr. Giannetto also contradicted something Dr. Mancia said. Dr. Mancia said Mr. King did not appear to be intoxicated, but Dr. Giannetto said Dr. Mancia told him that Mr. King was being transferred to County-USC Medical Center because he needed to be observed for PCP intoxication.

The various doctors seemed to be contradicting each other on this issue, but it was obvious that Mr. King must have been under the influence of something. I wasn't sure what difference it made whether or not he was on PCP, or whether the officers just thought that he was. They would have to act in accordance with their perceptions.

The next witness was Sergeant Richard S. DiStefano, the Assistant Watch Commander the night of the incident, who had been on duty from 11 p.m. to 7:45 a.m. He said before going on duty that night, the officers had participated in a baton practice at the end of roll call. He said he had required Officer Powell to repeat the practice on a wood post ringed with tires, because he was applying the baton in an ineffective manner. He said that Officer Wind, on the other hand, was very good in the use of the baton.

Mr. Stone asked the witness how long the roll call training was and he replied that it lasted about forty-five minutes and that the training had been on the use of the PR-24 baton. He repeated that Officer Powell was ineffectual and weak in his application of the baton during training, and that Officer Wind had pristine form. The training concluded sometime before midnight, he said.

During Mr. Mounger's cross-examination, the witness said the police officers were told to use enough force to break bones, in order to immobilize the suspect. I was shocked that this was condoned. I had assumed that the purpose of the baton was to inflict pain to assist in subduing a suspect. This was the first of several times we would be told that officers are taught to deliberately break bones. I had known it was brutal work, but this was startling and distasteful to me.

Mr. Mounger, who was once a police officer himself, demonstrated baton swings.

"Did you tell officers if they chose to use this weapon, it is an impact weapon and they must use as much force as possible?"

"Yes," Sergeant DiStefano said.

"The officers are taught to not tap lightly, to use force and that's the training?" Mr. Stone asked.

"Yes," Sergeant DiStefano replied.

Mr. Yochelson asked if the officers were taught to use baton blows on a person lying on the ground and the sergeant answered, "No."

The judge dismissed the jury with the same admonition about refraining from discussing the case or looking at news reports.

For some time, the jurors had been talking among ourselves about Juror Number 10, who claimed he had inherited Elvis Presley's voice. One day, he wore a very skimpy tank top that exposed a lot of skin. At the end of the day, the bailiff called us all together to say the judge wished the jury to use good taste in our dress. It was obvious who he was talking about, but the admonition was given to all of us.

I sat next to Juror Number 10 and sometimes he made grunting noises and long sighs while testimony was being given. He seemed to look out at the audience more than he looked at the witnesses. Once he took his pencil and made scratching lines on the pages of his notebook very loudly. This went on for quite a while and was distracting to those close to him. Some of the other jurors had conversations with him that led them to believe his behavior was erratic.

This afternoon several of the jurors decided to call his behavior to the judge's attention. Several jurors signed the note. I didn't. It didn't seem to me that it was our place to decide whether or not another juror was suitable.

The note was given to Rhett to give to Jerry, the bailiff.


FRIDAY, MARCH 13, 1992

It was a long morning. The jury was not called in until 11:30 a.m., so we had the whole morning to entertain ourselves. At one end of the table, there were a couple of gin rummy games. One of the jurors managed to play cards and also knit. She completed one scarf about midway through the trial. When I admired it, she said if I would get the yarn, she would knit one for me. I didn't think there was enough time left for her to complete it, but she did.

One of the male jurors sat next to her and kibitzed and helped her with her hand from time to time. Whenever she was ready to win, she would always say, "Yes. That's do-able." We took turns winning, but she was the one who won most.

It was nearly noon when we finally were called into the courtroom.

The first witness was Lawrence E. Davis, the Charge Registered Nurse in the emergency room of Pacifica Hospital the night of the incident. He described Mr. King's demeanor as calm when he was brought in. He said there were four to six LAPD officers in the emergency room. The two CHP officers, Tim and Melanie Singer, were in and out. He said that Officer Powell asked Mr. King if he remembered the game that they played that night. Mr. King said that he didn't know what Mr. Powell was talking about.

Mr. Davis said that Officer Powell replied, "We had a pretty good hard ball game tonight. We hit a few home runs."

He said that Officer Powell said, "You lost the ball game, didn't you?"

During his cross-examination, Mr. Stone pointed out that Mr. Davis had told the grand jury there were two to four officers making comments. That was inconsistent with today's testimony when he only quoted Officer Powell.

Even though that inconsistency had been pointed out, I still thought that Mr. Davis was a credible witness. I was offended by what he said, but I believed him. It doesn't seem right to me that police would talk to a suspect in that condescending manner. I'm sure that it happens, but I don't like it. It seems like they are trying to reinforce the fact that they are the authority figures, to let the suspect know that they are in charge.

Mr. Davis testified that they removed three Taser darts from Mr. King's clothing. He said that there were no darts embedded in Mr. King's skin.

He said that the officers told him they thought Mr. King was on PCP because of the way he was moving around on the gurney.

He said there was no dirt or gravel in Mr. King's wounds.

He said he didn't recall seeing Officer Briseno in the emergency room, and did not see Sergeant Koon. He testified that Mr. Wind was in the room, but he didn't remember if he said anything to Mr. King.

Mr. Stone asked Mr. Davis if the officers told him that Mr. King was a paroled armed robber. The prosecution objected, and there was another sidebar before Mr. Stone withdrew the question.

On redirect examination by Mr. White, Mr. Davis said that Officer Wind held up his baton and said that Mr. King had resisted arrest. He also said that Officers Powell and Wind took Mr. King away from the hospital.

Toward midday during one of the breaks, the deputies told Juror Number 10 to bring all of his things with him; the judge wanted to talk to him in his chambers. We never saw him again. Apparently, the judge got the note the jury sent.

That afternoon, the judge announced that Juror Number 10 had been dismissed for personal reasons, by agreement of all parties.

The court clerk drew a number from among the alternates and chose a woman who worked as a groundskeeper for one of the county colleges. With her addition, we became a six-man, six-woman jury, with two minority members: one Latino woman and one Filipino woman. There were five alternate jurors left.

# Chapter Seven: More From the Prosecution

The next prosecution witness was Carol Denise Edwards, the emergency room nurse on duty the night of the incident. She testified that when she removed three Taser darts from Mr. King's clothing, one tip was missing. She said that none was embedded in the skin. She told Officers Wind and Powell that she did not believe the Tasers worked because they were not in the skin. The officers told her they didn't have to pierce the skin to work.

She testified that Mr. King had said he ushered at Dodger Stadium. She said Officer Powell said, "Where do you usher? I want to make sure I don't sit in that section."

Again, I thought the officers made inappropriate remarks to Mr. King. It wasn't necessary to talk to him like that. On the other hand, just because the officer had a bad attitude didn't prove to me that he had used unnecessary force when he was arresting Mr. King. I think the prosecution was trying to show that Officer Powell was callous, and that indicated he had done something wrong. I just didn't think that the remarks he made after the fact were that significant, one way or another. He could have been guilty of using excessive force and then been very polite and solicitous, and that wouldn't have proved he was innocent, either.

During Mr. Stone's cross-examination, Ms. Edwards said that someone asked the officers what Mr. King had been hit with.

"It wasn't a verbal response," she said. "Officer Powell sort of patted his baton and Officer Wind sort of pulled his baton up in the air."

She said that she got the names of Powell and Wind from the newspapers. She recognized them, but didn't learn their names until later.

The next witness was Glenda Jean Tosti, an LAPD Police Service Representative, working as a Communications Supervisor. Ms. Tosti said that the Emergency Board Operator (EBO) accepts calls from citizens and other law enforcement agencies; the Radio Telephone Operator (RTO) is the dispatcher. The Mobile Digital Terminal (MDT) is for one-on-one communication with other officers or units in the field. She identified on the master MDT log a message sent to 16FB9 at 1:12:32 that said, *Oops*.

At 1:12:57 a message was sent to Unit 16A23: *Oops what?*

At 1:13:53 a message was sent from 16A23: *I haven't beaten anyone this bad in a long time.*

The return message was, *What did he do?*

And the reply was, *I think he was dusted. Many broken bones later after the pursuit.*

It was stipulated that Officer Powell had sent the messages.

This information seemed significant to me. It could have been an admission of guilt by Powell.

Ms. Tosti also testified that Sergeant Koon had typed a message that read, *Unit just had a big time use of force. Tased and beat the suspect of a CHP pursuit big time.*

Ms. Tosti had replied, *Oh, well. I'm sure the lizard didn't deserve it. Ha ha ha.*

Obviously, Ms. Tosti had been making a flippant remark to the officers. This didn't have much significance, as far as I was concerned. I am sure that officers make those kinds of remarks to each other all the time. She wasn't accused of anything, so her attitude about it really didn't matter.

Court was then recessed until Monday. Friday the Thirteenth had gone without any obvious bad luck for the jurors.


MONDAY, MARCH 16, 1992

By this time, we had fine-tuned and honed our arrival routine so that the deputies eliminated the waiting in Courtroom Number 2 until we had all arrived. We were now met and escorted individually or in groups, handed over from deputy to deputy, until we were safely ensconced in the law library. Gerry brought in a toaster, bagels, cream cheese and jam. We were really making ourselves at home. I tried to avoid establishing the habit of eating a sweet every morning, but I couldn't resist the bagels. Boredom or lack of activity always invites me to overeat, and we certainly had a lot of time on our hands.

Reading had become very difficult for me. There were just too many things happening in that small room to be able to concentrate successfully. I had been reading *Still Life* by A.S. Byatt. I finished that and didn't bring another book to read. I did all my reading at home at night.

When we were called into the courtroom, Mr. Mounger continued his cross-examination of Ms. Tosti. She said that messages can be garbled from the buffer. She also said that officers can be disciplined for inappropriate use of words in their communications.

During Mr. Stone's cross-examination, Ms. Tosti said that personal messages are not monitored but the record is retained indefinitely. They are audited only for investigations.

The next prosecution witness was Mr. Byung Kukyun, who had worked for the city of Los Angeles for more than eight years for the Department of Information Services with computer systems. He said that messages from the MDTs are recorded only on magnetic tape. He testified that unless the message just sent is displayed on the MDT, the next message cannot be sent.

Mr. Mounger asked Mr. Kukyun if he had ever been out in the cars with the MDTs. He said he had not.

The significance of this witness was lost on me. I didn't know why they wanted us to know about the MDTs. It all seemed a little mysterious.

The next prosecution witness was Lieutenant Patrick Conmay, who was the Watch Commander at the Foothill Division, in charge of the entire station the night of the incident. Lieutenant Conmay said he monitored a radio broadcast at 12:50 a.m. so he knew that Sergeant Koon was at the scene. When Sergeant Koon returned about forty minutes later, he reported that they had backed up the CHP unit. He said that the driver had not complied with orders to get down on the ground, but that eventually he had. He said the driver had jumped up and charged at some of the officers, and he had used the Taser with little or no effect.

Lieutenant Conmay said that Sergeant Koon told him that the officers delivered a series of blows with their batons, but they were not effective. He said that he had directed the officers as to where they should deliver the blows. Sergeant Koon indicated that he felt the injuries were relatively minor, and that the driver had a split lip from striking the pavement while being swarmed.

"Did Sergeant Koon tell you that the suspect was on the ground when he was hit with baton blows?" Mr. Yochelson asked.

"No, he did not." Lieutenant Conmay said he assumed that Mr.

King was on his feet. "Sergeant Koon told me there was a combative, aggressive, violent suspect and these activities occurred as the person was resisting and being aggressive."

Under cross-examination by Mr. Stone, Lieutenant Conmay stated that he had met Sergeant Koon for the first time that night. He saw no medical reports at that time, just Sergeant Koon's observations that Mr. King was under the influence of PCP. He said he thought Mr. King should go to USC hospital because of the PCP. He felt he was a safety risk. Lieutenant Conmay said he never listened to the radio tape and never reviewed the reports.

Mr. White then questioned the next witness, Sergeant Robert Troutt of the Valley Traffic Division, who investigates traffic-related crimes. Sergeant Troutt's report was introduced into evidence.

Sergeant Troutt said that Mr. King was officially booked by telephone because he had been involved in an altercation where he received injuries and had to be transported to the hospital. He testified that the officers had not mentioned in the report that Mr. King was under the influence of alcohol or drugs.

The witness told Mr. Stone that a field supervisor was not available to go to Foothill that night for booking. He said that there was no conversation about PCP intoxication.

Mr. White next called Sergeant John Amott to the witness stand, who said that he had been on the day watch for the Valley Traffic Division and his job was to approve reports brought in for felony arrests. About 8 a.m. he received the report on Mr. King. The arrest report was submitted as Exhibit 304.

He said there had been no blood or urine samples taken from the suspect, because Mr. King was charged with felony evading, and intoxication had nothing to do with that charge. The prosecution seemed to be pointing out that if Rodney King was really on PCP, it was odd that nobody made sure that blood or urine samples were taken.

There were so many sidebars today that I kept track of how many there were. There had been eleven. While we waited for the attorneys to finish a sidebar conference, I looked at the audience. Officer Powell's father was usually sitting in the spectator section. I was sure that was who he was, because he looked so much like him, and there was a woman with him who must be Officer Powell's mother. There was another man who appeared to be Officer Briseno's brother, by his age and appearance.

I tried hard to neither like nor dislike the attorneys, because I didn't want my decision to be influenced by my personal feelings about them. But I couldn't help noticing some of their characteristics. Mr. DePasquale had a very deep voice and spoke very slowly and deliberately with almost no intonation. I thought that it was very effective for an attorney, not to speak so rapidly that someone might miss some of his meaning. He was the shortest of the attorneys, and I admired his direct manner of speaking.

Mike Stone was kind of the clown. He repeated things and irritated the judge. His questioning was a great deal more detailed, and took much longer than the other attorneys. He seemed to occupy the floor much more than the others did. His client was the one who had actually struck the most blows, and was most likely to be found guilty, so maybe he had more work to do than the others.

All of the attorneys, both defense and prosecution were very good speakers. I like to listen to a good speaker.

Terry White seemed to be given to theatrics. I thought that his explosions were intended to try to impress the jury, so perversely, I was not impressed.

TUESDAY, MARCH 17, 1992

St. Patrick's Day! The jurors all wore some touch of green, including me. I was wearing a green floral skirt.

Judge Weisberg said, "Well, I see you are all wearing green."

He never failed to say "Good morning" and "Good afternoon" to us. We would all chorus "Good morning," back to him, like a bunch of kindergartners.

The first prosecution witness was Mr. Ewing Kwock, an LAPD detective, robbery homicide. Mr. White questioned him about the reel-to-reel tape. He indicated that the time stamp on the second tape was not working that night. The last known transcription time was at 10:50:48 on master tape number three. He reconciled the time with his digital watch. There were errors in time on page four of the transcript. The corrected transcript was entered as Exhibit 28.

Mr. DePasquale questioned Mr. Kwock about parts of the tape

that were inaudible. Mr. Mounger cross-examined the witness about errors in the names of the streets. He said the reference to Sylmar Street should have been Fillmore Street.

When Mr. White questioned the witness in redirect, he said he thought it was Sylmar.

The last witness called for the prosecution was Detective Addison Arce of the LAPD robbery homicide division, who was an investigator in this case. His testimony just applied to Officers Briseno and Powell. The witness pointed out on the videotape Officer Briseno putting his foot on Mr. King, and Officer Powell speaking into a hand-held radio.

Under cross-examination by Mr. Barnett, the witness said the video showed other officers not charged in this case also putting their feet on Mr. King, particularly during the cuffing procedure.

The prosecution announced that this was their last witness. So far, we had heard testimony from twenty-one prosecution witnesses. There were several more exhibits introduced, including the boots confiscated from Officer Briseno's locker; a jacket, boots and a PR-24 baton recovered from Officer Powell's locker; boots recovered from Officer Wind's locker; and the Taser gun Sergeant Koon used.

There were so many stipulations that I wasn't able to note all of them. It was stipulated that a blood sample taken from Mr. King on March 3, 1991 was analyzed at 6:45 a.m., showing his blood alcohol level to be .086. It was also stipulated that Mr. King's blood alcohol level at 12:55 a.m. was .19. It was also stipulated that a urine sample taken at 6:30 a.m. showed no traces of PCP.

The jurors were excused close to noon with the usual admonitions by the judge and told to report back the next morning to start hearing testimony from the defense witnesses.

We had reached a milestone now, the end of the prosecution's case. I was surprised. I had expected more from the prosecution. I had certainly thought that Rodney King would testify. If I were the prosecutor, I would want the victim to say how much it hurt when they kicked him and beat him. Maybe he was just so drunk that he didn't even know that it hurt.

# Chapter Eight: The Other Side of the Story

It was time for the defense to begin presenting its side. Although I had been doing my best to keep an open mind, it was clear that a human being had been brutally beaten, and it was difficult to imagine any justification for that beating. As hard as I tried to remain impartial, I was fairly certain that these officers were guilty. I knew that it was their job to subdue a suspect, but at some point, those blows became excessive. I was eager to hear what the defense had to say. What could they possibly say? The evidence so far seemed to me to be so strong against them. I was curious about how they could explain it away. Maybe they couldn't.

The first defense witness was called by Mr. Mounger, Sergeant Koon's attorney. Kathleen Bosak was a paramedic who was called to Foothill and Osborne the night of the incident, examined Rodney King and put him on a gurney. She described him as being combative and uncooperative.

When Mr. Stone questioned the witness, she said she felt Mr. King was not hurt seriously enough to be transferred to a trauma center. She said that in the ambulance, Mr. King was spitting blood at the paramedics. Her partner told Mr. King to stop spitting blood, and finally he was placed in leather restraints.

Mr. DePasquale asked the witness who her partner was and she said his name was Cruz. She didn't know who the two LAPD police officers in the ambulance were. She said she cleaned Mr. King's face with a towel after he was put on the gurney. She said they had no red lights or sirens going on the vehicle on the way to the hospital, because they did not consider his condition serious. It took five to seven minutes for him to be transported and he fought the restraints on the gurney all the time. She said Mr. King was talking but she didn't know what he was saying.

Under cross-examination by Mr. White, she said that Mr. King had one cut on his right cheek, and was bleeding a little bit from the mouth. She did not observe the inside of his mouth. She said she did not think his injuries could have been caused by a baton blow.

She said that Mr. King appeared alert and oriented, not consistent with serious head injuries. Mr. Stone asked whether it was unusual to pick up a suspect who was hog-tied, and she said no, hog-tying is used for combative suspects who are a danger to others.

I thought that Ms. Bosak was a believable witness, but I didn't think that her testimony had much significance. It seemed to center around whether or not there was any dirt in Rodney King's wounds. I guess that being hit with a baton wouldn't cause dirt in the wounds, while falling hard on his face would. But he could also get dirt in his wounds when he was lying on the ground hog-tied, after he was hit.

Mr. Mounger's second witness was LAPD Officer Susan J. Clemmer, who testified that she and her partner, Officer Tim Blake, were called to the pursuit, and that she diverted traffic from the intersection.

She said that Officer Powell told her, "I was scared. I thought I was going to have to shoot him."

She told Mr. Mounger that Sergeant Koon had directed her to ride in the ambulance, along with Officer Wind, and she heard Mr. King say to Sergeant Koon, "I love you."

To me, that proved that he was drunk.

During Mr. DePasquale's questioning, Officer Clemmer stated that in the ambulance Mr. King was spitting blood on her legs and shoes. She asked him not to do it, but he laughed and continued to spit blood. She said that Officer Wind was also in the ambulance and that there was no joking and no bragging.

Mr. Stone asked her more about what Officer Powell had told her about being scared, and she said he was out of breath and said, "This guy threw me off his back. I thought I was going to have to shoot him." She testified that Mr. King was laughing; that he said "Fuck you," four or five times. She said he had a blank stare and a cut by his mouth, but he did not appear to be in pain. She did not observe the officers taunt Mr. King.

During Mr. White's cross-examination, Officer Clemmer said she did not see anyone strike Mr. King with a baton. She said she did not know if the spitting was intentional. She said that Mr. King was bleeding from the mouth and cheek and that no one was attending to his injuries in the ambulance. She also testified that after the hog-ties were removed at the hospital, Mr. King was cooperative.

The jury was dismissed for the day with the usual caution about keeping ourselves removed from other opinions about the case. I believe that it was right about at this point in the trial when the judge started adding to his remarks each day that we were not to form an opinion. It was too late for me. At this point, I was firmly convinced of the guilt of the officers, at least Powell and Koon. I had some doubt about Briseno and Wind. But after that, I made myself keep an open mind, and just tried to absorb the testimony and reserve my judgment. I really feel I was successful in that attempt. However, I believe that a phenomenon occurs in jury trials. You may consciously prevent yourself from forming an opinion, while your subconscious is busily forming the opinion for you.

THURSDAY MARCH 19, 1992

Mr. Mounger called LAPD Officer David Anthony Love, who testified that when he and his partner, Paul Gebhardt, arrived, Mr. King was on his feet and seemed to be charging one of the officers. He had already been tased, and had Taser wires hanging from his clothing. Officer Love said that the officer struck Mr. King in the front torso with a power stroke of his baton, in a strike that Officer Love considered consistent with proper LAPD procedure.

He saw Mr. King being hit two to four times, while he was busy watching the passengers at the rear of the suspect's car. He said that during the course of the arrest, he had placed his foot on Mr. King.

During Mr. Stone's examination, Officer Love said that he had used only necessary force when he stepped on Mr. King's shoulder. During Mr. DePasquale's examination, the witness demonstrated how close Mr. King was to the officer who struck him. Then Mr. Barnett questioned him and asked him to put his hand on his own shoulder at the point where he had placed his foot on Mr. King's shoulder.

When Mr. White cross-examined Officer Love, he asked if he had been served lunch while he was waiting in the defense waiting room at the courthouse. He asked him if there had been a Foothill Division reunion at lunchtime. The question sounded sarcastic, as though Mr. White was implying that Officer Love was backing up the defendants out of loyalty or because he got a free lunch. This prompted a sidebar conference.

It seemed to be a ploy of Mr. White's, to make it look like the police officers were all getting together and ganging up to get the others off. Officers do stick together. They aren't alone in that. There's nothing wrong with loyalty. That doesn't mean that they would deliberately lie.

The witness agreed with Mr. White that in his grand jury testimony he had said that Mr. King was struck in the side, and that he had staggered.

When Mr. Stone examined the witness, he was asked if he was slanting his testimony for anyone, and Officer Love said, "No."

"You wouldn't do that for a roast beef sandwich, would you?" Mr. Stone asked.

"No," Officer Love replied.

He also told Mr. Stone that before he appeared before the grand jury, he had only viewed the video four or five times, and that after that, he had viewed it about twenty times. He testified that the blows delivered by Officer Powell did not strike Mr. King on his face or head.

The witness told Mr. Barnett that the other officers had a better opportunity to see Mr. King than he did, as he was about two car lengths' distance from the scene. Mr. Mounger and Mr. Stone questioned the witness again about his position at the scene and his subpoena from the District Attorney for the grand jury investigation. Then Mr. White asked Officer Love if his memory was better when the defense was questioning him than when the prosecution questioned him. He also referred to the inconsistencies in Officer Love's current testimony and his grand jury testimony.

The next witness was Sergeant Stacey Koon. This was the first time we had heard one of the defendants speak, and it was good to hear it from the horse's mouth, so to speak.

Sergeant Koon was wearing a black suit and a red-striped tie and seemed extremely self-assured. He testified that he had been a police officer for fourteen years, and had two master's degrees: one in criminal justice and one in public administration. He said he didn't attend roll call the night of March 3, 1991. When he arrived on the scene, he positioned his car at a 45-degree angle from Mr. King's car. He said that Mr. King was on his knees by the open door and that he was upright. He observed that Mr. King was very muscular or "buffed out." His initial thought was that Mr. King was probably an ex-convict, because many prisoners work out a lot while incarcerated.

Mr. King was swaying back and forth and side to side, and perspiring a great deal. He put his hands on the ground and began to pat the ground. He went down and came back up again, all the while being given commands to lie down. Sergeant Koon said that he made eye contact with Mr. King while giving him commands, but that Mr. King had a blank stare in his eyes. Sergeant Koon got his Taser gun from the car.

At this time CHP Officer Melanie Singer was approaching Mr. King with a drawn gun. Sergeant Koon said he ordered her to stop. Mr. King was in sort of a starting block position, Sergeant Koon said, and talking "gibberish."

Sergeant Koon spoke with an air of authority and sounded well-educated and articulate. But he mispronounced "gibberish" as if he had seen the word written and knew what it meant, but had never heard it pronounced. He repeated the mispronunciation several times and no one corrected him.

Sergeant Koon said he directed his officers to flank Mr. King. At the time, Sergeant Koon only knew who one officer was and that was Officer Powell. He said that Officer Powell took Mr. King's left arm, and another officer, who he now knows was Officer Briseno, took his right arm. The two other officers who took Mr. King's legs he now knows were Officers Wind and Solano, he said.

The officers were attempting to pull Mr. King's arms behind his back to handcuff him. Mr. King fell flat-faced into the asphalt. Officer Powell had his knees on Mr. King's back, and got his handcuffs out. All of a sudden, Mr. King's arms came out, he swayed to the left, then swayed to the right and Officer Powell was thrown off on his behind, and Officer Briseno was struggling to get away.

At this time, Sergeant Koon concluded that it was a possibility that Mr. King was on PCP, because of his "Hulk-like" strength, his blank stare and his "gibberish," which he said were all traits he had come to associate with PCP intoxication. He ordered the officers to back away and he tased Mr. King. The taser darts hit him in the back and shoulder. Sergeant Koon said that it is not necessary for the darts to pierce the skin to be effective.

Sergeant Koon testified that Mr. King emitted a "bear-like" yell, but continued to rise. Sergeant Koon said that often the Taser gun will not work on a PCP intoxicated person or persons with a psychotic or nervous disorder.

Mr. King continued to rise and turned 180 degrees toward Sergeant Koon, who told him if he did not get down on the ground he would tase him again. Mr. King did not comply, so Sergeant Koon tased him once more. Mr. King groaned again and let out another yell like a wounded animal. Sergeant Koon said Mr. King seemed to be overcoming the Taser shots.

Mr. Mounger asked Sergeant Koon about the grip of a PCP suspect and Sergeant Koon said that it was a "policeman's nightmare," that you could not break the grip of a PCP intoxicated person. You could break his arm, but still not break his grip. He said the fear was that such a person could grab your gun.

Sergeant Koon said he was able to talk Mr. King into going down to the ground again. He told Mr. Mounger that this was the point at which the incident started to be recorded on Mr. Holliday's videotape. Sergeant Koon went through the entire video, giving his impression of the activities. He used a wooden pointer as he narrated.

He said that although Mr. King had several avenues of escape, he charged Officer Powell. Officer Powell struck Mr. King in the right shoulder. Mr. King went down, landing on his side. He hit his head on the ground, and Sergeant Koon pointed out on the video where Mr. King's head bounced up. Mr. King started to rise again, and Officer Powell delivered a series of blows.

Sergeant Koon said he told him, "Don't hit him in the head."

Mr. Mounger asked the witness if he felt at any time before he was subdued that Mr. King was defenseless and Sergeant Koon replied, "No."

He said the fact that Mr. King had not been searched for a weapon and had received a torrent of blows without succumbing, combined with the risk involved with a pursuit and a stop at that hour, the size of the suspect, and the possibility of PCP intoxication, had all led him to believe that Mr. King was not defenseless. He also told Mr. Mounger that all of the officers' activities were perfectly within LAPD policy and procedures.

"This was a managed and controlled use of force. It followed the policies of the LAPD and the training," he said.

Sergeant Koon then went through the video, pointing out positions of Mr. King and the threat that he perceived Mr. King posed to the officers. He told Mr. Mounger that when Mr. King said, "Please stop," he ordered the officers to handcuff him. He concluded that the blows used were "valid and practical" to control a combative and aggressive suspect.

He said that he perceived that Officer Powell was exasperated and in fear of his life.

I thought that Sergeant Koon was a good witness. He was clear and believable. It was the first time we had actually heard a complete, detailed account of what happened.

Mr. Yochelson then asked questions of the witness. Sergeant Koon said that he felt he was in charge of all the officers there, and that he assumed responsibility for the use of force, which he felt was "reasonable and necessary." He said that he felt the LAPD policies and procedures parallel the law.

Mr. Yochelson quoted the Sergeant's Daily Report stating that Sergeant Koon had perceived PCP intoxication "immediately."

Mr. Yochelson asked Sergeant Koon if he did not think it appeared on the video that Mr. King might be trying to run past Officer Powell, rather than charging at him. Sergeant Koon did not perceive that. He also said that the LAPD teaches that officers should hit somebody until they comply. He said that he saw Officer Briseno move toward Officer Powell on the video, but that he did not see it at the time.

He said he thought Mr. King reached for a weapon in his waistband, but he conceded that when seen in slow motion, the video proved that Mr. King's hand was actually going behind him, palm up.

"And Mr. King is moving his hands back in compliance with what you asked?" Mr. Yochelson asked.

"On the video, yes," Sergeant Koon admitted. He told Mr. Yochelson that he saw no head blows. He said Officer Wind struck Mr. King in the lower right back area but not in the spine. LAPD teaches officers to stay away from the spine and head, he said.

The jury was dismissed with the usual admonitions.

Mr. Yochelson continued his cross examination of Sergeant Koon, asking if Mr. King was ever in the felony prone position. Sergeant Koon replied that he was not.

Sergeant Koon demonstrated Officer Powell's baton blow to Mr. King.

When asked about the entry in the Sergeant's Daily Report about taking over the case from the CHP, Sergeant Koon said he believed the CHP officers implied they wanted the LAPD to take over.

Mr. Yochelson also questioned what the report meant about the "Taser going the entire time." Sergeant Koon said the Taser only operates fifteen seconds at a time, but he thought that anyone reading the report would understand.

Sergeant Koon testified that he hesitated to use a chokehold even though he felt that deadly force might have to be used. Under questioning by Mr. Yochelson, Sergeant Koon explained that the LAPD had banned using it except for certain circumstances, because some black suspects had died after being subdued with a chokehold.

"So you would have done him a favor by shooting him?" Mr. Yochelson asked sarcastically.

Many people in the courtroom gasped.

"No, sir. I personally would have applied a chokehold to Mr. King prior to ordering him to be shot. I, personally. I wouldn't have delegated that to any officer," Sergeant Koon said.

Mr. Yochelson played the entire video again, in 25 percent slow motion. Sergeant Koon insisted that the force used was both reasonable and necessary.

"In your years of experience have you ever seen a worse beating?" Mr. Yochelson asked.

"I have not seen anything as violent as this in my fourteen and a half years, no sir," Sergeant Koon said.

Under Mr. Mounger's questioning, the witness said that from the first blow to the end of the videotape was only eighty-one seconds.

Sergeant Koon's testimony had a definite impact on me. It was the first time that I had seriously considered the officers' perceptions and their possible fears. It was also significant that Sergeant Koon had said it was an unusually violent encounter. Up to this point, there was question in my mind as to the amount of violence police officers normally use when faced with a resistant suspect. There was still doubt in my mind, but at least I had some frame of reference.

Sergeant Koon's testimony was a turning point for me. I was starting to be convinced that the police had done what they had to do.

The next witness called by Mr. Mounger was LAPD Officer Ingrid Larson, who certainly did not look like a law enforcement officer. She was young and had a very long, feminine hairdo. I wondered what she might do with all that hair if she was in a fracas. Maybe she did not wear it loose and flowing when she was on duty. She probably was wearing it that way just because she was in court. If I had all that long, beautiful hair and was going to appear on national television, I probably would wear it that way, too.

The night of the Rodney King incident was Officer Larson's sixth day out of the Los Angeles Police Academy, and when she got there, Mr. King was on his knees on the ground. She said she had been taught not to hit a suspect in the head, and to avoid the kidney area if possible. She said she knew nothing about a swarm technique.

Mr. DePasquale questioned the witness, then Mr. White cross-examined. She said she did not see Mr. King kick, hit or scratch anyone. Mr. White brought up something about a meeting of the Police Protective League that she had attended a few days later. That prompted an objection and another sidebar conference.

The witness told Mr. Mounger that she did not participate in the incident because she was new.

I really didn't take anything Officer Larson said very seriously. She was just there to observe and hadn't really taken part. She wasn't an experienced officer, so it didn't matter what she thought about it, as far as I was concerned.

The next witness for Mr. Mounger was Officer Larson's partner, Joseph Napolitano, who had been an LAPD officer for seven years. He said that they had gone to where the pursuit ended, that there was a helicopter above, and that he could not see outside the area of light shed by the helicopter. He said he had gone to the scene because he wanted Officer Larson to see what was happening, for training purposes for her.

Under questioning from Mr. DePasquale, Officer Napolitano said he had seen about six or seven blows, and he wasn't certain how many of them were struck by Officer Wind.

He testified that Officer Briseno had asked him if he had a Taser. He said he did not have one, but he participated in handcuffing Mr. King, by holding him while other officers handcuffed him.

Officer Napolitano said he had never been trained in the swarm technique, which prompted another sidebar. Further questioning of the witness by Mr. Stone revealed that Officer Napolitano had been taught never to "tie up" with a suspect; never to get in hand-to-hand combat or get into a physical confrontation with one, especially if there was reason to believe he was on PCP. He said that after Mr. King was in handcuffs, he appeared to be laughing.

While being cross-examined by Mr. Barnett, Officer Napolitano testified that Officer Briseno had run up to him, excited and yelling.

The witness was questioned next by Mr. White, who asked him if he had ever heard of "stick time." An objection was raised by the defense counsel, and another sidebar conference lasted until 4:58 p.m., when court was recessed for the day and the week.

While the week had been particularly stressful in court, the gin rummy games continued during breaks and lunches in the law library. Now there was something new going on. One of the alternate jurors had been trying to find someone to play bridge. Since she could not find any experienced bridge players, she finally convinced several people to let her teach them.

She appeared to subscribe to the "idle hands" adage, because when she wasn't overseeing the bridge games, she always had some project going. For a few days, she brought some flyers about the summer's happenings in her small city, and enlisted the aid of all of us to paste a correction on one line and to fold them for distribution.

One of the regular jurors was trying to drum up support to buy gifts for the deputies whose duty it was to guard us and escort us. She thought that we should buy some token of appreciation to give them after the trial was over, and she lobbied for this for several days. Several of the jurors, including me, questioned whether this was a good idea. We thought that it might give the appearance of impropriety. She talked about it off and on, but finally she gave up trying to persuade the rest of us.

It was not the first time that I had been annoyed with this particular woman for trying to instigate something. I'd had my reservations about Juror Number 10, because he seemed so weird, but who am I to say that he would not make a good juror? It had irritated me when this woman took it upon herself to send the note to the judge about him.

A lot of us had coughs and colds during the trial, but she was a smoker, and she coughed a lot. She sent Mary, the female bailiff, out to get her a glass of water when she coughed in the courtroom. Everyone in the room watched as Mary brought the glass over and handed it to her. She seemed to enjoy being the center of attention.

MONDAY, MARCH 23, 1992

Mr. White continued his cross-examination of Officer Napolitano, who repeated that he had gone to the scene especially for a training experience for his partner. He said that he observed about six or seven strikes in the legs and the side of Mr. King's lower back by Officers Powell and Wind, but he did not see any kicks.

He testified that in his opinion, the suspect was under the influence of PCP. He thought a second pair of handcuffs should be put on Mr. King, because some PCP suspects break their restraints. He told Mr. White that he had participated in three prior PCP arrests. He said that sometimes PCP users take their clothes off. But he admitted that he had detected no PCP odor on Mr. King.

The witness was then questioned again by Mr. Stone, who showed him Exhibit 319, a training bulletin. There was a nine-minute sidebar. It was something about a cartoon that the prosecution didn't want the jury to see. It had to do with the strength of a person under the influence of PCP.

When they came back from the sidebar, Mr. Stone asked the witness to tell the jury what "sherms" were. He said they were cigarettes dipped in liquid PCP, and then smoked. There would be an odor on a suspect's breath if he smoked them. It wasn't clear to me whether they were implying that Rodney King had smoked sherms or not. My mind was not made up that he had done anything other than consume alcohol, which he obviously had.

The witness testified that a baton is used to inflict pain and to immobilize by breaking bones, and that a carotid hold would render someone unconscious and is considered deadly force. He told Mr.

Mounger that a policeman is concerned first with his own safety, second with the safety of his partner, third with the safety of the public, and fourth with the safety of the suspect.

When it was Mr. DePasquale's turn, he came back to the topic of sherms, asking the witness to give an example of "peak" time when smoking sherms. Officer Napolitano said that if you just took a couple of puffs it would peak out about fifteen minutes later. He also said that it can be stored in your fatty tissue and you can get a flashback later.

Since five and sometimes six attorneys got a chance to ask questions, it was not unusual for one lawyer to ask a few questions on a topic, move on to something else, and then for another lawyer to follow up.

Mr. Stone, citing a hypothetical situation where a suspect had been tased and showed evidence of intent to flee, asked the witness if use of the baton would be justified. The witness said it would be justified.

I was impressed with Officer Napolitano. He seemed to be intent on telling the truth, no matter who it favored, or who it hurt.

The jury was excused for lunch and told to return at 1:30 p.m., but like many other days, we were not called back until 3:20 p.m. More time for the card games and visiting.

When we were finally called back in the courtroom for the short time that remained in the day, Mr. Mounger called his next witness, LAPD Sergeant Charles Duke Jr., a member of the celebrated SWAT team, short for Special Weapons and Tactics team, which the LAPD used sometimes in hostage or other emergency situations.

Sergeant Duke was also an instructor at the police academy, and said he had received ninety commendations for bravery. He testified as an expert in the use of force.

Mr. Mounger asked Sergeant Duke to explain the various levels of the use of force—verbalization, firm grip, batons and kicks, and deadly force. He commented that police officers should use the firm grip level only when they have stature advantage. He testified on the practice of escalating force, stopping to evaluate, and de-escalating if the situation calls for de-escalation. If an officer uses the baton, he should stay at that degree of force until it works. He said that the baton is used to break bones, to incapacitate the suspect. "This sounds cruel, but it may come to the point where you must break a bone or so incapacitate a person that he cannot rise."

Once again I was hearing, and this time from an expert, that the police are trained to break bones on purpose. Again, this was very shocking. But it did tell me that it was possible for an officer to beat a suspect very badly, even breaking his bones, and not be in violation of the policy.

Sergeant Duke said he supported Sergeant Koon's actions in ordering Officer Melanie Singer to put her gun away. "It would be almost suicidal to approach a suspect with a gun in your hand. It is inviting disaster."

He also supported the officers' perception that Mr. King was under the influence of PCP, and said the LAPD's Use of Force bulletin did not authorize the use of the swarm procedure.

Sergeant Duke was taken through the video. It was his opinion that Mr. King was not hit in the head. He also stated that he saw nothing in the video that was outside the policies and procedures of the LAPD. He said that when an officer is attacked, he should take all precautions to prevent the suspect from getting to his feet.

"Looking at the videotape in its entirety, do you see anything that is outside the training and policies of the Los Angeles Police Department?" Mr. Mounger asked.

"No, I do not," Sergeant Duke answered.

We saw the videotape so often that we began to become inured to it. Every once in a while I would stop and remind myself that I was watching the beating of a human being. I didn't want to get used to it.


TUESDAY, MARCH 24, 1992

Mr. Mounger continued his questioning of Sergeant Duke, who cited other methods of controlling a suspect which were not available to the police officers the night of the incident. He said that if they had been allowed to use nets, leg grabbers or the chokehold, most of the baton blows would not have been necessary.

Mr. Barnett was next to question the witness on behalf of Officer Briseno. During this testimony, the burly sergeant demonstrated the proper and improper way to use the baton. He said that he believed

Officer Powell struck Mr. King in the upper chest area. This opinion was based partially on the fact that the video shows no backward movement of Mr. King's head. He said that a baton blow would not necessarily leave a mark.

Sergeant Duke was questioned next by Mr. Stone and again said that he did not believe the blow by Officer Powell landed on Mr. King's head. He also said that he believed that some of the swings of the baton seen on the video did not actually result in blows. He talked about the fatigue factor involved. When an officer is fatigued, he will not be able to function properly.

Sergeant Duke was again shown the chart listing the steps of use of force escalation accepted by the LAPD. He said that the sergeant at the scene determines the actions taken, and the officers' perceptions of force needed affects the actions.

Mr. DePasquale questioned Sergeant Duke about alternative tools, such as leg grabbers, nets and Velcro blankets. He repeated that the LAPD considered the carotid hold, or the chokehold, an improper use of force.

When Mr. White cross-examined, Sergeant Duke told him that if a blow was deliberately made to the head, it would constitute deadly force. He also defined "combative" as "the use of force against you or getting into a position to use force against you." He defined "aggressive" as "when an officer has been attacked and the officer has defended himself against the attack." Mr. White cited Exhibit 41, a Use of Force Guidelines training bulletin, as saying that the baton should not be used in the absence of combative or aggressive behavior.

The jury was excused for the day. It had been colder than a witch's thorax in the courtroom today and was to be that way every day of the trial thereafter. I suspect that the warmer temperature was not keeping the jury alert enough to suit the judge, particularly in the afternoon. He must have ordered the bailiffs to lower the thermostat, because from this day forward, all of the jurors either wore or carried a sweater or a wrap of some kind to ward off the chill.

The temperature in the law library was warm enough that the wraps came off there and had to be located and put on again each time we were called into court. I believe, also, that the cold courtroom caused the judge and eventually the attorneys, to catch colds.

*Moral Uncertainty*

Sergeant Duke was questioned again by Mr. Mounger. He said that in 1984 he had conversations with superiors in the department and had expressed concern about the tools officers were limited to using when subduing suspects.

Mr. Stone had the witness cite the Use Of Force Guidelines about the use of the baton for compliance with verbal commands. The point was clearly being made that use of the baton to subdue a suspect is in accordance with LAPD policy.

The next witness for Mr. Mounger was LAPD Police Officer Danny Shry. He testified that he went to the scene to impound the vehicle. When he got there, the Unified School District officer had his gun out and pointed at two individuals on the ground. Officer Shry said that he handcuffed Mr. Allen and the CHP officer handcuffed Mr. Helms.

Officer Shry said he was about twenty feet from Mr. King, and that his view was somewhat obstructed by the amber lights. He said Mr. King was crouched with his knees bent. He demonstrated the position.

He said that the first blow by Officer Powell landed in Mr. King's chest and left arm area. He said there were then a series of back and forth strokes, probably three or four. The second time he noticed Mr. King, he was rising. Again, Officer Powell delivered a series of power strokes to the buttocks and legs. He heard someone say, "Hit his legs" and "Get down, get down." He said the Taser had been deployed.

When Mr. Stone examined the witness, Officer Shry told him he had been trained not to hit a suspect in the head. He also testified that the Taser was not making any noise.

The next witness called by Mr. Mounger was Sergeant Agnes Brenda Gordon, who had the a.m. watch the night of the incident. She testified that she did not leave the station to attend the pursuit because she was working on an overdue audit. I wasn't certain what the significance was of her testimony.

Mr. Mounger's last witness in defense of Sergeant Koon was retired LAPD Captain Robert Michael, who walked with a cane, held a Ph.D. and had retired in June 1990. He was offered by the defense as an expert, and spent nearly thirty minutes citing his experience in use of force matters. He had published two books. I was quite impressed with his credentials and he was very logical in his testimony.

Captain Michael said he had viewed the tape at his home more than one hundred times, some portions more than three hundred times. He observed ten separate uses of force, with the officers de-escalating and evaluating. He said that it took many viewings of the video for him to put it all together. He said his opinion was based on the video and nothing else.

In answer to Mr. Barnett's question, he said the beating seemed brutal to him but that he had concluded that Mr. King was a credible threat to the officers and that the use of force was proper.

Court was adjourned for the day.

# Chapter Nine: More From the Defense

Mr. Barnett questioned Captain Michael about the portion of the video that dealt with his client, Officer Briseno. Hypothetically, Mr. Barnett asked, if Mr. King was not a threat or being aggressive, would the blows have been inappropriate? The witness said the blows would have been inappropriate if the suspect had been non-combative and non-aggressive.

"Assume that Mr. King at this point is not attempting to get up, would these blows be appropriate or inappropriate?" Mr. Barnett asked.

"Inappropriate if there was no effort to get up or resist," Captain Michael said.

"Then the appropriateness of the baton blows would depend on whether there was a perception that Mr. King was a threat?" Mr. Barnett asked.

"Yes," Captain Michael replied.

He said that the PR-24 side handle baton was intended to be an impact weapon, not a deadly weapon, but that it can become a deadly weapon in certain circumstances. When questioned about the Taser, the witness said that Taser darts are propelled high and low and it is not necessary for the darts to pierce the skin.

Mr. White cross-examined, asking several questions about the witness's resume. He said that he had been promoted to captain in 1980 during a leave of absence to obtain his Ph.D. He said that he went off duty in September 1982 after he was injured and never went back, retiring in June 1990. Mr. White made the point that for the last eight years of Captain Michael's service, he was not on active duty. Captain Michael responded that he carried a gun and a badge during that time. Under questioning from Mr. White about the nature of his disability, he stated that he was suffering from gastrointestinal problems and hypertension.

All the while Mr. White questioned this witness, he frequently called him "Mister" and then each time changed it to "Captain." It was obvious to me that Mr. White was trying to negate or reduce the credibility of the witness by not using his honorary title.

It annoyed me. I thought, "Okay, you've made the point that you don't think he deserves to be called Captain."

The witness was questioned by Mr. Mounger, Mr. Stone and Mr. Barnett about fatigue and the use of force. The witness said that it was well known that if fatigued, the officers can escalate force.

Mr. White again questioned Captain Michael, who said that fatigue, by itself, is not justification for escalating to a higher force. That concluded Captain Michael's testimony and all of the witnesses for Mr. Mounger on behalf of Sergeant Koon.

Mr. Stone started his defense of Officer Powell by calling LAPD Officer Louis Turriaga, who was assigned to the Foothill Division on March 3, 1991, and rode from the station that night to the scene at Foothill and Osborne, with Officer Gebhardt driving.

"I saw Officer Powell standing next to Mr. King with his baton raised, and I saw Mr. King in the asphalt on his knees, forearms and hands," Officer Turriaga said. "What I saw next was Mr. King making a lunging motion and Officer Powell doing a forward and reverse power stroke in the direction of Mr. King."

He heard the Taser and the helicopter and heard someone say, "He stopped moving. Cuff him." Officer Turriaga said he came within about two feet of Mr. King with the intent to handcuff him, but someone produced cord cuffs and someone said twice, "Put your hands behind your back." After the handcuffing, he moved Mr. King from his position to the side of the road. He remarked that Mr. King was heavy. He moved him approximately seven feet. He said Mr. King was lifted, not dragged.

He said that when Officer Powell requested the rescue ambulance unit, he was not breathing normally, that his breathing was labored.

Under questioning from Mr. DePasquale, Officer Turriaga testified that during the tasing there was a sound from Mr. King like a throaty groan. He said that after the first forward and reverse power strokes, Sergeant Koon said, "Put your hands behind your back." After the second power strokes, he heard nothing, no shouting. Then Sergeant Koon said, "Get an ambulance."

The jury was then dismissed for the day. Today had been a very busy court day. We did have a little time to play cards, however.

Mr. Barnett began his questioning of Officer Turriaga, who said his attention had been on Mr. King that night. He said approximately five or six officers moved in to cuff Mr. King. He also said the Taser was going the entire time.

When he looked at the video, he couldn't locate the blows he had described and said he could not find himself in the video.

When Mr. Mounger questioned Officer Turriaga, he testified that he had been taught the swarm, that each person should grab hold of an appendage.

Mr. White then questioned the witness, who told him that he heard Officer Powell calling for an ambulance, heard no laughing or chuckling, and that he heard nothing about PCP or "dusted" and did not see any injuries on Mr. King. He said he did not see Mr. King's face.

He also told Mr. White that he and two other officers carried Mr. King to the side of the road, but he could not identify any of those officers on the tape. When he listened to the audio tape, he said it sounded like Officer Powell talking.

The witness told Mr. Stone that seeing the video did not refresh his memory of what happened at the scene. He told Mr. Stone that he was interviewed by investigators before he saw the video and that his answers did not change after he saw it. He said the video did not depict what he saw at the scene. In the fuzzy part of the video Mr. King seems to be in the positions he recalls, except it seems backward. He testified that from the time he arrived until he moved Mr. King seemed to be about thirty-five seconds.

When Mr. DePasquale asked the witness where he learned about the swarm, he could not recall.

Mr. Stone's next witness was Officer Rolando Solano, who was with Officer Briseno, his secondary training officer, the night of the incident. Officer Solano was a very physically attractive man. He was hard to miss. In fact, there were many comments about his appearance after his testimony, particularly by the younger female jurors and alternates.

Officer Solano said that Mr. King was in the process of getting out of the car when they arrived. There were two officers with guns drawn, and there were sirens on. He testified that Officer Briseno yelled to turn off the siren. He also heard other officers yelling, "Step away from the car. Keep your hands up. Get down." The commands were very clear, he said.

He said Mr. King's hands fluctuated slowly from his head to his waist. The commands were for him to get in a felony prone position. At that time, the witness said he drew his gun and put his finger on the trigger. He said he held his gun in a low, ready position.

He testified that Mr. King stepped away from the vehicle and went down to his knees, with his hands spread out. He said that Sergeant Koon and the CHP officer started to move toward Mr. King. Mr. King then went down on his knees and hands and when the officers approached, he went back up to his knees.

Sergeant Koon then said, "If you don't start doing what you are told I am going to zap you."

Officer Solano said Mr. King had a crazed, hostile stare. Mr. King, he said, was a very large, strong man, and he finally went into a somewhat prone position. At that time, a group of officers ran toward Mr. King. The witness said that he also ran toward him, and held down his left leg in the calf area. Mr. King's arms were beginning to be placed behind his back and there was a struggle. Mr. King's arms were going backward and forward. The witness said that an officer was thrown off Mr. King's back. He testified that it all occurred very quickly.

He heard Sergeant Koon's command, "Back off. Get out of the way." Mr. King's arms were fluctuating. He jumped away from Mr. King's leg and heard the popping sound of the Taser. Mr. King was on the ground "kinda shaking."

Officer Solano said he backed off and watched. He was greatly concerned when Mr. King got up despite having just been shot with fifty thousand volts. He said Mr. King made kind of a moaning sound and then lunged in the direction of Sergeant Koon. Officer Powell stepped in and began to deliver a series of backward and forward baton strokes. Solano said he drew his baton, but did not use it. Officer Powell was facing Mr. King, who seemed to be flailing his arms. He thought the blows were striking high on Mr. King's shoulder. He said he saw a blow striking the left side of Mr. King's face off his shoulder. He said there were two blows within the same flurry, one stroke touched Mr. King's face twice: the right side and

*Moral Uncertainty*

left side.

Officer Solano expressed the opinion that these blows were deflected and that Officer Powell was not deliberately aiming for Mr. King's head. He said that he was trying to maneuver himself into a position to take out the legs.

"I didn't like what I saw, so I focused my attention to try to take out the legs," Officer Solano said. "I didn't like the sound that the baton made. I'd never heard that sound before."

I felt that Officer Solano's testimony about the deflected head blows was significant. This testimony, if accepted as true, would create doubt in my mind about deliberate blows to the head by Officer Powell. Maybe the facial injuries were a result of deflected blows rather than direct hits.

After Officer Solano's testimony, we took the lunch recess. We had gotten weary of the interminable time spent waiting and had asked if we could go for a walk, at least during the ninety-minute lunch recess. The bailiffs started letting us spend most of the lunch period in the auditorium, where we could walk or jog to music and do the Hokey Pokey.

I had taught the bailiff, Jerry, to do the jitterbug and one of the male jurors, had given us all waltz lessons. Today, however, we added something new. One of the jurors taught us to do the Electric Slide. It was a line dance and a lot of fun and good exercise.

After the noon recess, Mr. Stone called a witness out of order. He was Dr. Dallas Long III, medical director of Hoag Memorial Hospital in Newport Beach, California. He was a very large man, very imposing in appearance and after the trial was over, I learned that he had been a well-known football player in his youth.

Dr. Long said that blunt force trauma resulted from a focal application of force, or the use of a blunt instrument to inflict injury, but said that it could be from a fall rather than an instrument. He testified that he had reviewed Mr. King's medical records from Pacifica Hospital and USC Medical Center, including a CAT scan and an MRI. He cited the names of three neurologists, one dentist and four surgeons whose names appeared on the records as having treated Mr. King.

He said Mr. King had surgery for fractures of the face. He demonstrated with a skull provided by Mr. Stone the areas of the face where the fractures occurred. He pointed out areas of the facial fractures on photographs of X-rays of Mr. King's face. He also pointed out a leg fracture, which he identified as a single fracture with many components. He said it was five to six centimeters in length. He said the fracture was minimally displaced.

Dr. Long said it was most likely that Mr. King's facial injuries were produced as a result of his face striking against a broad surface. He said the facial fractures were significant, of the type usually seen in a motor vehicle accident. When he was allowed to hold the baton and examine it, he said it was highly unlikely that the facial fractures were a result of a baton blow.

Shown photographs of Mr. King's injuries, Dr. Long testified that there were no injuries to the left side of Mr. King's head or to his hands. Nothing in the photographs was inconsistent with his opinions, he said. He pointed out that there was a superficial abrasion under Mr. King's right nipple that was a few days old because it was scabbed. He had no opinion about the possibility that the Taser dart caused that abrasion. He said there was a marked elevation of CPK, an enzyme associated with a diffuse injury to the skeletal muscle. He said it was most likely from the use of the Taser.

In reply to Mr. DePasquale's questions about physical signs of PCP ingestion, Dr. Long said there was usually a lack of sensitivity to pain, an exertion of physical prowess or strength, changes in blood pressure, and profuse salivation. He also said that there would be mood changes from low to euphoria and a feeling of invulnerability.

Under questioning by Mr. Barnett, Dr. Long said it was likely a single event that caused the facial fractures, but physics of the injury was not his area of expertise.

Mr. Yochelson, the prosecutor, cross-examined Dr. Long about his areas of expertise. Dr. Long said he was not an oral surgeon and that he was not an expert in the treatment of maxillofacial traumas.

So now we had heard from two doctors, one who said that the facial injuries were caused by the batons and the other who said they were caused by a fall. Both were believable, so didn't that mean there was a reasonable doubt about which was true?

Mr. Yochelson continued his examination of Dr. Dallas Long III, who advanced two theories of the facial injury, again saying that he was not a biophysics expert. The first was that there were two separate linear vectors (applications of force), one laterally and one frontally. The second was that there was one single application of force with Mr. King's head rotating or coming down again. His preference of the choices was the single application of force because of soft tissue injury that would have occurred with the two vector theory.

He also testified that there was skin injury present in the leg fracture, which was not inconsistent with a blow from a baton.

Dr. Long told Mr. Yochelson that he did not have access to the CT or MRI X-rays that would show more details of the injuries. When asked about PCP, the doctor said it had been about eight to ten years since he had seen someone under the influence of PCP. He said that Mr. King's CPK enzyme level was very high.

In redirect examination by Mr. Stone, the witness said he was still of the opinion that it was a broad flat surface, not a baton, that caused Mr. King's facial injury. He also told Mr. Stone that PCP causes the user to have excessive strength. It reduces the feedback mechanism, reduces muscle contraction, and the pain mechanism is anesthetized. Mr. Stone asked if, hypothetically, injuries such as those sustained by Mr. King could be caused by falling forward to the pavement and striking the head while receiving a charge from the Taser. The witness said they could be.

Dr. Long spoke in technical terms a lot. It was not possible for me to copy in my notes all of the technical terms he used, but I felt I understood the points he was making.

After further examination by Mr. Yochelson, the witness was excused, and Mr. Stone called Officer Solano to the stand again.

Officer Solano told Mr. Stone that he had reviewed the tape about twenty times, and there were things he saw on the tape that he could not recall seeing at the scene. He saw Officer Powell deliver a series of power strokes, forward and reverse, across Mr. King's shoulders and collarbone, just below the top of his shoulder. The direction of the blows was downward with the long end of the baton. Mr. King was standing at the time. Officer Powell was standing about three feet in front of Mr. King. He said they were both moving and shifting and that Mr. King was flailing his arms. The witness said he was standing to the right of Mr. King. He said he did not see any direct blows to Mr. King's face or head.

He said that when Mr. King was on the ground Sergeant Koon was saying, "Get the knees." He said Officer Wind hit from the waist down. He continued to hear commands being shouted. Sergeant Koon appeared to be in charge, saying, "All right. He gives, he gives." Officer Solano said that at that time Mr. King had his hands close to the top of his head and was in a kneeling position. Several officers came in and started to place the cuffs on Mr. King. He heard someone say to double cuff. At no time did he see Mr. King lie prone and stop moving. He said he was unable to discern these events on the video, so it is his opinion that they occurred before the video started.

The witness told Mr. Barnett that there were sirens going when he first arrived. He said he did not rush in during the baton blows or when the Taser was shot, because it would have been unwise to approach.

Under questioning by Mr. DePasquale, Officer Solano said again that he did not enter the fray while the Taser was in operation. He said if you touch the person being tased, you will get part of the fifty thousand volts. He also said there were no deflected blows on Mr. King's face or head by Mr. Wind. He said he did not hear the clicking sound of the Taser at all. He said that he was not taught the swarm technique at the academy. He also told Mr. DePasquale that Mr. King was on his feet longer than he was on the ground.

The witness said that after Sergeant Koon said, "He gives," no other officer struck Mr. King.

Under questioning from Mr. White, Solano said that when Mr. King did not comply with the commands, several officers approached and they each grabbed a limb, using the swarm technique, which he had learned in the field. The witness said he grabbed the left leg. He said Officer Powell was kneeling on Mr. King's back. He said he felt Mr. King's left leg move, but did not feel any other movement. He heard "get off" or something like that. He quickly jumped back.

He said he heard only one Taser, and he did not know where the Tasers hit. He heard a groan or a moan and Mr. King got up off the ground and lunged toward Sergeant Koon.

*Moral Uncertainty*

He testified that he did not recall if it was the first blow that deflected off Mr. King's shoulder. He said it sounded like the baton had hit a hard area on Mr. King's face but he did not actually see the blow deflected off Mr. King's face. He said he was shocked and thought, *My God, I can't believe he is swinging the baton that high.* He said that hitting the shoulder was proper, but going into the face was wrong. He said Mr. King's arms were flailing at the time, trying to reach out after the baton hit. He said he felt the blows to the face were accidental.

He remembered Mr. King standing during most of the blows, but he did not see that on the video. He said he put his baton away after Mr. King was handcuffed. He again said that the video did not remind him of anything he had seen at the scene. He said that none of the blows he described in his testimony were on the video. He never heard anyone say that Mr. King was on PCP.

The witness told Mr. Mounger that when he was holding Mr. King's leg, he was "holding on for dear life." He said he felt they were "dealing with something like Superman."

When Mr. White questioned Officer Solano again, he said he felt he had control of Mr. King's leg while he was holding it. He said he was not thrown off.

The jury was excused for about an hour and when we returned, the witness told Mr. White about a conversation with Officer Briseno when they got into the car after the incident. He said that Officer Briseno was angry and upset, and said, "I thought we were going to be in a shooting." The witness also testified that Officer Briseno said, "Goddamn it, Sarge should have handled it better. He was there." Briseno was pretty scared and shaken by the whole thing, Officer Solano said.

This seemed to verify that Officer Briseno really was trying to protect King.

The witness told Mr. Stone that Officer Briseno did not say anything about Officers Powell or Wind. He could not say what should have been done better.

Mr. Mounger, Mr. Barnett and Mr. White questioned the witness about his previous testimony on April 5, 1991. There seemed to be some differences between that testimony and his current testimony.

Mr. Stone called Officer Robert Simpach to the stand next.

He testified that his partner the night of the incident was Officer Hajduk, and they were in the station when they heard about the pursuit and went to the scene. He said he backed up the female CHP police officer while she searched someone.

He remembered Mr. King being told to get down. He said he saw Officer Powell delivering three power strokes to Mr. King's thigh, and Officer Wind kicking him in the shoulder. He said Mr. King did not go down completely, then he came back up. He saw that repeated three separate times. The witness said that after the last kick, Mr. King put his hands up toward the back of his head while in a kneeling position. He said that one of the officers grabbed Mr. King's left wrist, pushing his hand toward his back. Then Mr. King and the officer toppled over and down to the right.

He said there was a lot of resistance and they used two pairs of handcuffs. After the first set of handcuffs were applied, someone asked for a cord cuff restraint. The witness got his out, and then someone said put a second set of handcuffs on. Then he walked out in the street to direct the emergency vehicle when it arrived.

Officer Simpach said he went to Pacifica Hospital to retrieve his cord cuff and handcuffs and saw Mr. King lying on his back grinning and looking around. He didn't hear anyone taunt Mr. King.

Officer Simpach may not have heard any taunting, but two nurses had testified that they did. Probably Officer Simpach was not in the room when it happened.

When the witness was questioned by Mr. DePasquale, he said there was a lot of noise at the scene. He did not recall a siren or a helicopter. He said the area was illuminated by the headlights from the police cars. He demonstrated the three swings he saw by Officer Powell to Mr. King. He did not hear any sounds from Mr. King after the blows. He thought there were four kicks by Officer Wind.

Each time Mr. King went down, he came back up again. Officer Simpach said that after Mr. King's hands were behind his back, he was not touched by Officers Wind or Powell. He also remarked on the relative size of Mr. King. He said he was a very large man with very large triceps.

He told Mr. DePasquale that he was never taught the swarm.

Officer Simpach told Mr. Yochelson that he did not remember seeing his partner after he got out of the car. He also said he reviewed the tape on a number of occasions and was able to identify what he had described on the video. Mr. Yochelson played the video for the witness and he was able to point out the events he had described. He testified that he was at the hospital only one or one and one-half minutes. He also said there was a period of time while there were no officers near Mr. King by the side of the road. He could think of no reason to leave him on the side of the road unattended.

The next witness called by Mr. Stone was Officer Christopher John Hajduk, Officer Simpach's partner the evening of March 3, 1991, who testified that he had received no swarm training at the academy and said he had no idea what the swarm technique was. They kept having officers testify that they didn't know what the swarm technique was, or that they had never been trained in it. I couldn't see what significance that had, because Sergeant Koon had ordered the swarm technique and they had tried it. It didn't work. So what difference did it make if some other officers said they had never been taught how to do it?

When Officer Hajduk arrived at the scene, he saw a cluster of vehicles and there was a lot of shouting. He saw Officer Powell striking the suspect with a power stroke that landed on Mr. King's left leg. Officer Powell struck Mr. King four or five times. The witness heard, "Put your hands behind your back," in a loud command voice.

He said Mr. King's "hands were in a pushup type position and he started to push his upper body up off the ground. His left leg started to come up in a kneeling position, and his right leg was lifting up off the ground." He said Mr. King got into a sitting position and put his arms behind his head. The officers moved in, brought his arms back, rolled him down onto the ground and put two cuffs on him. He said Mr. King's eyes were wide and he was making no noise. There was blood on the lower part of his cheek.

Under cross-examination by Mr. Yochelson, Officer Hajduk said he left his baton in the car, and stood with his arms folded because it was very cold out there. It seemed to me that Mr. Yochelson was trying to create a picture of an officer who was just standing by with his arms folded, doing nothing, while Mr. King was being beaten.

The officer also testified that he heard chants, not continuous commands. In response to Mr. Yochelson's questions, he said he did not see Mr. King jump to his feet, nor did he see Officer Wind kick

Mr. King in the back, and that he saw no blows after Mr. King was in a sitting position.

Court was recessed for the day.

# Chapter Ten: Powell Testifies

TUESDAY, MARCH 31, 1992

The judge obviously had a very bad cold and looked like he didn't feel well at all. Seemed a bit testy, also. The jurors, however, were in high spirits. We were always bringing goodies to share, and today someone brought a few fireballs, round pieces of hard candy that are very, very hot. Some of the jurors and Rhett, the deputy, started having contests to see who could keep them in their mouth the longest. There was a lot of laughing as some of the more stubborn jurors had tears coming out of their eyes from the heat of the candy.

When we were called into court, Mr. Stone called his client, Officer Laurence Michael Powell, as the next witness. I was very surprised to discover that he was only twenty-nine years old. He seemed much older.

Officer Powell testified that he was on duty at the Foothill Division the night of the incident and attended roll call where the officers were being trained on baton techniques. The actual practice was preceded by a ten-minute lecture by Officer Wind. They were taught the baton maneuver on power chops to smash the clavicle. The training also included the elbow and wrist. They were told to strike with all the force you can muster in an attempt to break the bones, Officer Powell said. "Sergeant DiStefano criticized me for not using enough power in the technique and he had me repeat the exercise. He told me to muster all the force I could."

Here it was again. More testimony about police being trained to break the bones of the suspects. Somehow, I had always assumed that they would only hit hard enough to knock someone down, or be able to get them under control. I had never thought that the police were intentionally trying to injure a suspect when they were trying to subdue him. I guess it makes sense that it is better to break a bone than to shoot him, but I had never thought about it that way before. I also had the nagging feeling that perhaps if Officer Powell had just been criticized for not doing it right, he might have been hitting harder than usual when he got out on the scene. He might have been trying to prove how hard he could hit.

Officer Powell said he and his partner, Officer Wind, heard on their radio that there was a pursuit and an LAPD vehicle involved. He said when they were at Van Nuys and Glenoaks, two cars had to put on their brakes when the Hyundai made a left turn on a red light. He said the vehicle accelerated rapidly up Van Nuys Boulevard. Officer Powell was driving, and they activated the emergency light and siren and started following the Hyundai. He told Officer Wind, a probationer that he was training, to broadcast that they were in pursuit.

Officer Powell said that two or three other cars on the road yielded to the patrol car. He said he saw the driver of the Hyundai and a passenger look back, their heads moving like "little dolls." At Foothill, a car had to put on its brakes to avoid hitting the Hyundai, Officer Powell said.

Mr. Stone had his client identify the intersections in a series of blown-up photographs of the pursuit route, Exhibits 305 through 309. Officer Powell said the vehicle finally stopped about two hundred feet past Osborne at Foothill. Because of their erratic behavior, and because of where they parked, the officers thought the occupants of the car might run.

Officer Powell kept turning around in the witness box to look directly at the jury as he answered questions. He seemed very sure of himself.

Mr. Stone asked him to list the steps taken in a felony stop. The suspect is told to:

1. Put your hands on your head.
2. Get away from the car.
3. Get down on your knees.
4. Get your arms stretched out with palms down.
5. Put your forehead on the ground with your head turned away from the officer.

Officers are taught not to approach until the suspect complies, Officer Powell said.

He said the CHP officers were the primary unit and were giving commands, and had their guns out. He said Officer Wind had his gun drawn, also. He testified that Mr. King had no seatbelt on, and that getting out of the car took him thirty to forty-five seconds. He said Mr. King was moving real slow, real stiff. Mr. King turned his head and looked in all directions, and then walked over to the

*Moral Uncertainty*

white car and slammed both his hands on the roof of the car. Then he looked up at the helicopter and waved his hand with a circular motion and was laughing, a low guttural laugh. He took his left hand off the roof of the car and put it in his pocket.

Officer Powell said he yelled to Officer Wind, "Watch out, I think he's dusted." CHP Officer Melanie Singer directed Mr. King to take his hand out of his pocket. Mr. King then turned his back in their direction, grabbed his buttocks and started shaking it all around.

Officer Powell said that his training had taught him that when someone is on PCP they make unnatural sounds, are unresponsive to stimuli, have superhuman strength, and there is a chemical odor. He said you can become intoxicated from touching the skin of a PCP suspect. He said that Mr. King had a blank stare, moved slowly, was not complying with verbal commands and sweat was glistening on his face. His strange behavior and the erratic pursuit made him believe Mr. King was on PCP.

He said King turned around, facing away from his car and started walking away from the car, stiff-legged. Officer Powell said he yelled to Mr. King to put his hands up, to get on his knees, and get on the ground. Officers Solano and Briseno were also giving him commands. Mr. King got down on his knees and patted the ground. Sergeant Koon told Mr. King to "lay down on the ground or I am going to shock you." Mr. King looked up at Sergeant Koon. CHP Officer Melanie Singer approached Mr. King with her gun drawn. Sergeant Koon yelled, "Get back," and Officer Singer retreated.

Sergeant Koon told Officers Powell and Wind to go in and cuff him. Powell said he holstered his gun and approached the suspect, who was still on all fours. He said he approached cautiously and slowly, and gave Mr. King an order to lie down on the ground. Mr. King leaned forward on his arms, in a pushup position. Powell said he tried to pull Mr. King's arm out from underneath him so that he could be handcuffed. He pushed down on Mr. King's neck with his right hand, but Mr. King resisted. Another officer was pulling his right arm. Mr. King's head then slammed into the asphalt. Officer Powell said he got his handcuffs out and put his knee on Mr. King's back. Mr. King broke free of their grasp, raised up his torso, and threw Powell off of his back. He landed on his rear, and Mr. King went into a pushup position. The witness said that King was a very big man with very powerful arms.

Officer Powell said that Mr. King then raised up on his haunches and stood up. Officer Powell said he put his handcuffs in his back pocket as Mr. King rose. Then he saw Sergeant Koon shoot Mr. King with the Taser, but Mr. King did not go down.

Sergeant Koon yelled, "Back off, back off." Mr. King started moving in the direction of Sergeant Koon, and Powell heard a popping sound and saw him tased. The darts were on the left side of Mr. King's back. As Mr. King dropped to one knee, his body was convulsing, his face was convulsing, he was gritting his teeth and groaning, but the Taser was still not dropping him to the ground.

King got up onto his feet and took two steps in Sergeant Koon's direction. Then Sergeant Koon shot the other cartridge and hit Mr. King in the front torso, and he dropped to his knees. Sergeant Koon ordered Mr. King to drop to the ground. Powell had drawn his baton after the first Taser shot. Mr. King "got up, turned, and came right at me," he said.

Officer Powell said he did not remember the events clearly and that instead of refreshing his memory, the video had confused his memory. He tried to correlate the events with his memory and could not.

He said he did not remember facing Mr. King and striking him with power blows. He said Mr. King collided with him. He said he delivered a "checked swing" with his baton, aiming for the chest. Mr. King's right side collided with Officer Powell's right side, and Mr. King fell down like a rag doll, falling from a standing height with his face on the pavement.

His face struck the pavement first with no protection from his arms, Powell said. I wondered if this could have caused the facial injuries? Mr. King's head bounced, and his arms came up beneath him. He was in a pushup position.

Powell said he hit Mr. King with back and forth power strokes several times and told him to get down. He testified that he did not hit him in the head. He said Sergeant Koon yelled at him, "Don't hit him in the head."

Mr. King continued to get back up. The witness said he looked at Sergeant Koon, who said, "This isn't working. Go for the knees, go for the legs, keep him down." Powell then delivered a series of power strokes to the legs. He said he stopped when he saw some semblance of compliance.

He said his purpose for striking Mr. King was to keep him down. He said he feared for his own life and was doing everything he could to keep Mr. King down on the ground. He testified that Officer Briseno pushed him away from Mr. King, but didn't say anything. He thought it was to keep him from being shocked by the Taser.

Officer Powell said he was prepared to handcuff Mr. King as soon as he stopped getting in a position to get up. He said he reached back for his handcuffs but they were caught in his pocket, and he had difficulty getting them out. His baton was in his left hand. He saw Mr. King's legs cocked again in a moving position. He said he did not see Mr. King's upper body, and he did not see Officer Briseno put his foot on Mr. King. He hit him in the legs again, somewhere between his thighs and his ankles. He said Mr. King got all the way up, and he struck him again.

Sergeant Koon said, "Do you give?" and Mr. King put his hands up to his head.

Officer Powell said he was extremely fatigued, was breathing heavily, hyperventilating, and was very tired. He said he had not yet adjusted to sleeping during the day.

After this point, he said he did not hit Mr. King again. He said he handed his handcuffs to Officer Briseno, who grabbed Mr. King's arms. Several other officers assisted Officer Briseno in handcuffing Mr. King. Sergeant Koon said, "Get an AR here." Officer Powell said he took out his ROVER and made the call. He said he recognized his own voice on the audio tape of the call, sounding out of breath. He said he heard no laughing, but was breathing very heavily. He said he had no further contact with Mr. King at the scene.

Sergeant Koon asked Powell to complete a Use of Force report. The policies and procedures for the report require that a supervisor fill out the report. Sergeant Koon said he would fill out the face sheet and attach it to the arrest report, and Officer Timothy Wind filled out that report.

Officer Powell said that Melanie Singer asked him questions about the Taser and seemed very excited. Sergeant Koon instructed her to tell Officer Powell what had happened in the pursuit. She told him Mr. King was driving 110 miles per hour and running a red light, speeding on Paxton, all this mixed in with the conversation about the Taser. Powell said he asked her about her best estimate of the speeds and about pedestrians. She said there was north- and south-bound traffic that had to stop during the pursuit.

Powell said that Officer Wind went along with King in the rescue ambulance and he drove the patrol car to the hospital. He said he was still feeling the stress of the situation. He said he typed a message to a friend, Officer Corina Smith, in another patrol car. He said they were very good friends, that they lived close to each other. He did not remember what the message was that he had sent to her. He said he saw the words in a newspaper about a year ago, and did not recognize the words.

He said he assisted the paramedics in taking Mr. King into the hospital when they arrived, and filled out the admitting forms. This took him five to ten minutes, he said, and then he went back to the room where they had Mr. King. Mr. King told him he was an usher at Dodger Stadium. He said he heard no discussion about baseball.

He went out of the room for a conversation with the emergency room doctor to arrange a transfer to the jail. He said he went in and out of the room, and then walked Mr. King to the car, took him to Foothill Station, then to the USC jail ward. He walked Mr. King up to the jail ward, where he filled out the necessary papers for medical treatment.

He spoke with Dr. Giannetto about the contusions and abrasions on Mr. King. He asked if there were any broken bones and the doctor said there was no indication of any. Powell said he completed the report in the waiting room of the jail ward. Information on the extent of injuries came from Dr. Giannetto and his personal observations, he said.

Mr. Stone asked Officer Powell to identify the original arrest report (Exhibit 304) and a blow-up (Exhibit 303). The report consisted of seven pages. The first page was the face page, then there were four pages of continuation sheets, then Officer Timothy Singer's two-page narrative. Officer Powell said most of the report was based on his own perception but he did incorporate Melanie Singer's statement into the report. He said he believed that the report was accurate, and he did not intend to mislead anyone.

Prosecutor White then cross-examined, questioning Powell about the remark he had made to Corina Smith. Officer Powell replied that the *Oops* remark did not mean he had made an error or a mistake.

Mr. White read from a hard copy of the MDT transmission.

Smith: *What are you up to? Sounds almost as exciting as our last one.*

Powell: *Almost right out of gorillas in the mist.*

Smith: *Let me guess who be the parties.*

Powell: *Good guess.*

Officer Powell denied that it was a racial remark.

But clearly it was. However, just because he made a racial slur does not mean that the beating was unlawful. Because someone has a bad attitude doesn't mean they have committed a crime.

Mr. White questioned the witness about the call for the rescue ambulance. Officer Powell said that he had heard the audio tape of the call for the first time in court, and identified the sound on the tape as heavy breathing, not laughter.

Mr. White referred to Nurse Lawrence Davis's testimony at the hospital when Mr. King said he was an usher at Dodger Stadium. He quoted Powell as saying, "What section do you work in? I don't want to sit there." Officer Powell said this was merely common banter between an officer and suspect.


WEDNESDAY, APRIL 1, 1992

It was still very cold in the courtroom. The court reporter had a blanket around her legs to ward off the chill. The blankets she used were very colorful and usually matched or coordinated with her outfits. The judge's voice, his face, and his demeanor still demonstrated that his cold was going strong.

Mr. White continued his cross-examination of Officer Powell, who reiterated that some of the symptoms of PCP intoxication are muscle rigidity, sweating, blank stare, and unresponsiveness to pain. Officer Powell said he did not ask for PCP tests to be made, but there was no doubt in his mind that Mr. King was under the influence of PCP.

Mr. White cited the Use of Force report on the Taser (Exhibit

49) as not having the block marked "PCP" filled out. The block marked "Alcohol" was checked. Powell said he had detected a faint odor of alcohol on Mr. King. He said the report was inaccurate.

Mr. White also cited the baton Use of Force report (Exhibit 50) as not having the "PCP" block checked, but the "Other" block: "Possibly under the influence of unknown drug." Mr. Powell said the report was inaccurate.

He told Mr. White that he knew of no such thing as the swarm technique. He said they were trained on the "team takedown technique" after this incident. He said Sergeant Koon told him to put in the report that they were using the swarm technique.

Mr. White asked Powell if he didn't consider the treatment of King to be inhumane, dragging him to the side of the road and leaving him there like an animal. Officer Powell said he did not consider Mr. King an animal.

Officer Powell said he does not put down all of the details in an arrest report. Those are covered in the Use of Force report. When Mr. White questioned him about items such as "Officer Wind and I drew our batons," and "suspect was kicking and swinging his arms and attacking," he stated that the report was not a complete synopsis of what happened.

Mr. White questioned the witness on responsibility for his own actions and the following of orders from Sergeant Koon. Officer Powell said he took orders from Sergeant Koon, but he was also responsible for his own actions. He said it was his judgment to do what Sergeant Koon said. "When he tells me to do things and they're in department policy and I feel they're reasonable, then by all means you do them or you're in trouble."

Mr. White was putting pressure on Officer Powell, asking if he was just a "puppet" for Sergeant Koon. "Even if there was excessive force used out there that night, you wouldn't say it, would you?" Mr. White shouted. "You wouldn't testify here in court in front of this jury that this man was responsible, would you?"

Mr. White was very emotional. He walked all the way around the table, right up to Sergeant Koon, pointed at him, and shouted, "This man is responsible for what happened, isn't he?"

Officer Powell answered that everyone out there was responsible for his own actions. "If there was excessive force used that night I would have reported it to another supervisor."

"That is not the question," Mr. White shouted. "I'm saying if there was excessive force out there that night, is this man responsible?" again pointing to Sergeant Koon.

"He didn't hit anybody," Officer Powell said. "How could he be?"

"Was he controlling it?" Mr. White asked.

"He was controlling it," Officer Powell admitted.

As usual, I was annoyed by Mr. White's theatrics. They seemed contrived to me.

Mr. White asked the witness about the use of the Taser. He reiterated that the Taser had dropped Mr. King to one knee but then he got up and headed toward Sergeant Koon, who shot him the second time. He testified that, in his experience, the Taser works usually three out of five times. He testified that before the first baton blow, Mr. King was hit with the second Taser shot.

Mr. White asked Powell if he considered what had happened a fight, and Officer Powell said that in his mind it was a fight, that Mr. King had attacked. Mr. White said, "You wanted him to get up, didn't you? You wanted to hit him in the head with a baton."

Officer Powell said, "No."

Officer Powell said Mr. King's body actually made contact with him. He said he moved very quickly. He said he was moving out of the way as he swung the baton. At the time, he estimated Mr. King to be about six feet, three inches tall and about 265 pounds.

Mr. White seemed to be badgering Officer Powell, asking his questions in a very rapid and emotional fashion. He questioned Officer Powell again about the "checked swing." Powell said he saw things on the video that he doesn't remember happening. He said he remembered Officer Briseno pushing him back, but he doesn't remember hearing Briseno say anything. He also said that he felt the baton blows were keeping Mr. King down on the ground.

Mr. White asked Officer Powell if Mr. King was a human being, Officer Powell answered, "Yes."

Asked if Mr. King was an animal, Officer Powell answered, "No. Just acting like one."

Mr. White questioned Officer Powell about the report again. He said it did not mention lacerations or cuts, just "contusions and abrasions." Officer Powell said his definition of abrasions included scrapes and cuts, and that he did not consider Mr. King's injuries to be major at the time. However, Officer Wind's report reflected that there were major injuries, and Officer Powell acknowledged that as Officer Wind's training officer, he reviewed the report.

Mr. White seemed to be indicating that the fact that Officer Powell didn't mention the lacerations meant that he deliberately attempted to minimize the degree of injury. In my opinion, that didn't prove there was any deliberate attempt to falsify. The doctors had not considered the injuries major, so why would Officer Powell?

Mr. DePasquale questioned Officer Powell next. Officer Powell demonstrated the position of the baton when Mr. King was coming toward him. He said the baton was squeezed between them when they collided.

He said that the fall to the ground might have been the cause of the cuts to Mr. King's face. He did not see Mr. King's face contact the ground during the final handcuffing. He also said that Dr. Giannetto at the USC jail had told him that the injuries were minor and there appeared to be no broken bones.

When Mr. White re-examined Officer Powell, Powell said that no fluid samples were taken to determine whether or not Mr. King was under the influence of alcohol. He also told Mr. White that he did not remember swinging his arms. He said that Mr. King fell like a rag doll. He did not feel that Mr. King fell from the baton blows.

Officer Powell conducted himself rather well on the stand. He answered the questions straightforwardly. He didn't seem cocky at all. He might have been coached, but he seemed almost remorseful.

I had started out thinking that there was excessive force. When I heard defense witnesses say that King had charged Powell, I started thinking that maybe Powell wasn't guilty after all. But after his testimony, I still had a vague, gut feeling that he might be guilty. He was the one I had the most ambivalence about.

*Moral Uncertainty*

# Chapter Eleven: The Defense Wraps Up

The next witness Mr. Stone called was Sergeant Joseph Vondriska, a CHP traffic control officer who supervised Officers Melanie and Tim Singer. He testified that he had received a call from Timothy Singer to telephone him at Pacifica Hospital. He told Melanie Singer in a telephone conversation to relinquish the incident to the LAPD. She told him that she had observed Mr. King struck five to seven times around the head and legs with a PR-24. She said she was not sure if the blows to the head were intentional.

Mr. Stone indicated that he would have more witnesses later, but at this time, he had no further witnesses. Then Mr. DePasquale called his first witness, Officer Paul Gebhardt, who had been Officer David Love's partner the night of the incident.

When they arrived at the scene, Mr. King was standing up, his arms stretched out in front of him. Sergeant Koon was holding the Taser gun. Officer Gebhardt said he looked around and when next he looked at Mr. King, he was on the ground, with his hands on the ground as if he were trying to push up, the Taser wires still attached to him. He said he saw Officer Powell strike Mr. King maybe eight blows, Officer Wind four blows. He said both officers were screaming and shouting to Mr. King to put his hands behind his back.

"He wasn't listening to the commands and he was moving about," Officer Gebhardt said.

He heard Officer Powell say, "Watch out. He's dusted." He also heard Sergeant Koon say, "Hit him in the knees. He's trying to get up."

Officer Gebhardt then told Mr. White that he heard Officers Powell and Wind screaming, "Put your hands behind your back." He also said there were other commands by Sergeant Koon.

Mr. White asked Officer Gebhardt about disciplinary action against him that came out of this incident. The witness did not reply.

During Mr. Stone's further examination, the witness pointed himself out on the video and had the video stopped at the point where Officer Powell turned and told the witness, "Watch out, he's dusted." At this point, there was an objection and a very lengthy sidebar.

Mr. DePasquale called as his first witness Officer Jerry L. Mulford, an instructor at the Los Angeles Police Academy for nine years. He explained what a felony prone position is, and spoke of academy training of levels of force and escalation/de-escalation, starting with verbal commands and going to deadly force, including training in use of the Taser. He spoke of teaching recruits about vehicle pursuit and stops. He said a stop after a pursuit is a high-risk stop. He said if the pursued vehicle stops and then starts again, the risk is increased.

He explained what the recruits were taught about the positions of the police cars as they arrive at the scene of a high-risk stop, to prevent putting a police car in the line of crossfire.

The witness then described the swarm technique, or officer takedown. He said it could take two to seven people to handcuff an individual. There is usually a "designated shooter" should it come to deadly force. He also said the swarm technique was not routinely taught at the academy, but rather in the enrichment phase of training at the discretion of the instructor, if time allowed.

Mr. Stone presented a hypothetical situation where there were three people in the car being pursued who kept looking back at the officer. The vehicle stopped, then started again, then finally stopped next to a park in a dark area. Officer Mulford said this would be a danger signal, and that the officers should use as much force as possible to prevent escape.

Officer Mulford said that in his experience, officers in stressful situations can react with laughter, giggling or crying. He has seen them stand and look at the wall and he has seen them urinate and defecate on themselves.

Officer Mulford was verbalizing my own thoughts, that Officer Powell's laughter was a nervous response to tension, and did not indicate that he was amused.

Mr. Barnett questioned Officer Mulford about LAPD policy on baton use. He said that the policy is that maximum force can be used until the suspect complies. It could be one blow or one hundred. He also replied to Mr. Barnett that if a suspect is under the influence of alcohol and is hit in the head, that it might affect his ability to respond.

Mr. DePasquale gave the witness a hypothetical situation where there had been an unsuccessful attempt to handcuff a suspect, and he said the officers would be justified in using the baton if the suspect kept trying to get up. Mr. DePasquale referred to an LAPD training bulletin on kicks and on PCP. The witness said the cartoon on the PCP bulletin was not meant to be amusing.

Earlier, there had been a sidebar following mention of this cartoon. This apparently was the cartoon that they didn't want the jury to see.

After further cross-examination of the witness by Mr. Stone, Mr. Mounger and Mr. White, court was recessed.

FRIDAY, APRIL 3, 1992

The first witness called by Mr. DePasquale was Ms. Marcelline Burns, a psychologist who directs the Southern California Research Institute. Her work includes research on the effects of alcohol and other drugs on driving and driving skills. She testified that it would take about fourteen or fifteen twelve-ounce bottles of beer to reach a .19 blood alcohol level, assuming the person weighed 230 to 250 pounds, there was no food intake, he was not obese and the alcohol was consumed starting five hours prior.

Mr. Stone questioned the witness about a suspect's ability to respond to verbal commands if under the influence of alcohol. She replied that there had been no studies on that issue, but that a person under the influence of alcohol often fails to perceive or might misperceive.

Mr. Yochelson asked the witness how body fat distribution pertains to alcohol. She said that alcohol is distributed in body water, and that fat tissue has less water. She said someone under the influence of alcohol would be slower in responses, that they usually respond to only part of what is happening.

I found this technical testimony about the effects of alcohol to be rather interesting, but it didn't change my mind about anything. I had already concluded that Rodney King had been drinking and that he was impaired. How much he had to drink or how much alcohol was in his fat tissue didn't make much difference to me.

That concluded Mr. DePasquale's witnesses.

The next witness, Officer Theodore Joseph Briseno, was called by Mr. Barnett. He testified that he was thirty-nine years old, was five feet, eight inches tall and weighed 140 pounds. He said that the night of the incident his partner was Officer Solano.

When they arrived at the scene Officer Briseno said he shouted, "Turn off your siren."

He observed that the suspect, Mr. King, was very, very muscular. He said that Sergeant Koon told the CHP officer with the gun to get back. Briseno said he grabbed Mr. King's right arm, tried to move the arm, and couldn't. Mr. King then hit him in the chest, knocking him back and he lost control of the arm.

He saw Officer Powell being pushed off of Mr. King. When Mr. King started to get up, Sergeant Koon yelled to get down or he would shoot him. Then Sergeant Koon shot the Taser gun. Mr. King got to his feet, but the second Taser shot took him down to the ground. Then Mr. King headed for Officer Powell very quickly. He said Officer Powell hit Mr. King on the right side of his face. Mr. King went down.

Officer Powell was standing over Mr. King hitting him with a series of power strokes. Briseno said he saw that on the video, but he did not remember Mr. King getting up and down as shown on the video.

He said that at this point he thought Officer Powell was out of control. He said he did not see Mr. King getting up. He couldn't understand why it was continuing. He thought it was wrong. He remembered thinking that they must have seen something he didn't see.

"I just didn't know what was going on out there. I couldn't see it. I didn't understand it," Officer Briseno said. "It looked like they were just hitting him everywhere. I thought the whole thing was out of control. It was wrong."

Mr. Barnett played the video and asked Officer Briseno to point out where he put his hand on Officer Powell's baton. When asked by Mr. Barnett why he did this, Officer Briseno replied that he was trying to stop him. When shown the place in the video where he put his foot on Mr. King, he said that he was trying to keep Mr. King down with his foot.

Officer Briseno said he put his foot on Mr. King's left shoulder. He said he then went over to Sergeant Koon and asked, "What the fuck is going on out here?" He said Sergeant Koon told him to get another Taser gun. Then Mr. King was handcuffed and Briseno told Officer Solano to get in the car.

Officer Briseno said he was angry, upset and frustrated. When he got in the car with Officer Solano, he said to him, "Goddamn it, Sarge should have handled it a lot better," and "The officers should have their asses reamed." When asked if he had a better solution, he said he did not. He said he had thought they were going to have a shooting.

He said they headed back to the station, where he saw a message that said, *Big time use of force, victim beaten and tased.*

Mr. Stone then questioned Briseno, who said there was a collision or near collision between Mr. King and Officer Powell. He said he believed that the blow to Mr. King's head was accidental. He also said he did not know where on Mr. King the back and forth blows landed. He did not see them land on Mr. King's head.

Under cross-examination by Prosecutor White, Officer Briseno said that eventually Mr. King complied with the verbal orders. He testified that he was not taught the swarm, or team takedown, did not recall seeing Mr. King hit the ground and did not know if his arms broke his fall.

He said he heard a sound as the baton hit Mr. King's face. He said the second series of blows were toward Mr. King's back, but he couldn't say if these blows hit the head or neck.

He told Mr. White that he did not think Mr. King was combative, threatening or aggressive. When asked if he thought it was improper use of force, he said he thought it was. He also said that a lot of force was used, but he couldn't say it was excessive. He felt the situation was fast approaching use of lethal force.

Mr. White then asked Officer Briseno about the "code of silence." Officer Briseno replied that he had heard a training officer telling another officer not to inform on fellow police officers.

There was a recess and we returned at 3:15 p.m. After a sidebar that lasted from 3:16 to 3:21 p.m., we were told not to report on Monday until afternoon. Mr. Stone then examined the witness again.

Officer Briseno told Mr. Stone that, based on his recollection at the scene, the elapsed time from the first blow until Mr. King was handcuffed was forty to fifty seconds. He said that Mr. King was very strong and that he couldn't have handled him. He said he never saw Mr. King trying to get up.

I noticed that he was contradicting himself. Earlier he said that Mr. King was starting to get up.

He told Mr. Stone that he was concerned that Officer Powell was fatigued. He said he thought Officer Powell might shoot Mr. King.

"Officer Powell had a look I'd never seen before. It was just a look of pure exhaustion. His eyes looked like they could explode, like they were coming out. And he was constantly gasping for breath."

He testified that he had left his baton in the car, but even if he had it, he would not have used it. He said he did not tell his probationer to put his baton away. In answer to Mr. Stone's questions, he said Officer Powell was not laughing. He said he was not looking at Mr. King, that he did not want to get hit. In analyzing the situation, he said he could not think of anything else that could have been done. He said he didn't know if King broke his fall with his hands. He said Mr. King was not in control of his body, that he went straight down.

Mr. DePasquale then questioned Officer Briseno about his foot on Mr. King's shoulder. Briseno told him that he was trying to push him down to keep him from rising, but that it didn't work. He didn't accomplish his purpose.

When Mr. White questioned Officer Briseno again, Briseno said that he had never seen a beating like this one.


MONDAY, APRIL 6, 1992

When we were brought into court, it was again very, very cold. Chris, the court reporter, was sitting with a blanket around her lap and legs. The judge was at the stage of his cold where you could hear it in his voice and breathing.

Mr. Stone continued calling his witnesses in defense of Officer Powell. His first witness was Ms. Leslie Wiley, an LAPD Police Service representative at City Hall East in downtown Los Angeles, who said that on March 3, 1991 she was assigned to the Foothill Division. She assisted officers in the field and manned the Watch Commander's Area Command Console (ACC). If an officer sends a message from the MDT in the field, it appears on the ACC screen. Near 1 a.m., a message appeared from Sergeant Koon and she responded. During the next hour, until she finished her shift around 2 a.m., she was in the Watch Commander's office running stats, she said.

At this point, her testimony was interrupted by a sidebar that lasted eleven minutes.

When questioning resumed, she said the MDT message from Sergeant Koon read, *Big time use of force, beat the suspect of pursuit big time.* She said she read the message to Lieutenant Conmay.

After one minute, she said she cleared the screen and sent the following message in response, *Oh well, I'm sure the lizard didn't deserve it. I'll let them know.*

She said once a message is cleared, she can't bring it back up on the screen.

Ms. Wiley said she knew nothing about the suspect, nothing about his background. She told Mr. Stone that the word "lizard" refers to a criminal.

She testified that she was acquainted with Officer Briseno and that he did not come in at any time before she went off duty and there was no way anyone could have read the message. So if she was telling the truth, then Officer Briseno was lying.

Mr. Mounger then questioned the witness. She said her response to the message was sarcastic. There was another later message from Sergeant Koon, saying he was going to the hospital and that he wanted a fresh Taser when he came back to the station. She said she was there when Sergeant Koon had a conversation with Lieutenant Conmay, who asked about the use of force and injuries. Sergeant Koon said Mr. King had a cut lip probably from falling on the asphalt, that the Taser had not worked, and that there was a lot of baton use. He said that he thought the suspect was on PCP.

Ms. Wiley was then questioned by Mr. DePasquale, who established that the message from Sergeant Koon was at 00:56:04 and that her response was at 00:57:02. She looked at Exhibit 19 (ACC printout) before she replied. She said she had picked up the term "lizard" from the instructor at a class she had attended on "Verbal Judo" in January 1991.

When questioned by Mr. Barnett, she said that Sergeant Koon

was not a particular friend, that she joked with all the officers. She said she knew that Mr. King was felony evading. She also testified that she had told the District Attorney in an earlier interview that prior to the lizard message she knew that Mr. King was a suspect in a robbery. She also defined a lizard to the District Attorney as a "low-life criminal."

After another four-minute sidebar, Ms. Wiley told Mr. Barnett that she felt use of force was provoked or it wouldn't have taken place. She also said that the lizard message had been left on the screen until 1:10 a.m. She said that in her June 1991 interview with the District Attorney, she said the 211 might have been the reason for use of force. She also said she did not recall anything being mentioned about Officer Briseno in the interview.

When Mr. White examined the witness, he asked her about her comments on felony evading. He asked her again what her position was and she said she was a Police Service Representative (dispatcher), not a police officer. She said she had no facts other than what she heard on the broadcast. She said that it was not her job to protect the image of the LAPD or to protect the officers.

Mr. Mounger questioned the witness about the audio tape. She said no one in the District Attorney's office had played the audio tape for her, and that her interview with the District Attorney was from her memory. She said she was just trying to tell the truth. She testified that an operator cannot send a message with another message on the screen.

Mr. Stone questioned the witness next. She told him the District Attorney had asked her to explain the term "lizard." She said when she sent the message she was not expressing a judgment of the suspect. She said it was impossible for Sergeant Koon's message to stay on the screen more than fifty-eight seconds. She testified again that she knew Officer Briseno and that he did not walk into the Commander's office between the messages. She did not see Briseno at any time before 2 a.m. come in looking for the Watch Commander.

At 3:10 p.m. the jury was excused for the day, unusually early. The judge watched the time very carefully and most days, it was either 5 p.m. or very close to it before court was adjourned. He said he was going to continue the hearing with the attorneys and would be discussing the schedule for the rest of the trial. It was a short day.

*Moral Uncertainty*

We had very little court time, and a lot of time to spend in the law library waiting.

We waited all morning. Finally we were called in to court. Mr. Stone's first witness was Officer Dennis Watkins, who had been with the LAPD for twenty-six-and-a-half years. Mr. Stone had Officer Watkins make the point that he had not been subpoenaed. He said that after viewing Officer Briseno's testimony on television, he contacted Mr. Mounger about a conversation he had with Officer Briseno at about 10:45 p.m. on March 4, 1991 in the Watch Commander's office.

He said he told Officer Briseno there were a number of officers and investigators from Internal Affairs at the Foothill Station collecting data and analytical documents. He said Officer Briseno replied, "We didn't do anything wrong, let them investigate all they want. We had to kick a little ass last night."

Mr. Barnett asked Officer Watkins why he did not come forward after he heard Officer Solano's testimony about how upset Officer Briseno was. He replied that he didn't connect it at that time, but he did connect it after Officer Briseno's testimony. He said he did not report the incident to any official, but that he talked to Officer Williams on Saturday night. They had been coworkers and Williams had been retired since last May.

Mr. Barnett asked him about the "code of silence." He said it was something the media said was a code between police officers to maintain secrecy in their activities.

After a nine-minute sidebar called for by Mr. White, Mr. Stone questioned the witness again on redirect. He told Mr. Stone that in his conversation, Officer Briseno did not say that anyone had used excessive force or that the Sergeant did not handle it right or that it was out of control. Officer Watkins said he had no ax to grind; he did not feel angry with Officer Briseno, he just wanted to get at the truth of the matter.

The witness then told Mr. Barnett that his loyalty to the LAPD was strong, but that he was not thinking about whether benefit or harm would come to the department because of his testimony. He said he came forward because he felt Officer Briseno was lying.

In answer to a question by Mr. Stone, the witness said that perjury would make the LAPD look bad also.

The next witness was Gerald Williams, a retired LAPD officer who worked for the department twenty years. He didn't look like a law enforcement officer. He had long hair pulled back in a ponytail and was wearing a jacket and a western type bow tie.

He told Mr. Stone that on March 4, 1991 he was present at the Watch Commander's office. He said he had an independent recollection of the conversation between Officer Briseno and Officer Watkins. He said they had watched the video at 10 p.m. Internal Affairs had invaded the Foothill Station collecting reports. He said he had asked Internal Affairs for their identification.

He said that Officer Watkins walked away after his conversation with Officer Briseno and that he, Mr. Williams, continued the conversation. He testified that Officer Briseno said, "We didn't do anything wrong, the asshole deserved it, anyway."

He also said he had no ax to grind with Briseno, but thought that he was lying in his testimony. He said that he and Officer Watkins had done nothing to get their stories together.

When Mr. Barnett questioned Mr. Williams, he said that both he and Officer Watkins were upstairs waiting to testify. He admitted it would have been wrong to talk about their testimony. When questioned about the effect of the trial on the LAPD, he said it was his opinion that the LAPD will look the same no matter what the outcome of the trial.

Mr. Stone next called Officer Glen Robert King to the stand. He said he was assigned Unit 16A99 on the night of the incident. He arrived at the station at 10:30 p.m. and changed into his uniform before roll call.

He said he and his probationer, Officer Graybill, responded to the Foothill and Osborne pursuit when he heard it on the radio.

He said "stick time" was "archaic jargon" for hitting someone with the baton.

He said that the night of the incident he had called Officer Briseno over to his car and had a conversation with him. Officer Briseno told him that four officers tried to handcuff Mr. King and he threw them off his back. He also said that Mr. King was tased and it had no effect. He said that Powell came out of nowhere and took Mr. King down with his baton.

Officer King said he had another conversation later when Officer Briseno said that Rodney King had "reared back on us." Officer Briseno said he had kicked the suspect while he was on the ground. He said that Officer Briseno told him that he was afraid if Mr. King got up, they would have beaten him to death.

WEDNESDAY, APRIL 8, 1992

We were called in late again. Mr. Stone continued his examination of Officer Glen Robert King. Mr. Stone referred to a conversation at the station after court yesterday. The witness had recalled another statement by Briseno in the locker room conversation. Officer King had said to Officer Briseno that with that one prior complaint, it wasn't going to look good.

Mr. Barnett objected, and after a nine-minute sidebar, the jury was told to disregard that last statement. The jury was sent out and called back at 11:30 a.m.

Mr. Stone questioned the witness about his interview by police investigators in mid-March 1991 when he was asked to review his daily log for accuracy. He pointed out omissions on the log and inaccuracies concerning his visit to the scene of the pursuit.

Officer King said he was Officer Briseno's partner for twenty-eight days and considered him a friend. When he arrived, Officer Briseno was just standing there, and he called him over to the car.

The witness was reluctant to say whether his memory was clearer in March 1991 than now. The investigators had asked him to tell them what was said by the car. They also asked about other conversations and he said there was a conversation later that night at a doughnut shop, during which they did not discuss the incident.

In a second interview with the same investigators, he said the doughnut shop conversation was the night of the incident. Later, he said it was the next night. He also told Mr. Stone that during the interview he told the investigators that at the car that night Officer Briseno acted as if there was nothing out of the ordinary.

The witness rarely answered with a yes or no. He would say, "I believe so," or "I don't believe so." It seemed like he didn't really know.

Then Mr. Stone would say, "Would it help to listen to a tape of the interview?"

Officer King told Mr. Mounger that he was a personal friend of Officer Briseno, on and off. He said that in his locker room conversation, Officer Briseno had told him that he "kept yelling at Sergeant Koon the whole time this was going on."

Mr. Mounger asked the witness if he had been a training officer, and if he taught the officers to take their equipment with them when they leave a car. His point was that Officer Briseno had failed to take his baton out of the car.

There was another three-minute sidebar and Mr. Mounger continued questioning the witness. Officer King said when he was interviewed by police investigators that he didn't believe his locker room conversation was relevant, so he did not tell the investigators that Officer Briseno said he had tried to stop the event.

After lunch, Mr. Stone said he had decided not to call any further witnesses. Mr. DePasquale stipulated that Rodney King was on parole on March 3, 1991 and that one condition of his parole was that he obey all laws.

The judge announced that the prosecution would begin its rebuttal evidence. He said there probably would be some testimony heard early next week, but that we would not be in deliberation until after the Easter weekend.

# Chapter Twelve: Rebuttal from the Prosecution

The prosecution's first rebuttal witness was Mr. Turhan Folse, who photographed Rodney King's injuries on March 6, 1991 in the Beverly Hills office of King's lawyer, Stephen Lerman. He told Mr. DePasquale that it took him about thirty minutes to take the pictures, without any special lighting or makeup, and he made no attempt to accentuate the injuries. He said he dropped the film off at a lab and picked up the prints a week later. He said it was not his concern why the lawyer wanted the photos.

Mr. Stone questioned the photographer further but just about every question he asked drew an objection and the judge admonished him that he was covering subjects that had already been covered or that were beyond the scope of direct examination.

The judge seemed to be getting a little testy and trying to hurry counsel along. He excused the jury at 2:25 p.m. for a conference with counsel requested by the prosecution. We returned more than an hour later at 3:35 p.m.

Mr. Yochelson called Mr. Robert F. Packard, an Engineer of Survey for the Los Angeles Bureau of Engineering, who researched records of measurements of the distances between intersections and streets involved in the pursuit. Exhibits were entered into evidence showing the distances on a map. Mr. Packard said he figured the distance from Tamarack and Van Nuys to Glenoaks and Van Nuys was close to a mile.

The prosecution apparently wanted to prove that Officer Powell could not have traveled far enough to see Mr. King's car during the pursuit, in the amount of time he cited.

Under questioning from Mr. Stone, the witness said he didn't do the measuring himself but based his calculations on measurements that were taken maybe twenty years ago.

Mr. Yochelson then questioned Mr. Packard again, and he said that the survey principles he used had been developed over hundreds of years.

Next was Ms. Shaton Denise Brown, the Emergency Board Operator for 911 calls at the LAPD Communications Dispatch Center on March 3, 1991 from 11 p.m. to 7:30 a.m.

Mr. White played a tape of a call from CHP and Ms. Brown said she was the operator who took that call and that she was the only one who heard it at the time. She testified that at no time before she brought up the frequencies to broadcast the call to Foothill Division did she transfer calls to LA police officers' vehicles.

She told Mr. DePasquale that the broadcast was sent before midnight to all units that the CHP was in pursuit. But when she was questioned by Mr. White, he established that the first time the message was broadcast to police officers was 12:46 a.m.

Mr. White then re-called Glenda Tosti, a Senior Police Services Representative for the LAPD. Ms. Tosti said that it was not possible for Los Angeles police officer vehicles to hear conversations of CHP dispatchers, to her knowledge.

The judge called a sidebar that lasted for three minutes, then court was recessed for the day.


THURSDAY, APRIL 9, 1992

The day's first witness called by the prosecution was Dr. Norman Shorr, an ophthalmologist who performed eye surgery on Rodney King on March 14, 1991. Dr. Shorr said King had suffered muscle and nerve damage and that the entire cheekbone had been broken free. He called the injury a blow-out fracture, which he said would not be caused by hitting a broad, flat surface, but would be consistent with pressure being put on the eyeball itself, not the structure above and below the eye.

Dr. Shorr used a skull to demonstrate the anatomy of the eye, pointing out the zygomatic arch, the maxillary sinus and the orbital floor, and showed X-rays of King's injuries. The injury was consistent with more than one impact, he said, and it "seems logical" that it was not caused by just a single fall.

When questioned by Mr. Stone, Dr. Shorr said he could not rule out impact from one fall or a number of falls causing the injuries. But he said there were a lot of orbital floor fractures and that he sees that kind of injury often from a handball hitting the eye.

Mr. Stone allowed Dr. Shorr to handle the police baton to assess the weight. He said that he did not know how many pounds of force it would take to cause an injury. He said he would have to look to literature in the field for that.

Mr. Stone had the doctor examine a photograph of Mr. King's injuries. He said he talked with Mr. King before performing the surgery and he had looked essentially like the photograph, but the sutures had been removed.

The judge declared a lunch recess at 12:05 p.m. and we were called back in at 2 p.m.

When Prosecutor Yochelson questioned the doctor, he testified that he didn't recall ever seeing anyone fall straight to a flat surface and sustain an injury like this one.

The witness was excused and the attorneys had another five-minute sidebar. The judge then told the jury we would not be in session at all on Friday.

Mr. White's next witness was LAPD Commander Michael Bostic, who was quite imposing in his meticulously tailored and well-fitting blue uniform. He had a commanding presence, as might be expected from a man in his position.

He explained that the hierarchy of upper management of the LAPD started with the Chief. Directly under him are the Assistant Chief and the Deputy Chief, both on the same hierarchical level. Under the Deputy Chief are seventeen Commanders, of which he is one. Commander Bostic gave a history of his experience with the LAPD, including his part in developing the Use of Force training bulletin and the Use of Force guidelines still being used. He also cited his experience as an investigator of use of force incidents. He was currently chairman of the LAPD's Use of Force Board, and taught use of force policy at the academy to new recruits as well as in-service training. He was presented to the court as an expert in use of force.

Bostic was shown Exhibit 320, a stair-step diagram teaching aid used by the academy training staff. He discussed the escalation/de-escalation policy as a way of describing to police officers the minimal force necessary. He said that force must be applied in direct response to some action by the suspect, or a perception the suspect may be about to do something. He said that the baton could be used when there is aggressive action from a suspect, or a perception that there is about to be. Reasonable force has to be based on reasonable fear, he said.

Commander Bostic was asked to look at the videotape, and to

have it stopped at the point where he felt the actions of the police officer were unreasonable or unnecessary. He had the tape stopped at 3:42:20 (just after Officer Briseno put his hand on Officer Powell's baton) and said that from that point forward, it was outside the policy of the LAPD. He also said that after that point, all use of force was unreasonable and unnecessary.

Under questioning from Mr. Barnett, Commander Bostic said he based his opinion on his personal review the previous week of Officer Powell's police report, Sergeant Koon's daily log, the Singer testimony and the video. He had considered nothing else, no other evidence. He told Mr. Barnett that he had looked at the video three to four times in real time, one time at twenty-five percent speed, and one time at six percent speed.

Mr. Barnett asked the witness many questions about his involvement in the development and writing of the use of force policy. Commander Bostic talked about the elements in response to danger: consideration of the fear factor, the ability or potential of the suspect to carry out the perceived threat, and the relative size of the officer compared to the suspect. He said the perception could differ among officers.

The more reasonable fear you have, the more force you can use, he said.

He said there is disagreement within the department about the use of force policy, and the interpretation of it. Mr. Barnett asked the witness about the background and responsibilities of Sergeant Duke, a previous witness. This elicited objections and a short sidebar conference.

Commander Bostic said that his nineteen years of experience included duty arresting suspects for approximately five-and-a-half years, during which time he probably made five to six hundred arrests. Although he was present for a lot of fights, he did not need to use the baton often. He said he had his baton out and hit somebody maybe ten or twelve times. He said he had actually seen maybe another twenty-five uses of the baton by other officers. He considered all of those instances to be within policy. He said he was in only one life-threatening circumstance where he feared that he might be killed.

Mr. Barnett continued his questioning of Commander Bostic, who testified that he met with the prosecutor for the first time the previous Monday for about two hours to discuss his testimony. The prosecutor told him they were looking for someone to determine if the use of force was in or out of policy. He said he had viewed the tape probably six times. (Last Thursday he said five times.)

He told Mr. Barnett that he had not been in a fight in his duties since 1978, and that he had never even witnessed an incident where excessive force was employed.

After his testimony on Thursday, he said he had talked to the District Attorney. There was some concern that he might have made some mistakes on Thursday.

Mr. Stone examined the witness next. He told Mr. Stone that when developing the Use of Force training bulletin and Use of Force guidelines in 1977 and 1978, he was one of three final draftspersons and they also got input from the Chief of Police and others. He said the Use of Force Board of Review consisted of five members who acted as advisers. They do not give opinions, but they do listen to what the officers involved have to say.

Commander Bostic said a Use of Force Review Board on this case had not been convened. He had a meeting with high-ranking LAPD officers right after the Foothill incident and the official position of the department was to wait until all the facts were in to make a judgment. He denied that he was influenced by Chief of Police Daryl Gates's remark that the incident was an "aberration."

After a recess, Mr. Stone continued his questioning. He had Commander Bostic point out that the swarm, or team takedown, was missing from the Use of Force step chart. He then introduced Exhibit 344, the Training Analysis, and referred to Page 131, which was the Use of Force chart that was still displayed on the tripod. He pointed out that it was current policy as of October 1991. Swarms and leg restraints were not included. The witness verified that there were no training bulletins on these techniques.

Commander Bostic said the department policy was that officers must follow the orders of the supervisor at the scene. Officers are trained to function like a team and the sergeant is the team leader.

Under questioning by Mr. Mounger, who showed him Exhibit

41, the training bulletin on Use of Force, Commander Bostic said the "policy is the overriding guideline of conduct for officers." Mr. Mounger then introduced Exhibit 413, a 536-page manual. The witness said that every officer is issued a copy of the manual, and they must sign for it. He also said that the policy is tighter than the law. You can violate the policy without violating the law in some cases.

Commander Bostic was then questioned by Mr. DePasquale, who asked about the significance of an officer's perception. The witness said that if the suspect had apparent capability to carry out a threat, an officer would not be penalized for using force. When Mr. DePasquale spoke of the banning of upper body holds, Mr. White objected, and there was a two-minute sidebar. When they returned, the witness testified that there were more tools available now to the line officer than thirteen or fourteen years ago. He said that some of the tools that used to be considered below the level of deadly force had now been elevated to deadly force.

Mr. DePasquale introduced Exhibit 504, a bulletin on Use of Force for the side handle baton. It said that the baton was not only to protect, but it can be used to decrease the likelihood of people getting killed. It is one of the tools just below deadly force, which includes the upper body hold and the gun. The baton is used to prevent situations from escalating to deadly force, he said.

Mr. DePasquale introduced Exhibit 505, an educational and training tool on deadly force in particular firearms. It said that in an effort to minimize the amount of force, alternatives to deadly force are to be used. The baton and the chokehold can be used instead of shooting a suspect.

Under questioning from Mr. White, Bostic said that the first time he saw the Foothill video on television in early March 1991, his reaction was shock at the amount of force being used. He had learned in fighting as a kid, that if the gang tackle was employed, if you had enough people to jump on them, you could get control of the other party. He said the officers should have handcuffed Mr. King when he was down on the ground instead of using the baton. He said they had three opportunities to do this.

He said it was unreasonable to believe they could get a PCP or alcohol suspect into a felony prone position. He said the officers should physically wrestle a suspect. There was an objection and a two-minute sidebar, then a recess.

After the recess, Mr. White again played the video for the witness, who repeated that the force was not reasonable after 3:42:20. On the first part of the tape, he said, it is hard to tell. He could see that Mr. King stands up. He said the first blow looks like it was within policy. The tape was fuzzy. He couldn't tell for sure.

He said if he had been in the officers' place that he would have felt fear, but the fear would not have been enough to justify continued use of the baton. He then pointed out places on the tape where he thought handcuffing could have taken place. At 3:45:24 he believed Mr. King could have been taken into custody if the officers had moved quickly. At 3:55:04 and 4:03:27 on the video, he believed Mr. King could have been taken into custody using the swarm technique. He said there was another opportunity at 4:21:06, when Mr. King was prone.

Commander Bostic pointed out that Sergeant Charles Duke had testified for the defense, not on behalf of the LAPD, and that he felt that Duke didn't understand the police department's use of force policy.

Mr. Stone asked the witness if reasonable minds could not differ in this matter or was he the only one who is correct, and the witness answered, "Yes." He said he did not have to seek advice from experts. He said the only thing the officers could say that would influence him is that the suspect had a weapon or that he was about to use a weapon.

He also said that it was his testimony that all police officers at the academy are taught the swarm technique during the enrichment phase. He said he found it very difficult to believe that some officers alleged they had not been taught the swarm technique.

The witness said that a pursuit was a particularly volatile situation because the officers are "pumped." Mr. Stone cited a hypothetical situation where a suspect is not cooperating and PCP is suspected. The witness said they should first try verbalization to calm the suspect, and then all options are available to the officers all the time. If the Taser does not work, get another one. When Mr. Mounger examined the witness again, Bostic reiterated that training bulletins are given to all employees. He repeated that Sergeant Duke did not understand department policy. When Mr. Mounger asked if that is being corrected, the witness answered, "Yes."

Mr. White questioned the witness who said that under some circumstances, a suspect can be hit with a baton while on the ground.

The witness was excused and after a sidebar, Lieutenant Patrick Conmay was recalled by Mr. Barnett. Lieutenant Conmay testified that on the night of the incident, he was Watch Commander. He denied having a conversation with Leslie Wiley and said she did not tell him at any time that the message had been transmitted. That appeared to be the only thing the prosecution wanted clarified because we were excused after that.


TUESDAY, APRIL 14, 1992

The jury was not called in until 2 p.m. The first witness, Officer Annette Olivas, was called by Mr. Yochelson. She testified that she has been an instructor at the LAPD Academy since September 1988 and teaches physical training, baton use, upper body control holds, twist locks. She said she taught the swarm technique as part of the curriculum in the enrichment phase, which occurs after the self-defense test.

She recalled Officer Wind going through the academy and said she taught the swarm technique during the eighteenth week, probably in September 1990. She could not say for sure that Officer Wind was present because she taught four groups the takedown on the same day. There was a demonstration in classroom format of the takedown procedure, she said.

She said she instructed groups not to tie up with a suspect but to use the baton instead.

She said that she might possibly have told officers that a PCP suspect has the strength of ten men. Mr. Yochelson objected and there was a sidebar. She then said that part of the training of recruits was that different suspects can pose different levels of danger to an officer; that a PCP suspect was difficult to deal with.

Mr. DePasquale asked Officer Olivas a series of questions about what the officers were taught to do with their gun during a team takedown. She said it was optional. He asked the same question about the baton. She said it should be left in the ring. She said

*Moral Uncertainty*

that during the instruction she did not bring up the possibility of a suspect getting the gun or baton during the team takedown, unless someone asked the question.

She did not recall drilling it into the recruits that it is better to break bones with the baton than to physically tie up with them.

Mr. Mounger then asked the witness if she had taught Sergeant Koon the swarm technique and she said she had not.

Officer Olivas told Mr. Stone that the swarm technique is referred to officially as the team takedown. She said proficiency in the use of the baton, pain compliance holds and weapon retention are taught as part of the self-defense course. If trainees do not pass the self-defense test, they are given remedial classes before work or after work and go on to the enrichment phase. She said the team takedown is a two-hour block in the enrichment phase The team leader must assign a limb to each officer and they grab the limbs simultaneously, and they are told, "Don't let go." They are taught not to allow a kneeling position. They must keep the suspect prone. If a suspect is pushing up, the officer might not have control.

Mr. Stone conferred with the prosecution attorneys and then there was a short sidebar.

Officer Olivas told Mr. Stone she was not present at all of the instruction of the enrichment phase, but that all of the officers should have gotten the training.

Mr. Yochelson next called Officer Matthew Lindholm, an instructor at the California Highway Patrol Academy. He has taught the technique of using a gun when approaching a suspect. In a high-risk felony stop, he said if a suspect is on the ground, you approach him with a shuffle step or slide step, weapon out, close to the body. The weapon remains out until a control hold has been achieved. He said a "forward shuffle" is used to maintain your balance. This method has been taught for about ten years and is still being taught, he said.

The witness then told Mr. Stone that at some point the officer grasps with his free hand the hand or wrist of the suspect, prone or kneeling. Once they have achieved moderate control, they put the gun away.

The witness was questioned by Mr. Mounger and told him that he had never taught at the LAPD.

The witness was excused and there was a sidebar, after which Mr. Yochelson offered two stipulations regarding the photographs of Rodney King, and they were accepted by the defense. The prosecution said they had no further rebuttal witnesses, but they might have further rebuttal evidence later.

Mr. Barnett recalled Ms. Glenda Jean Tosti and showed her Exhibit 223, a printout of the ACC terminal at the Foothill Division March 3, 1991. It contained incoming and outgoing messages to and from the ACC terminal. It recorded times of the messages. He also introduced Exhibit 224 which was a blow-up of the document. He placed it on the easel and pointed out the 00:56:04 entry, which was a message from Unit 16L140 (Sergeant Koon's unit) to the Foothill ACC.

It read, *U just had a big time use of force, tased and beat the suspect of a CHP pursuit big time.*

Ms. Tosti said a message could be preserved by a command from the operator, and could be re-displayed at any time.

He pointed out the reply from ACC to 16L140 (The "lizard" message). The witness testified that by sending the message in two steps instead of one step, it would leave the 00:56:04 message on the ACC screen.

The only way to really know when the message was wiped off the screen is to talk to the ACC operator, she said.

Mr. Barnett then introduced a Daily Work Sheet printout as Exhibit 325, listing deployment of officers for that evening. 16L170 was Sergeant Wilson. The ACC operator had sent a message to 16L170 at 01:26:25 that said *Good-bye I'm gone. X's and O's.* That was the last entry on Exhibit 223.

Obviously, this was all intended to prove whether or not Officer Briseno could have seen the message.

Mr. Mounger then questioned the witness, and she told him that it was a personal preference as to whether the operator normally cleared the screen after each message. They are not taught one way or the other. She said the first time the message could have been gone was 00:57:03. It could have been left on the screen as late as 01:07. The witness was briefly questioned further by Mr. Stone about times of the messages. Mr. White questioned the witness about messages from ACC to Sergeant Wilson about the pursuit and a Code 415.

Mr. Stone then questioned the witness about Code 415. She said it could mean anything from a fight to a loud disturbance. The witness was excused and there was another sidebar. The jury was told to report for duty tomorrow at 1:30 p.m. The jury was excused and court recessed.

WEDNESDAY, APRIL 15, 1992

The first witness called by Mr. Stone, LAPD Officer Jace Burton Kessler, said that he had attended the academy with Officer Powell through conclusion in December 1987. He said they took the self-defense test and training in use of force together. After the self-defense test, toward the end of the class, they participated in the enrichment phase, but they did not learn the swarm technique, gang tackle, or team takedown, he said.

Mr. Yochelson showed the witness Exhibit 502, the Recruit Officer Syllabus. Officer Kessler said it did not look familiar and it may or may not have been given to them. He said they were given weekly schedules. He said they had been taught weaponless defense (if the gun is taken away) during the original phase of training. He said that during the enrichment phase they were taught martial arts type weapons, knives, and techniques in long-rifle and shotgun take-away. They were also taught to use the leg restraint or cord cuff. He said the enrichment phase was for a period of one or two hours, and consisted of one class.

There was a short sidebar, after which it was announced that there would be no further testimony. The judge said court would be recessed until Monday, April 20, to allow the attorneys to prepare their closing arguments and to allow him to prepare his instructions to the jury. We were dismissed for a four-day Easter weekend.

# Chapter Thirteen: The Prosecution's Final Argument

The long weekend provided a nice break. I was feeling refreshed and eager to get on with it, but true to form, we were left sitting all morning, and not called into court until after lunch. Apologizing for the delay, the judge explained that the next step would be for the attorneys to present their arguments. The arguments were not evidence, he said, but simply an opportunity for each side to interpret the evidence in the best possible light from their point of view, and to try to put it into the perspective that they hoped we would share when we got into the jury room. The prosecution would go first, then the defense counsel, with the prosecution getting the last chance to speak before we began deliberating.

Mr. White began. Apparently he had finally caught the cold that the judge and the attorneys had been passing around. His voice was raspy and he obviously was not feeling well. He started out by apologizing in advance about how long he planned to talk, saying he needed to show us about sixteen charts. Because he had been losing his voice, he said he would take it slow, and not raise his voice.

It would be our duty, Mr. White said, to decide the case strictly on the basis of what we had seen and heard in the courtroom, to be impartial, and not to be an advocate for one side or the other. Neither the Los Angeles Police Department, nor Los Angeles Police Chief Daryl Gates, nor Mayor Tom Bradley was on trial, Mr. White said. There were only four defendants to judge, and it was up to us to decide if what those four men did was against the law.

He said we should not be concerned that we hadn't gotten a chance to hear what Rodney King himself had to say about what happened. He said it would be improper for us to draw any conclusions about why he didn't testify, but added that the defense would have called him if they had thought it would help their case.

He pointed out that other witnesses had described for us what happened. Besides, he said, the best evidence was the videotape itself. "This videotape is the central piece of evidence in this case. We don't need to rely on the word of the defendants. The videotape shows conclusively what occurred that night, and it's something that can't be rebutted. It is important that you realize just how important the videotape is. Without it we wouldn't be here. Without it, Rodney King would be facing the false accusations of Stacey Koon and Laurence Powell based on the false reports they wrote that night," Mr. White said.

Mr. Mounger had been coughing relentlessly, and Mr. White stopped to comment that he wasn't the only sick one.

"Police officers have a tough job to do," he continued. "They are dealing with an element of society that most of us would rather not deal with. Their life is always potentially on the line. We recognize that these defendants had a tough job to do, but recognizing that tough job, we also expect and I think we demand, that a police officer follow the law.

"We expect them to treat criminal suspects fairly, honestly and like human beings. Even though they might not be someone you want to invite home for dinner or even though they might not be someone you want as your neighbor, they should be treated like human beings, not like animals. And when they have done something wrong and you write a report, you write truthful facts in that report."

Mr. White propped up a chart on an easel in the front of the courtroom, listing the counts and special allegations in the case, and indicated which defendant was charged with which counts. If we found Sergeant Koon guilty on Counts 1 and 2, then he couldn't be guilty on Count 5, Mr. White said. It had to do with whether he was a principal or if he was an aider or abettor. He couldn't be both, so we had to decide which. The prosecution wanted us to find him guilty of Counts 1 and 2 and not guilty of Count 5, Mr. White said.

He talked about Count 2, explaining what elements were necessary for us to find the defendants guilty on that count. He showed us the PR-24 side handle baton, and said the prosecution was alleging that this was a deadly weapon, capable of producing death or great bodily injury. He said the prosecution was alleging there had been great bodily injury to Mr. King's face, which they believed was caused by deliberate head shots by Officer Powell. They also alleged that Mr. King suffered great bodily injury when his leg was broken. He pointed out that there didn't need to be an actual bodily injury as a necessary element of the crime in Count 1. The only thing the prosecution had to prove was that the force used was with a means that could produce bodily injury. Unless it was proved that there was a lawful reason for the blows and for Officer Briseno's stomp, that is unlawful force.

The only time a peace officer is allowed to use force is in self-defense or in defense of others, or in effecting an arrest, overcoming resistance, or preventing escape. The force must be reasonable force. Unreasonable force is unlawful, Mr. White told us.

Officers Powell and Wind were charged in Counts 3 and 4 with Filing a False Report by a Police Officer. In order to find them guilty of filing a false report, we had to find that they knowingly and intentionally made a false statement in the report on a material matter.

We were looking at two kinds of crimes, Mr. White said. The first, assault with a deadly weapon and assault under color of authority, are general intent crimes. No intent to violate the law is necessary. These officers did not have to intend to violate the law when hitting Mr. King with the baton, but if their conduct did violate the law, they are guilty.

The second kind, accessory after the fact and filing a false report, are specific intent crimes, he said. In order to be guilty of those crimes, there needs to be a specific criminal intent. When an officer writes a report, he must specifically intend to make a false statement regarding a material matter.

Mr. White told us to put ourselves in the shoes of a reasonable police officer and determine what we would have done. He said as triers of fact, we have to determine at what point the right of reasonable force ceases. When we reach the point on the tape when we say, "enough is enough," then everything else is unreasonable, Mr. White said.

Mr. White said we had to decide the case against each of the four officers separately.

He then set out methodically to outline the evidence against each of them, starting with Officer Powell.

The videotape, he said, showed "unnecessary, unreasonable brutality by Mr. Powell." "From the first moment until Mr. King is handcuffed, Officer Powell is relentless in his baton blows, even though there are points in time when Mr. King is on the ground not doing anything, but Officer Powell continues. He strikes Mr. King the most with the baton for no apparent reason; the man is not resisting or trying to escape, there is no reason for it."

He said that Officer Powell wrote a report "totally contrary to the facts," because he knew what happened was excessive force.

"He knows what he did was wrong, White said.

Mr. White said that Officer Powell's laughter when he called for the ambulance proved that he was not afraid of Mr. King.

"Why would he be laughing if he was in fear for his life? He's laughing for one reason: he just punished this man and he thinks it is funny."

Mr. White called Officer Powell's typed message to his friend Corina Smith, "I haven't beaten any one this bad in a long time," as "close as you are going to get to a confession in this case."

"He has to tell someone, he has to brag about it," Mr. White said. "This man laughs, jokes, goes to the hospital and taunts Mr. King. Does this sound like someone who has just used reasonable force?"

Mr. White said that Officer Powell's "gorillas in the mist" remark was clearly a racial slur and might explain his motivation.

He placed another chart on the easel, showing what he claimed were discrepancies in Officer Powell's testimony that a southbound car had to slam on its brakes to keep from going through the green light at Foothill and nearly smashed into King's Hyundai.

"Tim and Melanie Singer said they never saw that, they didn't tell him that. He wants to make this situation seem more dangerous than it actually was."

Mr. White said Officer Powell lied in his report when he wrote that Mr. King got out of and back into his car.

"Even Officer Powell testified this didn't happen. What is he trying to tell the reader of this report? He is trying to establish that things were a little bit more dangerous out there than they really were. So does he say he leaned out and leaned back in? No. He says, 'He exited the vehicle then got back in and then exited again.' That sounds like a very serious situation. That would be something very dangerous, but that didn't happen. But that didn't stop Officer Powell from writing it in his report."

In Powell's testimony, Mr. White pointed out, "he has Mr. King throwing him off. Again, he is trying to make things seem a little bit more dangerous out there. Then he says, 'Defendant recovered almost immediately (this is after the tasing) and resumed his hostile charge in our direction.' Well, the video clearly shows there was no 'our' there. It was just Officer Powell. If you have an individual who is willing to attack two officers, it is more dangerous situation than if Mr. King moved in the direction of one officer."

Mr. White said he had found a total of twenty-six lies in Officer Powell's testimony or in his report. He propped up another chart, listing the lies. Officer Powell claimed he smelled a chemical odor on Mr. King's breath, but nobody else smelled it. Officer Powell wrote in his report that Mr. King had abrasions and contusions, but didn't mention lacerations. Mr. White said Officer Powell didn't want anyone to know that Mr. King had been cut.

Mr. White said it wasn't the jury's job to worry about whether or not Mr. King was guilty of felony evading. There was a failure to yield, and at some point that night it became felony evading. He pointed out that when Tim Wind filled out the Use of Force reports, he did not check the PCP box, and he did not note any lacerations. He suggested that might be because the officers knew that Mr. King was not under the influence of PCP. He said Sergeant Troutt's report, which said that the suspect would have to be booked because of the injuries he received during the altercation, also did not mention anything about PCP.

At this point, Mr. White asked for a recess, which the judge granted.

When we came back, Mr. White summed up the prosecution's case against Officer Powell. He said that the videotape alone was enough to convict him, but we also needed to consider the lies in his report, the taunts to Rodney King at the hospital and the "gorillas in the mist" comment he had made just after the incident. He called those factors circumstantial evidence, and he said that the judge would instruct us that circumstantial evidence is just as valid as direct evidence.

He said that the only reasonable interpretation was that Officer Powell knew that the force he used was unreasonable, and that's why he lied about it. He said we had both direct and circumstantial

*Moral Uncertainty*

evidence not only that Officer Powell filed a false report, but that he was guilty of Count 1 and Count 2.

Mr. White then turned to the case against Sergeant Koon. Someone who aids and abets a crime is as guilty as someone who directly commits the acts, he said. He displayed a chart explaining why the prosecution believed that the evidence showed Sergeant Koon was guilty of aiding and abetting.

Koon was in charge the whole time and everything that happened was at his direction, he said.

Mr. White said the judge would instruct us that mere presence at the scene of a crime is not enough evidence to convict someone, "but this is more than mere presence at the scene," because the other officers looked to him, and assumed that if the use of force was excessive, he would stop it.

"By him saying nothing, he allowed it to continue. He was the one who instructed them where to strike Mr. King. When Mr. King was down on the ground they were still striking him in those same areas. He allowed this to continue. There is no doubt that he is an aider and abettor."

Mr. White posted a chart entitled "Sergeant Koon's Lies and Inaccuracies."

"Sergeant Koon started out his testimony and he said, 'Well, the first thing I heard was there was a pursuit at Paxton and Foothill and then about a minute later I heard the pursuit was at Paxton and Glenoaks.' " He said Sergeant Koon said that told him that meant Mr. King must be going sixty, seventy or eighty miles per hour.

"The only thing wrong with that was he never heard this first transmission. That's why we called in the Emergency Board Operator who actually transmitted this information over the audio. Now it starts out where the EBO, Miss Brown says, '911 Emergency Operator Number 812.'

"CHP then says, 'Hi, this is CHP. We're in a pursuit right now.'

"And the EBO comes back with, 'Okay, what's your location in the pursuit?'

"CHP says, 'Southbound Paxton and Foothill.'

"The EBO then says, 'Southbound Paxton?'

"CHP then says, 'Yeah.'

"EBO, 'At Foothill?'

"CHP, 'Yeah.'

"EBO says, 'What are you in pursuit of?'

"CHP says, 'Uh, just a second. It was a failure to yield at this time. It's a white Hyundai.'

"EBO says, 'White Hyundai?'

"CHP says, 'Two King Frank Mary, 102. We are approaching Glenoaks southbound Paxton approaching Glenoaks.'

"EBO, 'Okay, let me broadcast this to our units.'

"CHP, 'Thank you.'

"EBO then broadcasts, 'All units CHP advises they are in pursuit of a vehicle southbound Paxton approaching Glenoaks, a white Hyundai, Two King Frank Mary 102, Two King Frank Mary 102. Vehicle wanted for failure to yield.'

"When the Emergency Board Operator was having this initial conversation with the CHP, this did not go out over the air. He never heard it. This was a lie. Never heard it. She even testified. At the point in time where she said, 'Okay, let me broadcast this to our units,' that's when she opened up the Foothill frequency. That's when Sergeant Koon could first hear about this pursuit. And even Officer Powell says that's when he first heard of it. Right here at the bottom of page one. So he never heard this. He lied. Never heard it at all.

"When you go through this entire transcript and this is a transcript of the Foothill frequency audio tape, there is nothing in here about CHP requesting LAPD or Foothill unit because they have an LA Unified with them. So when he testified to that on the stand, he was lying," Mr. White said.

"Next, his time of arrival at the scene. He says when he got to the scene, Mr. King was already out of his vehicle, on his knees, glassy-eyed. However, going back to this transcript, at 00:50:18 a Code 6 on Foothill east of Osborne goes out. 00:50:18. That means they're stopped east of Osborne, on Foothill east of Osborne. And the RTO, Mr. Frierson, comes back and says, 'Suspects are Code 6, the units are Code 6 on Foothill, east of Osborne.' Eight seconds later, you hear Sergeant Koon's voice saying, 'L140 there appears to be sufficient units here.' He arrived at the scene approximately eleven seconds after Officer Powell puts out a Code 6. Well, did Mr. King get out of that car in eleven seconds? Well, if he did he was a lot more cooperative than they're trying to make him appear to be. No, I just think Sergeant Koon lied to you about what time he got to the scene. Now why he needs to lie about that, I don't know, I have no idea. But his statement is, 'When I got there Mr. King was out of the car on his hands and knees.' Well, he got there a little bit before that, but he wants you to believe he got there later. He got there eleven seconds after Officer Powell and Officer Wind, irrefutable evidence, by his own voice, he was there eleven seconds later."

Mr. White put up a blow-up of Sergeant Koon's daily log.

"He testified that the officers were flung off of Mr. King in this initial swarm. He says they were flung off, they were thrown off. All the officers. Well, Rolando Solano, who was one of the officers out there said that was not true. 'I wasn't flung off. I felt a little wiggle. I was holding onto the leg, I had a hold of the leg, and I felt a little wiggle.' He wasn't flung off, but again, he wants to make you think Mr. King is superhuman, he's Superman. Four officers on him and he just threw them all off. That's not true. It's not true at all."

Mr. White said, "You think to yourself, 'Wow, this is quite a suspect they have here, not only is he receiving all these power strokes and jabs, but he's also fighting off the effects of this Taser, this device that is supposed to cripple someone.' Well, that's not exactly true. That's the impression he wanted to leave with the reader of this report. Not only was he receiving these power strokes and jabs but the Taser was going the entire time.

"But Sergeant Koon said, 'Well, the Taser wasn't really going the entire time. It was only going about fifteen seconds or so, and actually, I turned it off.' The Taser wasn't going the entire time. He knew the Taser wasn't going the entire time when he wrote the report, but again when you write this report, you want to make this man seem a little bit more dangerous, a little bit more of a threat, a little bit more of an individual whom you need to use this great amount of force on, you write things like 'Taser going the entire time.' "

White said that clearly Rodney King did not comply immediately, but considering that he was under the influence of alcohol, being given commands from various directions from three or four officers, with a helicopter hovering overhead, "it is amazing to me that he was able to comply at all, but he did put his hands where they could be seen, he did put his hands on top of his head, he did get down to his knees like he was instructed, he did get down on the ground like he was instructed. Officer Briseno said he did."

Mr. White said that Sergeant Koon wanted to write a report himself so he could cover up the fact that there had been excessive force used.

As Mr. White put up a chart entitled DEFENDANT WIND, he said the jury should not dread that each attorney would talk as long as he did, because he had to describe the case against all four defendants while each defense attorney only needed to defend his own client.

The key piece of evidence against Officer Wind, he said, was "the video which shows unreasonable baton strikes by Officer Wind, unreasonable kicks by Officer Wind. These are clearly shown on the video at a point where there is no resistance by Mr. King, he is on the ground."

The prosecutor said, "Mr. King has the right, once unreasonable force is being used, he has the right to defend himself, he has the right to try to get away, he has the right to try to cover up. So at a point in time where you believe or you think that unreasonable force is started, if there is any movement by Mr. King, he is justified in making that move, he is justified in moving around because he can defend himself."

Mr. White said, "So there is a point in time, clearly, in this video, I believe, where everyone can agree an unreasonable force started. And that's real late in the video and I think everyone can agree on that, but when you look at the video you'll see unreasonable baton strikes, you'll see unreasonable kicks by Defendant Wind."

Mr. White pointed out that Officer Wind heard Officer Powell taunt Mr. King at Pacifica Hospital, "but not only did he remain silent, those taunts directed at Mr. King said, 'we.' 'We played a pretty good game of baseball. We hit quite a few home runs.' As this was said, Officer Wind stood silent. The court is going to read to you an instruction called 'Adoptive Admission.' An adoptive admission is one where, by your behavior, you adopt the comments or you adopt the statements of another person. By his silence, by him standing there, sitting there, being in the room while these comments were being made to Mr. King, about we did this, we did that, we won the game tonight, you lost the game, by him standing there or sitting there doing nothing, he adopted those comments. He is agreeing with those comments by his silence."

Mr. White also pointed out that Lawrence Davis testified that Officer Wind held up his baton and patted it when he was asked how Rodney King got hurt.

In comparison to Officer Powell and Sergeant Koon, Officer Wind's actions might not seem so bad, Mr. White said. "But if you look at the tape and you determine at some point that unreasonable force has begun and Officer Wind strikes Mr. King after that point, Officer Wind kicks Mr. King after that point, he is just as guilty as any of the other defendants, just as guilty."

Then Mr. White turned his attention to Officer Briseno. He said he didn't have a chart for him because the only thing Officer Briseno was charged with doing was stomping on Mr. King with his foot and that was clearly visible in the videotape.

When Officer Briseno's foot goes down on Mr. King, there is an obvious reaction, he said. "This man's body, 250 pounds, violently reacts, every part of his body violently reacts to this stomp."

Mr. White then showed the tape again, at what he said was twenty-five percent slow motion, so that we could see how Mr. King responded to the stomp.

"At the time where Mr. King was the most compliant, at the time where Mr. King is the least resistant of any moment on this tape, is the time that he delivers this forceful stomp to Mr. King."

Mr. White said that Officer Briseno's contention was that he was trying to help protect Mr. King from further injury. "You have to ask yourself, you have to determine whether or not a reasonable person in the same or similar circumstances would believe the force that was used there was necessary to prevent this further infliction of bodily attack on Mr. King. Officer Briseno said that's what he felt, that's what he thought. But when you see that force being used there, that force is unreasonable."

Mr. White pointed out that the prosecution didn't have to prove that the stomp actually hurt Mr. King, just that it was enough force to be likely to hurt him.

"Now why did Mr. Briseno do that? Maybe he just got caught up in the frenzy of this event."

Mr. White put up a new chart. He said that both sides agreed that any blow to the head was unreasonable use of force, and that the prosecution admitted that it was permissible for the officers to use the baton in the beginning of the incident, to subdue Mr. King.

"It is our assertion that the evidence shows that this incident went on too long. That at some point, enough was enough, they should have stopped." Mr. White said that after Mr. King was deliberately hit in the head, they should have stopped.

"The importance of this first blow is that if it is a deliberate and intentional baton strike to the head, every use of force after that deliberate and intentional baton strike to the head is unreasonable, every one. Once that first blow is unreasonable use of force, Mr. King has a right to defend himself. So if you find that that first blow is a deliberate and intentional baton strike to the head, that's unreasonable force. No reason for it. No reason for it, because remember this is not a self-defense case anymore, or according to the defense, it never was, but there was no reason to hit this man in the head with a baton even if he was moving toward Officer Powell. That is unreasonable."

The chart listed the names of the witnesses who contended they saw a head shot, including Melanie Singer, Tim Singer, Ted Briseno and Rolando Solano, who said he saw high swings which might indicate head shots.

Mr. White said that the medical evidence indicated there were baton blows to the head. Mr. King's head would have to be in an unusual position to break those bones in his face by falling.

"I mean, look at this tape, you have a man on the ground, rolling around and they continue to strike him. Why? What is he doing to be a threat to them? What is he doing to be aggressive toward them? What is he doing as far as escaping? And I never heard anyone mention escape, in fact Sergeant Koon said hey, he wasn't escaping, he was attacking. And remember again, self-defense isn't an issue. So you have to figure, what is this man doing that justifies the continued use of this baton?"

Mr. White said if the situation was as dangerous as Sergeant Koon and Officer Powell said it was, then the other police officers on the scene would not be "standing around, non-responsive, casual, nonchalant attitudes, arms folded."

"If it was as dangerous as they are saying, wouldn't these other officers also appear to be in fear? They're not in fear. No one was in fear."

Mr. White said that the defense's position reminded him of a cartoon film he had seen with his daughter. In the movie, there was a cat disguised as a mouse, chasing another mouse. "All the other mice say, 'Look, a cat, a cat.' And the cat says, 'No, no, you can't trust your eyes.' Then the mask comes off, and the cat says, 'Who are you going to trust, me or your own eyes?' "

Mr. White said, "And that's what the defendants are trying to tell you. Who are you going to trust, them or your own eyes?"

He then played the whole videotape for us yet again.

"Now, who are you going to believe, the defendants or your own eyes? Thank you."

# Chapter Fourteen: Closing Arguments for Officer Powell

TUESDAY, APRIL 21, 1992

Attorney Michael Stone was the first of the defense attorneys to present closing arguments on behalf of Officer Powell. He began by joking that the previous day he felt sorry for Mr. White because he had an awful sore throat, and for Mr. Mounger because he had a cough.

"And then it occurred to me that we all came to court this week with some things we would rather not have come to court with. Mr. White came with that awful sore throat, Mr. Mounger came with his terrible cough, and I came with this awful haircut."

Everyone laughed. I must remark that Mr. Stone was right; he had a terrible haircut, very short, with non-existent sideburns. It was good he could laugh at it.

Mr. Stone said he wanted to talk about a police officer's duty. He said Officer Powell could have ignored the CHP request for help, but he didn't. There were "many opportunities for Officer Powell to avoid the risk and the threat to his own personal safety . . . But he determined to stand his ground, he determined to take the necessary steps to do his duty, and as a result of those choices that he made that night on March 3, 1991 early in the morning, he is sitting here as a defendant before this jury. It's not Rodney Glen King who is sitting here. It is Officer Laurence Powell, Sergeant Stacey Koon, Officer Ted Briseno and Officer Tim Wind."

Mr. Stone went on. "What do we, ladies and gentlemen, as members of the community, expect from our police? What is it we want them to do? What is it that we would want Officer Powell to have done on March 3, 1991? The answer is simple, isn't it? We want them to do their duty. We expect them to do their duty. Indeed, as Mr. White mentioned, we demand that they do their duty.

"Duty required Officer Powell to act, not run away, and he was faithful to that charge. Duty did not require Officer Powell to end up on a gurney himself in the emergency room of some local hospital. Duty did not require Officer Powell to end up toes up on a slab in a morgue."

He said that police officers "don't get paid to roll around in the dirt with the likes of Rodney Glen King. That's not their job, that's not their duty, and if we, as members of the community, demand that they do that, the thin blue line that separates the law-abiding from the not-law-abiding will disintegrate."

Officers, Mr. Stone said, are "not robocops. They hurt, they feel pain, they bleed and they die just like everyone else. And we leave it to them to take care of the mean streets, so that we can safely enjoy our lives."

Mr. Stone said the case boiled down to "whether or not Officer Laurence Powell acted as a courageous, faithful, responsible police officer, or whether he acted in the manner of a brutal thug in a uniform who abused and beat another human being with no justification."

"It has to be one or the other. Either he acted as a responsible police officer or he acted like a uniformed hoodlum and that's all there is to it," Stone said.

Although the videotape was violent, he said, it does not depict uncontrolled police brutality. "You see, rather, a controlled application of baton strikes for the very obvious reason of getting this man into custody."

Whether they did it precisely the right way, he said, might be arguable, "but the main purpose of what they did is obvious and it's uncontradicted. It was to take this man into custody. It was not to administer summary punishment."

Mr. Stone said that Sergeant Koon had taken responsibility for the actions of his officers, and that he was impressed by Koon's "courage and his guts. He didn't come into this courtroom, sniveling, back pedaling, turning on his own men one bit. You didn't see or hear one bit of that in an effort by Sergeant Koon to save his own skin. He was a police supervisor out there on March 3, 1991 and he was a police supervisor in this trial."

He said "from start to finish," Rodney King controlled his own destiny. "He chose to drink, he chose to get in the car, he chose to drive 100 to 115 miles an hour on the freeway, he chose to run from the CHP on the freeway, he chose to ignore the red light and siren. He chose to run red lights. He chose to drive eighty miles an hour on city streets, in an effort to get away."

Mr. Stone said that King was on parole and knew he was

violating the conditions of his parole by being drunk and speeding. "He knows what's going to happen if he is taken into custody. This is not a new drill."

At the scene, he said, the two passengers understood what was happening and got out of the car. "They are both black people, African Americans. Nobody beat them up."

He said, "Rodney Glen King had 7.8 miles to stop. Rodney Glen King had 7.8 miles to comply. At the scene, Rodney Glen King had four minutes to submit to arrest. Rodney Glen King made the choice every time he had the opportunity to make a choice. And every choice Rodney Glen King made was the wrong one. Now whose fault is that?"

Mr. Stone said the evidence could be broken down into eight categories, which he had summarized on a chart displayed on the easel. He said the first "pocket" of evidence concerned Officer Powell's remarks prior to the incident about "gorillas in the mist." He said those remarks had nothing to do with what happened at the scene and he drew a big X through that part of the chart.

He said when lawyers don't have a strong case, sometimes they offer distractions, "throwing stuff on the wall to see what sticks. Other lawyers refer to it as opening up a box of butterflies before the jury and handing all the jurors a butterfly net and saying, 'Go chase that.' Don't go chase it, ladies and gentlemen. It's not connected to this case."

He said the second pocket of evidence concerned use of force and the LAPD policies, which he said was important, because Officer Powell's actions reflected what he had been taught by the police department.

Testimony about Rodney King's injuries was important, he said, because knowing the type of injuries that Mr. King had or did not have has a direct bearing, a direct connection with, what happened at the scene in terms of use of force. "But again, the issues are not whether department policy was followed here or whether Mr. King got good medical treatment."

The fourth pocket was what Mr. Stone called "Rodney King issues." He said Rodney King had no obligation to testify, but since he didn't, we couldn't help wondering what he would have said if he had testified.

The next three issues concerned the Koon/Powell reports—the Sergeant's log, two pages written by Sergeant Stacey Koon and the seven-page police report written by Officer Powell. "Now both Sergeant Koon and Officer Powell are charged with Penal Code Section 118.1, which is 'Writing a False Police Report,' so that's a real important issue for you to decide."

But if the officers told the truth or did not intend to be untruthful, "then it's just another pocket of free-floating evidence out here. It doesn't tell us anything about the main issue in the case, the use of force."

"The next green circle, number six, is 'Post-incident MDTs.' What are we talking about here? Well, this is the MDT message where my client said to Corina Smith minutes after the Rodney Glen King encounter, 'Oops.' 'Oops what?' 'I haven't beaten anyone this bad in a long time.' "

Stone said those messages could show Powell's state of mind. "But what state of mind? Is it an admission of an unlawful assault and battery on Mr. King, or is it an expression of disbelief about how much force it took to take Mr. King into custody?"

Mr. Stone said the message was like a comment made at a doughnut shop, just casual conversation between offices, and had no bearing on the case.

The seventh pocket concerned the remarks made at the hospital, Mr. Stone said. He characterized the remarks about "hitting a few home runs," as "the kind of banter that goes on all the time between persons in custody and police officers." Stone said neither of the nurses had used the expression "taunting."

Mr. Stone said that CHP Officers Tim and Melanie Singer caused a problem at the scene when they let suspects climb out of both sides of a car. He said it would have been prudent to have all of the occupants of the car get out on the same side so they can all be observed at the same time.

"But Mr. Helms and Mr. Bryant, they got out of the car without any problem, got out, proned out, and they lay there and they had no problem. They chose to do what they were told to do. And they didn't have a problem."

Mr. Stone continued. "When people don't get out of the car and then they make funny motions and then they start out of the car and then they get back in, that's a danger signal. You don't know whether the driver is arming himself, whether he is trying to get a position of advantage. It is a danger signal, and whether or not he got technically all the way out of the car or not is, to me, irrelevant."

Mr. Stone stopped to take a drink out of one of the red paper cups the attorneys used.

"Picking the spot. Why did Mr. King choose to stop where he stopped? Always something that the officers have to think about . . . It was right next to the Hansen Dam Park. It's dark, it's open, there's cover to hide, a foot pursuit in that area to the right of the car stop would have been a real control problem.

"Mr. King chose this, not these police officers. These officers weren't out looking for Mr. King, laying in the weeds. He found them . . . Now at that point, every officer at the scene concluded, 'We got a duster on our hands.' There's no doubt about that. There's no doubt about that. Their perception was this guy's under the influence of PCP. And oh boy, look at how big he is. We've got problems. All right. That's what confronted these officers at that time."

Mr. Stone said Sergeant Koon took charge to prevent Melanie Singer from firing her gun.

"What do you think would have happened? You would have had a shooting. Either that or that gun would have been taken away. So this is what confronted Sergeant Koon. This is why he said, 'Get back.' It wasn't because, 'Hey, CHP, get out of this. LAPD is here, we're going to beat this black man.' "

Mr. Stone said that Ted Briseno at 140 pounds and Laurence Powell at 193 pounds were no match for Rodney King.

"What did Mr. King do with Laurence Powell on his back? He did a pushup. Do you know how much strength that takes? And Powell rolled off. It tells you just how strong this man was. The swarm technique, ladies and gentlemen, would have been a disaster."

At that point, Mr. Stone said, Sergeant Koon used the Taser gun and Mr. King lunged at him. Mr. Stone pointed out that Timothy Singer had testified that King was " 'like something out of a monster movie. This man, Rodney King, got up and I could see the muscles in his face convulsing from the electricity and it was like right out of a monster movie.' Well, that's what these officers confronted out there that night."

Mr. Stone asked the judge if this was a convenient time to break and the judge declared a recess, saying we would resume at twenty minutes to the hour. After the break, Mr. Stone said that before he started commenting again on the issues on his chart, he wanted to talk about a point Mr. White had made about Mr. King and Officer Powell.

"Mr. White said that Officer Powell wanted to hit Mr. King, that he planted his feet, he saw that he was rising up and he wanted to strike Mr. King with the baton. He said that in his argument and he tried to imply that in cross-examination of Officer Powell. Now there's a couple of reasons why this ought to be rejected. Number one, there is nothing to indicate that Officer Powell ever wanted to strike Mr. King with a baton until Mr. King made the choices he made.

"The testimony, in fact, is that Officer Powell's baton was in the ring until this point in the video where Mr. King gets up and turns. Secondly, I made the remark about a linebacker. This is a man who is large by all descriptions and definitions, six-three, somewhere between 230 and 250 pounds, maybe six-four, has just been zapped with fifty thousand volts of electricity from this Taser which momentarily felled him, and yet he is able to turn and move in the first few frames of that video, in a period of less than two seconds from on the ground to a full charge in the direction of Officer Powell.

"Now the suggestion is that Officer Powell is able to intake all of that information, to respond to that, to plant his feet and get ready and say, 'Okay, big fellow, come on.' I mean, it defies logic and if you look at the video you can see that's not what happens."

Mr. Stone stepped around the lectern and closer to the jury while demonstrating his perception of Officer Powell's actions. "Powell's movement is very quickstep like this because he doesn't know which way to go. And he steps this way, Mr. King comes this way, and they have what Powell describes as a collision."

Mr. Stone went back behind the lectern. "Now it's a fact that Mr. King did not bowl Officer Powell over, thank God for that. But it is incorrect to say that there is no evidence that they collided. Mr. King overcame the strength of four police officers so it escalated once again to the Taser, again a very appropriate, classic escalation of force. And the Taser worked momentarily and then the Taser didn't work anymore. Rather than escalate at that point, the officers then went to a different type of the same level of force, intermediate force, the so-called impact weapon, the baton."

Mr. Stone reached down and brought out the baton and held it up very high in the air.

"And the people would like to say that Powell belted Mr. King so hard in the head with that baton that he just collapsed," Mr. Stone said, suggesting that perhaps Mr. King really toppled from the combination of his own intoxication and the continued effects of the Taser.

"I can tell you this, that he was still hooked up to the Taser. There is witness testimony that the Taser clicking was heard after that point in time, which means, logically, that there was still some juice left in the batteries.

"Now, Sergeant Koon's report talks about the Taser going all the time. But the testimony has been from every witness who testified about the Taser that you turn it on and when it does what you want it to do, you turn it off. You don't sit there and electrocute somebody who is on the ground and has no control over his muscles. So it stands to reason that Sergeant Koon fires Taser number one cassette; it does what it is supposed to do. Then Mr. King recovers. He fires cassette number two; it does what it is supposed to do. The video starts. Mr. King is on the ground. Suddenly Mr. King is up, he turns, he moves. Doesn't it make sense that Sergeant Koon standing there with the Taser would turn it on again?

"Of course. That is to me the only logical explanation for the rag doll like fall that you see in that video."

When he fell, Stone said, King's head struck the pavement. "This is not Mr. King hitting the ground, it is hitting the pavement, hitting the asphalt. And you can see very clearly in that video that head is moving very fast and when it hits the pavement, that's where I think we got the major injury."

Once King was on the ground, Stone said, Officer Powell was able to keep him on the ground by striking his arms, shoulders and legs with the baton.

Mr. Stone brought out a series of still photos from the blurry part of the video that he said showed Mr. King getting up. "But you can see this, after you examine the still frames and then you look at the video and here on the final, at 3:33:11, he's back down again. The baton has worked. He's on his feet, he's coming up again, and he's knocked back down. The baton is working. We don't need to escalate again to a carotid hold or to a shooting. The baton is working."

In coming back to the lectern, Mr. Stone knocked over the tripod holding his charts. He picked up the tripod and replaced his charts and said, "I hate it when that happens."

Almost everyone but the judge laughed.

"Now the next thing that happens in the video is that the tape clears. And what's happening there? Mr. King is flat on the ground, he's on his elbows, his head's up, and Officer Powell is doing this."

Mr. Stone moved around in the well with the baton held in his arms in a ready position. "He's moving around like this and he's moving pretty quickly. You can see his feet moving and he doesn't look like he's really calm. I mean, to me he looks like someone who is very scared. You make your own decisions about what you see. But you can see him very clearly. He is assessing the situation."

Mr. Stone let the baton drop to his side and he walked back behind the lectern again.

"Even Commander Bostic said that it would be within policy and it would be within the training to use the baton to keep an actively resistant suspect from getting to his feet again, for the very logical reasons that once he gets to his feet, now you've got a real problem. Because if you can't get him back down with the baton, what are you going to do? Either he's going to get in his car and leave and you're going to go back to the police station for coffee or you're going to have to shoot him. So that's why these officers determined to keep Mr. King down on the ground. And that's why it looks so awful to see this man rolling around and these officers continuing to strike him. And just looking at that video tape, you'd say, 'That's terrible. That makes me sick,' just like it did the President of the United States. Because he doesn't understand. He's not looking at this through the perception of the officers."

Mr. Stone said there were no head shots shown on the video, eyewitnesses had contradicted one another, and Officer Powell denied hitting Mr. King in the head.

"Now we don't know about Mr. King because he didn't come in to testify. We don't know what he would say, and it would seem to me that if we can't decide whether Mr. King was hit in the head with a baton, maybe we would want to ask the person who owns the head."

Mr. Stone once more came closer to the jury with the baton in his hands. Swinging the baton like a baseball bat, Mr. Stone said that Melanie Singer had said the blow split open Rodney King's face from ear to chin.

"I want you to handle that baton in the jury room. I want you to pick it up and I want you to feel it and I want you to imagine Officer Powell delivering that kind of head blow to a human being with this instrument," Mr. Stone said, throwing the baton to the floor, toward the jury. It was very dramatic, it made a startling sound.

"And whether or not Mr. King would be alive today, or whether Mr. King would lose consciousness, or whether Mr. King would suffer a skull fracture."

Mr. Stone said the video distorted the reality of what happened from the perspective of the officers who were on the scene. The jury was "going to have to stand in their shoes. You're going to have to be able to say, 'What were the perceptions of these officers?' And what are the reasonable perceptions of reasonable officers standing in their shoes? And the video doesn't show you that at all."

Stone pointed out that the whole incident unfolded "in super real time, super fast. Remember, only eighty-two seconds. That's not a long time."

Mr. Stone again retrieved the baton from the lectern, walked closer to the jury and emphasized his words with the baton.

"That's not what these officers were doing. They weren't saying, 'Mr. King put your hands behind your back. Oh, you're not going to do it? Bam! Mr. King put your hands behind your back. You're not going to do it? Bam!' That's not what was happening out there. They were trying to keep Mr. King on the ground so they could forcefully handcuff him, because he wasn't going to go any other way. Again, it was his choice."

Mr. Stone took another sip and a quick look at the wall clock. He asked the judge if it was a good time to take a break for lunch. The judge declared the noon recess, to resume at 1:15.

After lunch, Mr. Stone finished his comments about the baton saying, "You must accept that clavicles, arms, shoulders, elbows, wrists, knees, ankles are the preferred targets. The objectives they are taught is to inflict pain and to immobilize if the pain doesn't do the job."

He said it was not the jury's job to decide how Rodney King was injured, just whether excessive force was used. He said it is hard to demonstrate specific intent to make a false police report, pointing out that there were also discrepancies in the Singers' reports. "Is it just a good faith mistake or is it a false police report?"

Mr. Stone used a chart labeled THE BIG LIE to discuss whether Officer Powell was lying when he said he was at the intersection of Glenoaks and Van Nuys when he saw the pursuit. "It would be ludicrous for a police officer to say something on the stand that's so easily impeached if he's not telling the truth. I think it's a fair statement that Officer Powell estimated the distance."

Mr. Stone had another chart he titled OTHER STUFF.

"The first of these is Powell's call for the rescue ambulance. And you hear Officer Powell in the tape recording say that the ambulance is needed for the victim of a . . . and then there's a pause and someone else says, 'beating,' and he says something like 'heh, heh'. . . you call it what you want, you listened to the tape."

Stone said that the jury had heard testimony that Powell was panting and breathing hard.

"Officer Briseno talked about his eyes bulging out, total exhaustion, all of these things. Officer Clemmer talked about how he was running around, Powell, saying, 'This guy threw me off his back, I thought we were going to have to shoot him.' He was breathing hard.

"Everyone said that it was a serious situation at the scene, it wasn't high comedy, officers were not running around high-fiving each other over this glorious use of force. There is nothing to indicate that anybody thought anything out there was funny."

Stone said the so-called *Oops* message to Corina Smith after the incident could be "just stuff."

"You might not be comfortable, ladies and gentlemen," he said, "with the term beating or beat. Maybe you don't think police officers ought to say things like that but it's something else again to say they are admitting crimes when they use those expressions. Maybe you don't like 'lizard' either. Unfortunately it's a part of police work and I'm not saying it's professional police jargon. It's jargon associated with the profession of police work. And that's all it is."

Stone said that the nurses at Pacifica emergency room did not use the word "taunting" to describe what Powell had said to King.

"It's Mr. White's twist on the testimony," he said. "It was a conversation."

He discussed circumstantial evidence, the burden of proof, and the concept of considering someone innocent until proven guilty. Then he talked about reasonable doubt.

"There's a jury instruction that's going to be given to you at the close of argument about what it means. And it goes like this: 'It is not a mere possible doubt because everything relating to human affairs and depending on moral evidence is open to some possible or imaginary doubt. It is that state of the case which, after the entire comparison and consideration of all the evidence, leaves the minds of the jurors in that condition that they cannot say they feel an abiding conviction to a moral certainty of the truth of the charges. An abiding conviction to a moral certainty of the truth of the charges."

Then, speaking more slowly than usual, in almost hushed tones, Mr. Stone said, "Ladies and gentlemen, the key to this case is this. Was that force used on March 3, 1991 so clearly excessive and unnecessary such that no reasonable officer in the same or similar circumstances would have done as these men did? You will be required to judge the propriety of the use of force from the perspective of the reasonable officer in the same or similar circumstances.

"Ladies and gentlemen, if reasonable minds could differ and if reasonable police minds can differ over the propriety of the use of force on March 3, 1991, then I suggest to you there is no proof beyond a reasonable doubt."

# Chapter Fifteen: The Case for Officer Wind

The judge called for a sidebar that lasted a couple of minutes, and then declared a break until 4:15 p.m. When court reconvened, it was Mr. DePasquale's turn to make the closing remarks for Officer Wind. He told us that he would be talking for another half hour today and would finish up in the morning.

There was no question, he said, but that the tape was violent and brutal. He recalled that Sergeant Koon had said on the witness stand, "Sometimes police work is brutal. That is just a fact of life."

Violence, he said, was outside the realm of our normal experience, so we couldn't view it with our normal standards. We needed to think about it from the point of view of a police officer. "It is a violent line of work that you are here to judge. And it is a line of work that Tim Wind chose as his own. He chose to be a police officer."

Mr. DePasquale said that while Officer Wind unquestionably was responsible for his actions, we also should bear in mind that he had "a position in a chain of command," and that he had only been working for the LAPD for ninety days as a rookie cop when the incident occurred.

An important point that he wanted us to keep in mind was that we were going to have to judge each of the defendants separately. "Please, if the point were to rise in argument, 'Oh, they all . . .' Any phrase that begins, 'Oh, they all' is not fair and is not fair to Tim Wind. Timothy Wind is entitled to your separate judgment as to how the law applies to him."

Mr. DePasquale said that he was not trying to place blame on Sergeant Koon or Officers Briseno or Powell, or to deny Officer Wind's responsibility for his own actions. And it was not his position that Rodney Glen King was a bad guy who deserved anything. But Rodney King presented a problem because he was such a large man, he was under the influence of alcohol, and it was the officers' duty to subdue him somehow.

He said the tape did not show what happened before or afterward. He said we should also keep in mind that the swarm technique was used and did not work, and a Taser was tried and did not work.

During all of today's arguments, there was still a lot of coughing, primarily by Mr. Mounger, but also by a couple of the jurors.

Sometimes it was disruptive to the point that we could hardly hear what the attorneys were saying.

WEDNESDAY, APRIL 22, 1992

The jury was called in almost on time today and Mr. DePasquale continued his closing arguments for Officer Wind. "The situation that these officers were dealing with was chaos. Their choices were very limited. Neither the Singers, as highway patrol officers, nor Stacey Koon and his LAPD officers had the choice of walking away from this problem, this crisis. If they did, if that were among their choices, then you would have unbridled chaos."

Mr. DePasquale said that we would receive a jury instruction that said, "A peace officer who is making a lawful arrest may use reasonable force to make such arrest, or to prevent escape, or to overcome resistance. It is lawful for a peace officer to use force in the arrest if a reasonable peace officer in the same or similar circumstances would believe that such force is necessary to make the arrest, or to prevent escape, or to overcome resistance."

Mr. DePasquale said, "If you have a reasonable doubt that the use of force was unlawful, you must find the defendant not guilty, and again, ladies and gentlemen, one at a time, not some mythical 'they' and please not guilt by association any more than innocence by association."

Mr. DePasquale showed us the tape again, asking us to look at the surrounding circumstances. "What would a reasonable officer perceive Mr. King's behavior to be and to be necessary?"

Mr. DePasquale said that a reasonable officer would have the right to use reasonable force to prevent escape or to overcome resistance. He said the prosecutor wanted to "gloss over" the fact that the officers had the right to use reasonable force simply to effect his arrest.

"The rational conclusion that would create a reasonable doubt, I suggest, is that force was necessary to effect the arrest of Rodney King. And another part of that same instruction reads, 'If the circumstantial evidence is susceptible of two reasonable interpretations, one of which points to the defendant's guilt, and the other to his innocence, you must adopt that interpretation which points to the defendant's innocence and reject that interpretation which points to his guilt.'

"Because this is a criminal case and the burden of proof is, as you have heard, beyond a reasonable doubt, reasonable doubt works in the favor of a defendant to make impossible a conviction if the circumstances can be reconciled reasonably with anything but the prosecution's interpretation of these facts."

Mr. DePasquale showed us the videotape again at twenty-five percent speed, and he wanted us to see the minute-long period when we might observe Officer Wind's interactions with Mr. King.

He put up a chart that listed various acts and the time frame during which they occurred. He had narrowed the activities down to thirtieths of seconds.

He also wanted to remind us that a prosecution witness, physical training instructor Annette Olivas, who was Wind's instructor at the police academy, testified that it's not proper to allow a subject on whom you are trying to effect an arrest to get into a pushup position, or to rise to his knees, "and heaven forbid, you do not allow him to get to his feet."

"And you do not have the choice of ending it easy, even with all the fire power that's out there, by shooting Mr. King. So those are the intolerable extremes. Somewhere in between those choices these police officers had to deal with Mr. King."

Mr. DePasquale posted a chart with a list of times.

During the blurry part of the tape, he said, we would see Powell using the forward and reverse power strokes and then we would see Tim Wind's participation.

Mr. DePasquale commented that Commander Bostic "didn't like this brutal violent police work he saw on this videotape and he suggested, in fact, that right about before Tim Wind got engaged in this is where he really starts to dislike what he sees."

Just before Tim Wind makes his first swing, he is standing right behind Powell when King charges at him, Mr. DePasquale said. "And as Powell comes together with King and King goes down you'll see this person I believe that you will deduce is Tim Wind move around to the other side. That is, when the picture comes back in focus, Wind is in essence behind King. And you watch when King is down on the ground, you watch Tim Wind, you watch his posture and how he is holding his baton. You don't see him drooling and you don't see him standing there like, 'Oh boy.' And remember what Annette Olivas said . . . You can't allow him to his feet, you can't allow him to his knees, you don't even want him in a pushup position. And you look at what Commander Bostic thinks is a good time to just be a nice guy and walk in there and handcuff Rodney King."

He said there was a seven-second delay "while Mr. Wind is observing, appears to be positioning himself, not just wildly participating in some orgy of violence, but watching."

Mr. DePasquale said that in a period of seven seconds from 3:54 to 4:01 on the tape, "you see six swings by Tim Wind, again not an uncontrolled orgy of force and violence, but directed blows. And then another period of seven seconds—posture—waiting—withdrawal."

Mr. DePasquale said to watch what Mr. King was doing while Officer Wind was observing him. It would be hard to miss the first time King rose up, and that "Officer Olivas would have no question about that. Not even Commander Bostic with his administrative naiveté would doubt the necessity to deal with Mr. King."

He pointed out that Wind appeared to be watching King's hands. "At 4:28 as Mr. King's hand reaches toward his right thigh, Mr. Tim Wind's head follows the hand, and you'll be able to see that Wind is watching the lower torso of Mr. King when Briseno makes a movement that Wind is not in a position to see."

Mr. DePasquale said that after nineteen seconds of "cautious observation, what Wind is in a position to see is the resumption of very strong, forceful, quick movement by Mr. King. And then there are five more swings by Mr. Wind. It may not be nice, it may be kinda brutal and violent but it is police work. It is what he was sent out there to do."

Mr. DePasquale ran the video, pointing to Mr. Wind with the wooden pointer, and commenting on his actions, as well as Mr. King's, emphasizing the checked swing, the periods of time that Mr. Wind waited, and the kicks pushing Mr. King back down when he was appearing to rise.

"The videotape isn't very nice. It has perspectives on it for everybody. You see George Holliday's perspective. Hopefully, with the assistance of this examination you can begin to put yourself in the position of Tim Wind."

Mr. DePasquale then discussed the notion of adoptive admission. "Nobody said Tim Wind smiled or laughed or prodded Mr. King or mocked him. Nobody said that Tim Wind participated in those statements at the hospital. But because he was there, that supposedly is what you might call an adoptive admission."

"We're not even talking about accusatory statements. We're talking about somebody being a jerk. And Larry Powell denies it was Larry Powell. But somebody, supposedly, according to the nurses Davis and Edwards, made some dumb comments about baseball. Well, obviously nobody was in a baseball game. And does the fact that Tim Wind was silent indicate some guilt on his part?

"What's he supposed to do about that? Deny? 'Well there was no baseball game, we didn't hit any home runs?' If somebody made a dumb comment, a tasteless comment in some poor version of humor, what does it show about Tim Wind who's silent? Nothing."

Mr. DePasquale said the nurses had said that Wind raised his baton, apparently indicating the injuries were the result of his baton. "Isn't the silent gesture actually rather more gentlemanly, rather more of a human response than any kind of words? It's certainly not an indication, 'Oh gee, we had our jollies. We had a lot of fun, we kicked the tar out of this guy.'

"What Tim Wind did is his job. You saw it on the videotape. In reply to a question at the hospital, in reply to a direct question, all he did was a gesture, not an indiscreet word out of his mouth.

"Because all Tim Wind did that night was his job. He didn't make jokes, he didn't have fun, he didn't take any cheap shots, not verbally, not physically, he didn't do it."

Mr. DePasquale said he was going to finish before the midmorning break at 10:30 a.m., but first he wanted to discuss what he called "the legal bottom line," the concept that a defendant is presumed innocent until proven guilty. He said we would get an instruction that a reasonable police officer has got no choice but to effect an arrest in a violent and brutal incident.

"What do you want from Tim Wind? He did his job. What's the alternative? This unpleasant incident is what we have police for. The burden of proof in a criminal case before you can convict my client, Tim Wind, is proof beyond a reasonable doubt, not to a preponderance of the evidence, as it would be in a civil case. Beyond a reasonable doubt to an abiding conviction and a moral certainty, to a moral certainty."

He said we would not be able to decide to a moral certainty that Wind violated the law, because he was just doing the job he was hired to do.

The judge thanked Mr. DePasquale, asked Mr. Barnett if he needed some time to set up and Mr. Barnett said he did. He then declared a recess to resume at ten minutes to eleven, with the usual admonitions.

# Chapter Sixteen: Barnett's Final Argument for Briseno

When we returned to the courtroom, Mr. Barnett told us that this was the last chance for the defense lawyers to present their case. He explained that the reason for the prosecution having the last word was that they bore the burden of proof. He said, however, this was not a contest between the attorneys, this was a search for the truth.

"Officer Briseno is presumed to be not guilty. He doesn't have to prove anything. The burden of proof is on the government. Now it may seem that this is a very high standard of proof, it may seem that it makes Mr. Briseno—gives him a leg up. And it does.

"If this trial, however, was conducted in Havana or China or someplace like that, he might have the burden of proving that he's innocent. But here in America we do things a little bit differently. You see, over the course of our two-hundred-year history, over the evolution of our judicial system, one tenet has come out, one basic tenet and that is, the worst thing that can happen in our judicial system is the conviction and punishment of an innocent man. So we take safeguards, and those safeguards include proof beyond a reasonable doubt. In other countries they say, well let's round up the usual suspects and if a few innocent people get convicted with the guilty, that's okay. We don't do it that way in this country.

"It's fair because you make it fair. You twelve members of the community who will decide this case, you make it fair. Against the power of the government, against all their resources, even against the co-defendants in this case, you make it fair. And you make it fair by following the rule of reasonable doubt and the presumption of innocence."

In everyday life, Barnett said, people almost never make decisions based on reasonable doubt. "In the most serious decisions you might make in your life, like buying a house, you have reasons to doubt whether you should do that, substantial reasons. You might lose your job, interest rates may go up, the economy may go down. They are serious, very serious doubts that you have, but you make those decisions anyhow. You go ahead, you buy the house. And there's a change in presidents, interest rates go up, your business goes down, you lose the house. You made a decision, a personal decision, in the face of reasonable doubts, a very substantial one. It didn't work out.

"In a criminal trial, however, when you're making a decision that affects somebody else's life, his life . . ." Mr. Barnett pointed to Briseno. "You cannot make a decision about guilt if you have any reasonable doubt. Your decision affects his life, not just your own, and the law, our law, does not permit you to make a decision in the face of a reasonable doubt. If you have a reasonable doubt you must vote not guilty. You can't come in here a week after your decision or a month after your decision or a year later and say, gee, I thought about it and you know Officer Briseno, I think you were innocent. You can't do that. You have to have an abiding conviction."

Barnett said Officer Briseno was charged with one count of assault with a deadly weapon or force likely to produce great bodily harm, and one count of assault under cover of authority. Both charges require that an assault be proved. He said the judge would define what an assault is and would tell us, "An attempt to apply physical force is not unlawful when done in the defense of another."

Barnett said the prosecution had the burden to prove the negative, that beyond a reasonable doubt, Ted Briseno was not trying to help Rodney King. "If you have a reasonable doubt whether that attempt was not in the lawful defense of another you must find the defendant Briseno not guilty."

Mr. Barnett placed the chart with the instruction about circumstantial evidence on the easel and read aloud the third paragraph: " 'If the circumstantial evidence as to any count is susceptible of two reasonable interpretations, one of which points to the defendant's guilt, and the other to his or her innocence you must adopt that interpretation which points to the defendant's innocence and reject that interpretation which points to his or her guilt. If, on the other hand, one interpretation of such evidence appears to be reasonable and the other unreasonable you must accept the reasonable and reject the unreasonable.'

"What does that mean? If you look at the facts and there are two reasonable interpretations of the facts—both must be reasonable— and one points to innocence, the other points to guilt, you gotta reject that which points to guilt, if they're both reasonable. It doesn't matter if one is more reasonable than the other, if they're both reasonable."

The jury had to look at the direct evidence and figure out what was in Officer Briseno's heart and mind, "and then determine the reasonableness of his perception, the reasonableness of his actions when he performs that single application of force. You gotta take the direct evidence, what he did, what he said, what he saw, and then you have to put it through the filter of circumstantial evidence."

He pointed out that Wind and Powell were both charged with a special allegation of specific intent to cause great bodily injury, but Officer Briseno was not. "The prosecutors are not even alleging that the application of force by Mr. Briseno was done with the specific intent to inflict great bodily injury. Now think about that. That puts Mr. Briseno in a completely different category, doesn't it? They're not even alleging that he did that act with specific intent to cause great bodily injury."

He pointed out that a great deal of evidence and many of the exhibits did not pertain to Mr. Briseno. "For instance, the prosecution says or alleges that Mr. Koon aided and abetted or helped Wind and Powell perform criminal acts. That theory of liability is not available as to Mr. Briseno. You know, it may seem unusual that a series of instructions would apply to one defendant and not another and evidence would apply to one defendant and not another but that's the law. And you might agree or disagree but you have taken an oath and you have promised." The judge interrupted Mr. Barnett with a brief comment, but his microphone was not turned on and we could not hear it.

Mr. Barnett continued, "I've been told to get through by noon, so I apologize for speaking so fast. I know that the first lawyers took up all of our time . . ."

There was some laughter, and Mr. Barnett said, "I'm teasing, I'm teasing. The judge is going to allow us as much time as we want as long as it doesn't go past noon.

"You gotta go back to March 3, 1991 and you've gotta get into Officer Briseno's shoes at 12:45 and judge his actions from that perspective. What did he do? What act did he commit to get here? More importantly, what was he trying to do? He was trying to put his foot in the back shoulder area of Mr. King so that he could control Mr. King, so that he could stop the beating. That's what he tried to do. Whether he hit the shoulder or the base of the neck, that really doesn't matter. You are to determine what was in his head, what was in Officer Briseno's heart, what was in his soul when he did that?"

Mr. Barnett retrieved the baton from the lectern and held it as he spoke. "He heard the terrible sound of metal against flesh even as Officer Solano had described. How is Officer Briseno to stop this beating? How is he supposed to do that? He's supposed to do that by using his foot instead of his hand. He's gotta keep his own head out of the strike zone. As he steps, he sees Mr. King move and move slightly. He puts his foot down and he is thrown off balance, Mr. Briseno is thrown off balance. Mr. White says this is a stomp, an unnecessary stomp. Remember what Mr. Briseno is thinking about. He has Mr. Wind in front of him cocked and ready, he's got Mr. Powell behind him who has been swinging and is huffing and puffing. He doesn't have the luxury that Mr. White has to stop the film and say, well look you should have known this or you should have known that.

"What did Mr. Briseno know, and what did he do? Did he go and kick him like a professional football player? No, he didn't do that. He used his left foot, his weak foot, not like Mr. Wind, he used his weak foot. He's right-footed. Would he do that if he was trying to harm Mr. King? Would he use his weak foot if he was trying to harm Mr. King? Would he do that if his purpose was to apply unnecessary force? Is that something he would do?"

Mr. Barnett put the baton back in the lectern.

He said that compared to Rodney King, Officer Briseno, at 140 pounds, looked like a midget.

"What is perhaps the most compelling evidence in this case, however, as to Mr. Briseno's state of mind is the actions he took seconds before he tried to cuff Mr. King. After Mr. King runs toward Mr. Powell, after Mr. King is hit by several baton strokes, Officer Briseno grabs Mr. Powell's baton and he tries to push Mr. Powell away. Even as he is doing this, Mr. King is getting up, but Officer Briseno does not see that. Officer Briseno is trying to put an end to the baton usage and nobody can get around that. He grabs the baton. He pushes Mr. Powell. Is this the activity of a police officer who is trying to use excessive force? Is this the activity of a person who is trying to mete out punishment, to beat someone? I don't think so."

Pointing to Officer Briseno, Mr. Barnett said, "Of all the police officers at the scene, one officer steps forward and tries to stop his fellow officers. He is the one, he is the only one who tried to stop this beating. It's kind of ironic, isn't it? Ted Briseno seeks to intercede on behalf of Mr. King and his reward is an indictment. In the panic, in the confusion, with helicopter blades screaming, with cops wildly swinging batons, he tries, Officer Briseno tries to put an end to the violence. He didn't have any legal obligation to intercede. He could have stood by as dozens of officers stood by and done nothing, but he interceded. I suppose he could have done nothing and let them just beat Mr. King to death. He could have done that. Or I suppose he could have drawn his revolver and shot Powell and Wind. It's darned easy months later to suggest a better course of conduct would have been preferable. It's not unlike when Joe Louis was the champion of the world. Young, tough men would go up to him and say, 'Hey Champ, I can beat you, I could do it.' And Joe Louis responded correctly, 'It's not enough that you say you can do it. You gotta do it at eight o'clock at Madison Square Garden on Saturday night.'"

Mr. Barnett said that in order to indicate that Officer Briseno had not disapproved of the actions of his fellow officers, the other attorneys had distorted his actions. "Mr. Stone announced in his opening statement that when Briseno pushed Powell away, Briseno said, and I'm quoting now Mr. Stone's opening statement, 'Don't touch him, you'll get shocked.' That's what the opening statement was. Briseno wasn't pushing him away to stop him, Briseno was pushing him away so that Powell wouldn't get shocked. Now that puts kind of a helpful spin on the video, doesn't it? It kinda makes you think Briseno didn't think Powell was doing anything wrong, he was trying to protect Powell. That's a nice little spin on this. The problem is, it isn't true.

"There was no evidence, no evidence at all, that Ted Briseno said, 'Don't touch him, you'll get shocked.' Sergeant Koon didn't say, 'Look out, the Taser is working.' Sergeant Koon didn't say, 'Briseno said, look out the Taser is working, you'll get shocked.' Not even Officer Powell said, 'Look out for the Taser' or anything like, 'you'll get shocked.' Nobody said that."

Mr. Barnett said that Officers Briseno and Solano "were

appropriately shocked and concerned. Mr. Briseno was upset, just look at that. He was upset about this. That gives you a window into his mind and heart. It shows his attitude was one of anger and frustration and this is in stark, stark contrast to the others in this case, particularly Mr. Powell.

"Seconds after the beating, seconds after the beating you've got Powell on the Rover, and he's giggling about it, he's giggling about it. Officer Briseno didn't say that at the scene nobody was giggling. He didn't say that. He said at the time of the beating, around that time, Powell was huffing and puffing with his eyes bulged out. He didn't say what was going on on the Rover."

Briseno's behavior showed "a lack of callousness, a lack of viciousness and a legitimate belief that the force he used was necessary," he said.

"You heard Officer Briseno testify. You saw his face and his eyes as he described his fear and he described his frustration at what he saw. You felt the emotion as he transported all of us back in time as clearly and as accurately as Mr. Holliday's video. You felt the shock and horror as he described the blow after blow, the terrible scene. He was thrust into a crucible of cross-examination. He was vilified, he was defamed, he was labeled a liar for telling the truth, belittled and accused of not taking more action, not taking a more active role."

Barnett pointed to Briseno. "Ted Briseno stood and stands alone against the power of the state and against the cruel weapons of slander, deceit and perjury and the extortion of his former comrades. It's easy to lump everybody together, to say they were all wearing LAPD uniforms, that they were all out there together, that they share responsibility, that's an easy thing to do. But it's wrong. It's not the law and it just isn't right.

"Ted Briseno stands in a different position from those with whom he stands trial. He stands in a different position because of what he did and because of what he did not do. He did not strike Mr. King with his flashlight though it was readily available, he did not beat Mr. King fifty times with his Monadnock, or one time. He did earlier in the event, grab Officer Powell's baton and push him away. That tells you something about his motives, that tells you something about his subsequent conduct. That puts into context the later use of his foot. It tells you he was not out there to use excessive force, it tells you he was trying to prevent excessive force.

"One officer that night took affirmative steps to try and put an end to the beating. That one officer was Ted Briseno. The very same Ted Briseno who stands before you accused of committing excessive force, the excessive force he sought to prevent.

"The truth of it is, if you believe there was some reason for Officer Briseno to believe that Wind and Powell are out of control, if you think that Officer Briseno had some reason to think he ought to intervene, then you've got a reasonable doubt and you've got to vote not guilty.

"In this connection, Mr. White was a far more effective defense attorney for Mr. Briseno than me. He was much better than me. For almost three hours he held your attention when he described why you should convict Wind and Powell. Think about that for a second. The problem with that argument is that the same reasons he argued so forcefully should lead you to convict Wind and Powell create more than a reasonable doubt as to Briseno.

"Even if you believe that there's insufficient evidence to prove guilt beyond a reasonable doubt as to Wind and Powell, Mr. White has certainly argued effectively so that reasonable doubt exists as to Briseno. A glaring and obvious departure from this well-reasoned argument of the prosecution team is this business that Officer Briseno stepped in when there was compliance, that Officer Powell was moving for his cuffs and maybe, maybe Officer Briseno just got caught up in the frenzy of the attack. Mr. White asked several questions. Where does his foot go, why did he do it, was this force needed? Mr. White challenges the defense for answers. He challenges the defense to answer questions that he has no answers for."

Barnett said it was not the job of the prosecution to ask questions but to answer them. "Maybe Mr. Briseno was caught up in the frenzy, maybe. These questions posed by Mr. White are more appropriately posed by a Commissar in Tiananmen Square as opposed to a counselor for the people of the State of California. I checked this morning. The flag still flies here. The American flag still sits in this courtroom, right to your left. And I don't apologize for invoking the flag, which represents all that's different between our jurisprudence and other countries'. I don't apologize for that.

"This is a symbol, a symbol of the difference between our country and other countries who make their citizens answer those questions, who make their citizens prove their innocence. That's not where we are . . . Mr. Briseno had to wait until there was a momentary break in the beating, he had to wait until he could avoid the onslaught of baton blows. He knew that every time Mr. King moved, he got hit.

"The prosecutor argued that. Every time Mr. King moved even slightly he got hit. The defendants say, 'Well, look, that's danger to us.' The prosecutor says that's not a danger. But everybody agrees: every time Mr. King moved, he got hit. Mr. Briseno had to wait, wait for his one moment where he could stop this beating. He knew, as everyone knew, that every time there was movement, Mr. King got hit. The slight movement that he saw prior to his stepping on Mr. King he believed would bring again the raining of batons. He tried to stop this. It didn't work, but at least he tried. Mr. White says, 'Mr. Powell was going for his cuffs. It was all over.'

"That ignores something kinda important and that is, Mr. Briseno was not in position to see that. Mr. Briseno testified and the film shows that he couldn't see that that's what Powell was doing. And he certainly couldn't predict that the baton blows would stop. Ted Briseno was in a frenzy all right, but that frenzy was born out of the actions of Mr. Wind and Mr. Powell that Mr. White has so bitterly complained of. Ted Briseno put himself in harm's way. He tried to stop it. It just didn't work."

Barnett said that for more than a year, Briseno had labored under the false accusations and suspicions of this indictment, was an outcast in the LAPD, subjected to lies and perjury for telling the truth, whose kids go to school every single day and wonder why their dad who took heroic action the night of this event, who took heroic action, why is he being vilified and victimized for doing what was right?

"This was not a fairy tale, ladies and gentlemen, this was a nightmare. It was Rodney King's nightmare and it is Ted Briseno's nightmare. When you took your oath as jurors in this case, you became part of a centuries old tradition, a tradition of fairness. Our whole system of justice is based on the belief that if we get twelve people from the community to fairly and dispassionately decide this issue, devoid of prejudice and bias, then the truth will come out."

*Moral Uncertainty*

# Chapter Seventeen: Mounger's Summation

When court reconvened at 1:30 p.m., attorney Darryl Mounger told us that Stacey Koon had done more to save Rodney King's life than Mr. King had done for himself. If Sergeant Koon had not been there that night, there inevitably would have been a shooting. "Had Sergeant Koon not been there to control that situation, as ugly as it looks, Rodney King wouldn't have been home now. And maybe Sergeant Koon would have had to go tell some officer's family why they didn't come home."

He said the LAPD had not provided officers with the tools they need. "They certainly don't have tranquilizer guns. They do that with dangerous animals and they prevent injury to them. They haven't given them nets, they haven't given them leg grabbers, they haven't given them Velcro blankets, they have given them no tools. This same incident could happen again. The question is, at what point is it reasonable to go in and have bodily contact with this big guy?

"When I was a little boy, and my father would say, 'Darryl, come on,' and I'd say 'Okay, I'm coming' and if I didn't move fast enough, I'd get a belt on my little rear and I'd go, 'Okay, okay.' "

Mr. Mounger demonstrated by grabbing his rear. "I'll tell you something, a little pain makes you move real fast. It's a great incentive. But when a policeman hits somebody with a baton, a baton that is a tool of his trade, they don't give you that to make love to somebody, they give you that to do your job.

"The law gives officers the right to use any amount of force that is reasonable and necessary to accomplish that goal. At what point is it unreasonable? It's an interesting question and there's no right or wrong answer.

"After you've seen him attack once, at what point are you willing to go in and risk your safety, knowing that he could grab your gun belt, knowing he could grab your neck, believing and reasonably believing that this guy's under the influence of drugs, and they believe PCP. Mr. White says that they would have you believe he's superhuman. Well, real strong, stronger than your average man. Well, how much strength do they have to have before we don't touch them? How much risk does an officer have to go through? What do you expect, what can any of us expect? You can expect that once this starts, once Rodney King chose to attack at that policeman, he has told those officers what he is willing to do, and at that point he must either be restrained or he must submit. And all he has to do is comply. And although you may not like what you see on the video tape, before you can tell me that that's wrong, tell me what they should have done. Tell me what they safely could have done. Not just, my God, it's not necessary. I agree with Mr. White, none of this was necessary, none of it was necessary. All Rodney King had to do was be handcuffed. But he wouldn't do that."

Mounger said we didn't know why King didn't surrender "because he didn't come in here and tell you what he thought, just like he didn't tell Sergeant Koon what he was thinking."

Koon didn't want to use deadly force, Mounger said, so he tried bare physical force, and when that didn't work, he used the Taser, which he thought would cause the least injury, and that didn't work either. "Forget the reason. It didn't work. Now do you keep going back and doing the things that don't work?"

Mr. Mounger said nobody likes what they see on the tape, but that's not the question. The question is not whether or not it's brutal, the question is whether or not they are criminals. He said the police had no options to do anything else than what they did. No witness had said how they could have stopped King. "They just said, we don't like what we see and somebody should have stopped it. And my proposition to you, ladies and gentlemen is, I agree with you, somebody should have stopped it, the same person that started it."

Rodney King should have said he gave up or he should have complied. "Because when you look at the video tape when he's not being a threat, when he's not bringing his legs up and his arms up, he's not being hit."

Mr. Mounger noted that Sergeant Koon was also accused of being an accessory. "Well, Sergeant Koon told you that he believed his officers were doing the only thing they could, based upon the tools they had available to them. I'm not asking you to like it, I'm not asking you to say they're innocent. I'm asking you to say they're not guilty. I'm going to tell you the people have not proven beyond a reasonable doubt that there was a reasonable way to do this, another way to do it, a safer way to do it.

"I'm not asking you if this is humane. That's not the question. I don't think it is. I think there ought to be a better way, but until you give it to us, until you train these officers in it, then I don't think you can find them guilty of a crime when they're doing what's reasonable and necessary based upon the facts and the circumstances and the tools they have available to them at the time they act. I think that there's a problem there."

Mr. Mounger talked about the arrest reports and the prosecution's accusations that the extent of Mr. King's injuries were not properly reported. He said that when you cut yourself shaving, there can be a lot of bleeding even though the cut is very minor. When Sergeant Koon wrote the report, he thought the injuries were minor and it had not yet been discovered that Mr. King's legs were broken. The rescue ambulance report and the records from Pacifica Hospital said the injuries were minor.

Mounger pointed out that Sergeant Koon wrote, "Of important note for roll call training. Always have a backup plan with a use of force. It doesn't always work the way you are trained, the Taser doesn't always immobilize, PR-24 doesn't always cripple, etc. If you don't have a frame of reference, officers tend to panic when things don't work the way they're supposed to. A backup plan prevents panic, and it don't hurt to have lots of backup, especially with PCP suspects."

That showed, Mr. Mounger said, that Sergeant Koon believed Rodney King was on PCP.

Dr. Mancia wrote in his report that there was a possible PCP overdose. He said Sergeant Koon's experience and training led him to believe that he should not let his officers come in contact with a suspect on PCP.

Just because what was on the videotape was brutal "doesn't make it illegal and it doesn't make it unreasonable because there's no other reasonable way to do this. And if there would have been a more reasonable way, you can believe the prosecutor would have brought them in, and that's what his duty is, to show you that this was unreasonable. Not just to show you it's ugly, not just to show you it looks bad, not just to show you he doesn't like it, not just to show you, my God, somebody should have said enough is enough, but to show you that there was something different they should have done."

He also said that when three different people see an accident, they all see something different. "That's human nature. It doesn't mean they're lying. Some of them might try to color it and tell you that they saw more but it depends on how calm they were at the time. And I propose to you that Sergeant Koon's truth was the same on that night as it was when he testified. That he told you the best he could, that he took accountability for his officers and he said, 'I am responsible for my officers and I ordered that to prevent something else. I thought he was trying to get up and attack.' "

Mounger concluded by saying that when the jury deliberated, he hoped we would decide that Sergeant Koon was not a criminal and should not be criminally charged in the case. All he had done, "was to write a report that didn't state things the way the district attorney's office thought they ought to be stated."

# Chapter Eighteen: Prosecution Rebuttal

After a recess, Mr. White started his rebuttal. He said that after listening to three of the defense attorneys, Mr. Mounger, Mr. DePasquale and Mr. Stone, he was reminded of the comment that desperate men do desperate things.

"To have them hide behind the very badges they wear by talking about this thin blue line, by talking about these hordes of criminals out here that they're protecting us against, that is embarrassing. Men and women across this country do their job every day as law enforcement officers without resorting to the violence and the brutality that you have seen on this screen over the last six weeks," Mr. White said.

"They are not above the law. 'What kind of world would you have without cops?' That's what Mr. DePasquale asked. I ask what kind of world are you going to have where these cops violate the law, they fail to uphold the law and they fail in their duty? And their duty is to follow the law. That is their duty. Make no mistake about that. That is their duty, to follow the law, and they did not do that in this case."

Mr. White went on to try to refute some of what Mr. Stone had said. He pointed dramatically to the defendants. "These three defendants have been doing desperate things for the last six weeks. It is embarrassing for me to have to stand up here and tell you about the facts they left off. So what else does Michael Stone want to tell you? He wants to tell you that Timothy Singer in his testimony confirmed Laurence Powell's description of this Foothill and Van Nuys intersection, this alleged tire squealing, smoke, the whole show that Laurence Powell testified to. What he doesn't want to tell you, however, is that Tim Singer's directions are different than Laurence Powell's."

Mr. White put the blown-up copy of Officer Powell's report on the easel. "Tim Singer testified, 'I didn't see any tires squealing, I didn't see any skidding, I didn't see any smoke.' He's talking about a different direction. He didn't confirm anything Laurence Powell said."

Mr. White said that Mr. Stone wanted to mislead us. "Why is it every time, every piece of evidence regarding Laurence Powell that's bad, it's somebody else's fault? It's Terry White's fault, it's Alan Yochelson's fault, it's Ted Briseno's fault, it's Lawrence Davis' fault, it's never this man's fault." He pointed to Officer Powell. "Why not?"

Mr. White was actually shouting. He walked around the defense attorneys' table, and continued to point his finger, getting right up in Officer Powell's face, and still shouting.

"This is the man, and look at him. This man laughed, this man taunted," he roared.

Mr. Stone objected and the judge said, "Mr. White, get back to the podium, please and confine your argument to the podium."

"I'm sorry, your Honor," Mr. White said.

Up to this point in his closing argument, Mr. White's voice had been very strong and he exhibited a lot of anger and emotion, but this outburst was still unexpected and more than a little disturbing to me.

"This man laughed, this man taunted, and he's denying it, he's denying it? How many times did we play that tape in here and was that not laughter, was that not chuckling, was that not giggling? Well, what was funny out there? But he's denying it? Everything that's bad, everything that looks bad against Laurence Powell, everything that is bad, he denies, he denies. And it's always somebody else's fault, somebody else's fault. Well, it's nobody else's fault. That's Laurence Powell up there using unreasonable force, that was Laurence Powell having a good laugh afterwards, that was Laurence Powell on the MDT saying, 'Oops. I haven't beaten anyone this bad in a long time.' That was Laurence Powell who was taunting him at the hospital.

"Desperate men do desperate things. So CHP is to blame, Terry White is to blame, Lawrence Davis is to blame, Rodney King is to blame. Everyone is to blame except the person who should be sitting here shouldering the responsibility. And that's Laurence Powell. He is the man responsible for his actions. He is the man who beat Rodney King on March 3, 1991.

"Even if you want to give him the benefit of the doubt, even if you want to say what he has said is true, let's look at it for a second. We have a man on PCP, who they say is impervious to pain, who they say is unresponsive to verbal commands. And then the video starts and this man attacks. But Mr. Powell doesn't hit him in the head, he barely even contacts him and maybe he trips and he falls

*Moral Uncertainty*

and he hits his head on the pavement without putting his arms out. Okay. Let's say that's true. Look at that videotape. Not more than a second after this man allegedly falls and hits his head, face first on the pavement, a serious injury, Mr. Powell is on him like that (a snap of the fingers) with the baton.

"Now is that reasonable use of force? I asked Melanie Singer, 'What commands did they give him after that initial movement?' 'None.' 'What did they say to him?' 'Nothing.' Mr. Powell was on him right away. Is that reasonable? Maybe he shouldn't have moved toward Mr. Powell. Maybe he shouldn't have done that. Okay. We'll give him that. He shouldn't have done that. But then this man falls face first into the pavement, fractures nine bones in his face, falls without any protection, and you immediately jump on him and start hitting him with a baton? That is unreasonable."

Mr. White said we would get an instruction that when an officer was arresting a person, and they knew they were being arrested, it was the duty of the officer to refrain from using force. When Mr. King stopped resisting, the force should have stopped. "That is the duty. Once you see Mr. King refraining from using any force or any other means to resist arrest, the force has got to stop. That's the law. He doesn't have to say, 'I give, I give.' He doesn't have to say, 'Please stop.' That's not the law.

"They treated this man, that night, that early morning hour, like an animal, they treated him like an animal. And yet Michael Stone does not want you to call his client a thug, or he doesn't want me to call his client a thug."

Mr. White turned and looked at Laurence Powell. "Okay, you're not a thug, but you were acting like one. Just like Mr. King wasn't an animal but he was acting like one, according to Mr. Powell, so you're not a thug, you were just acting like a thug.

"I'm going to take up Mr. Mounger's challenge and I'm going to tell you what the reasonable method was, and I'm going to tell you it was brought out in this trial and it was brought out by his client. As a matter of fact, I'll show you right now what the reasonable method was."

Mr. White pointed to Officer Powell's report on the easel. Sergeant Koon told Officer Powell to mention in his report that they had used the swarm technique, "because he knew according to policy, that's what they should have done. So you put it in the report. Even if it didn't happen, you put it in. Swarm technique. Stacey Koon told you. Swarm technique. That was the reasonable method, and he knew it, but he didn't do it. But he covered it up by saying he did."

Mr. White put the chart entitled STACEY KOON LIES AND INACCURACIES on the easel. "And how does Mr. Mounger want to explain these lies and inaccuracies? Well, right here he says, 'Well, my client, maybe he got mixed up.' He didn't get mixed up. He's a fourteen-year veteran of the Los Angeles Police Department, he knows he couldn't hear Paxton and Foothill, he knows he can't hear CHP audio, he knows that. He got mixed up? This is a man who was confident, who told you 'managed and controlled use of force. Everything was okay, I had everything under control' and then he lies about this. Time of arrival at scene. This is another embarrassment.

"I am really shocked Mr. Mounger did this. Mr. Mounger read off to you from this transcript, '49:36 Code 6 Osborne and Foothill' And then he says, 'My client wasn't there until 50:29.' That is as bad a misrepresentation as Mr. Stone's and I'll show you why."

Mr. White wrote on a clean sheet of paper on the easel, then continued, "49:36 Osborne and Foothill. Remember the testimony of Melanie Singer, Tim Singer and Laurence Powell? There was a stop at the light by Mr. King at that intersection and they thought the pursuit had ended. And that's what 49:36 is. Osborne and Foothill Code 6. The erroneous interpretation by Officer Powell and Officer Wind that the pursuit had ended."

Mr. White wrote 50:18 on the paper. "Code 6 Foothill east of Osborne. That's where the pursuit finally terminated, Foothill east of Osborne, 50:18. His client comes in at 50:29."

He wrote 50:29 on the paper, and crossed out 49:36. "That's the time where they first stopped at Foothill and Osborne. It is embarrassing to have to come and point this out, this bald misrepresentation of the facts."

Next, Mr. White displayed the chart with photographs of Mr. King's back injuries to the jury. "These bruises are on the back. This is not a rubber baton. Does it wrap around and make these bruises back here?" He picked up the baton and held it against his left shoulder area. "Sergeant Koon laid this baton like this. He said that's where it struck Mr. King. Well, how do you explain these bruises?"

He pointed to the photos. "There's no bruises on the clavicle, the front. This is the clavicle." He touched his right front shoulder area. "There's no bruises there. But he wants to tell you, well, this is close enough. Close enough? He's got to be kidding. This didn't wrap around the top of the shoulder and then got the back bruised over here. Who was he kidding?"

He held up the photo of Rodney King's injuries. "This shows the bruise of the clavicle the way Stacey Koon demonstrated that baton struck Mr. King? You have to wonder why all of the lies. Why? Because they know what's on that video tape. They know, they know it's unnecessary, they know it's unreasonable, they know it's excessive."

Mr. White said he wasn't going to play the videotape again because we could play it in the jury room.

"I want to talk about Officer Briseno. It is not the requirement of the prosecution to show you that Officer Briseno had an evil heart or an evil mind. You remember we discussed general intent." He read from notes. "Officer Briseno is saying that he used the force in defense of another. It's a very unique way to use this particular defense because usually it's used in cases where someone attacks another person and then an individual steps in and fights off the attacker or somehow uses some sort of force or action against the attacker. But that's not what's happening here. He's saying, 'I had to inflict damage on Mr. King in defense of Mr. King.'

"Ladies and gentlemen, the force Mr. Briseno used was unreasonable. He may not have had an evil heart, he may not have had an evil mind. It was unreasonable and you have to judge it under the reasonable person standard of the instruction the court is going to give you."

Apologizing for having walked around the table previously, Mr. White said that he was finished.

I had the distinct feeling that Mr. White had made a sudden decision to cut short his closing comments. During his argument, he had spoken with great fervor and energy. Now he seemed subdued, almost depressed.

I was glad the closing arguments were over. I was dubious about how useful they were to the jury. I know that the attorneys are being paid to put on the best possible case for their side, but at times they seemed to be carrying things too far. They were very theatrical, and their arguments seemed quite contrived. Since this was my first experience seeing a trial firsthand, I had nothing to compare it to except television courtroom dramas. On television, they get right to the point. That was not the case in real life, I discovered.

But it had been a very long trial, and we had listened to a lot of witnesses and seen dozens of exhibits. The closing arguments served as a refresher course, jogging my memory as to what had been said. It took a lot of separating the wheat from the chaff, but having done that, the arguments did answer some of the questions that had come up in my mind as I listened to the testimony. Listening to the arguments reminded me of what seemed to be the most important facts in the case.

The judge called the lawyers to the sidebar. When they returned to their seats, he warned the jury to resist the temptation to start discussing the case among ourselves or with others until tomorrow when jury deliberations would begin. He told the alternates the same rules applied to them because they might be called on to fill in for a juror who might be excused, and that they must remain untouched by outside influences. Once more, he repeated his admonition not to listen to, watch or read any of the news coverage, not be exposed to anything outside the courtroom, not to form any opinions about the case, and not to discuss the case with anyone.

# Chapter Nineteen: Sequestered

THURSDAY, APRIL 23, 1992

It was my sixty-fifth birthday. Things were pretty chaotic in the early morning as I threw together enough clothes to last the four or five days I thought we might wind up being sequestered. They had told us that we would be staying at the Travelodge. Dick hinted that he might send some flowers to brighten up my room since it was my birthday, but I asked him not to. On several occasions in the past, he had sent me flowers at work and it embarrassed me. Being the center of attention has always made me feel uncomfortable.

I drove up to the East Valley Sheriff's Station at eight o'clock, unloaded my suitcases from the car and locked it up. One of the other jurors ran over to me with a birthday card and a gift certificate for a box of chocolates. I was surprised and touched that she had been thoughtful enough to take time to remember my birthday. She had a lot on her mind because her husband had injured his leg the previous weekend playing softball, and was immobile. She had to make arrangements for him to be taken care of as well as pack her things and attend to all of the other details necessary to keep her household running while she was sequestered. The card she gave me had a picture of a pig sitting right in the middle of a birthday cake stuffing it in his mouth with both hands. Inside the card she had written, *This picture may bring back memories of your jury friends*. We did eat a lot of desserts during the trial.

We gathered inside the sheriff's station. Jerry, the bailiff, had also brought me a card, and several small gifts, including jelly beans and a little crystal soap dish, and he presented them to me while we waited for the bus to take us to the courthouse.

It was nearly an hour before the bus arrived, the same jail bus that had been used to transport us to lunch earlier in the trial. We would ride back and forth to court in it every day during the deliberation period. I never got used to riding like a prisoner, or to the attention that it attracted. People in passing cars always peered up at us, trying to figure out who we were.

The deputies loaded our baggage and we climbed aboard for the ride to the Simi Valley Courthouse, where we were escorted to the law library to wait another hour before we were called into the courtroom about 11 a.m.

Judge Weisberg informed us that he would read aloud the seventy-eight pages of jury instructions, and then give us a copy to refer to while we were deliberating. He was still stuffed up from his cold and stopped frequently to sip water. When he had finished, he explained that we would not be given a copy of the transcript of the trial proceedings, but if we wanted to hear any of the testimony again, the foreman should request it in writing, and he and the lawyers would decide whether the court reporter would read it to us in convened court, or up in the jury room. He explained that any communication with the court during deliberation would be done in writing on forms that would be provided to us. We were to give the communication to the bailiff, who would give it to the judge. He also explained that we would be given verdict forms, one not guilty and one guilty for each defendant for each count, and only one would be filled out by us, either the guilty form or the not guilty form.

We were not permitted to discuss the case unless all twelve jurors were present and the only place it could be discussed was in the jury room. Any discussion of the case with alternate jurors was forbidden.

Judge Weisberg told the alternate jurors that even though they would be taking meals with the regular jurors, they were not to talk about the case with us or among themselves. He explained that this was necessary in the event that one of the regular jurors should have to be replaced by an alternate.

The last instruction he read was: "You shall now retire and select one of your number to act as foreman. He or she will preside over your deliberations. In order to reach verdict(s), all twelve jurors must agree to the decision (and to any finding you have been instructed to include in your verdict). As soon as all of you have agreed upon a verdict, so that (when polled) each may state truthfully that the verdict(s) express his or her vote, have (them) dated and signed by your foreman and then return with (them) to this courtroom. Return any unsigned verdict form(s)."

The court clerk then swore in the five bailiffs who would guard us during the deliberation period. It was about 1 p.m. and Judge Weisberg told us to go upstairs and choose a foreman before going

*Moral Uncertainty*

to lunch. The twelve jurors were escorted into the jury deliberation room and the alternates waited in the two jury services rooms.

Since the beginning of the jury selection process, I had not been allowed to discuss my thoughts and feelings about this trial, not with my family, my friends, not even with the other jurors. I had been closeted with these people on a daily basis for almost two months and had been unable to discuss with them the one thing we had in common. It was frustrating. Each time we had a break from court, I had so many things I wanted to talk about. Now all of these thoughts that had been internalized could finally be voiced. It was a feeling of great relief and anticipation.

However we could not discuss the case unless all of the jurors were present. Within the deliberation room were two restrooms, one for men, the other for women. The only time we left the room was for breaks, lunch and when we quit for the night. However, whenever one of the jurors went into a restroom, we had to stop discussion, which greatly limited the amount of actual productive deliberation time.

The room was long and narrow, about twenty feet by twelve feet. A long, rectangular table and chairs took up most of the space, and a high, narrow window ran the length of the room. You could see other offices across the way if you looked out the window. We kept the metal blinds closed all the time and it became a little claustrophobic. On one wall was mounted a chalkboard. A cart with a television set and a VCR stood in the right rear corner. The exhibits, including the baton, were stacked on a card table.

The deputies had set up a table at the back of the room where we could make a pot of coffee every morning, which was available to the jurors all day long. I had brought a cup with my company name and my name on it, but had not brought it upstairs with me, so I drank from plastic cups. After the verdicts had been read, and we were gathering up our personal things, there was no time to go downstairs to the law library and retrieve my cup. So I left behind a cup in the Simi Valley Courthouse with my name on it.

We sat down at the table in whatever seats we chose, and wound up occupying the same seats for the entire deliberation period. Two of us were nominated for foreman, me and a male juror. We had started to vote when one of the women said she thought it would be appropriate for each of us to give some information about ourselves and why we thought we were qualified.

I was uncomfortable campaigning to be foreman. I have never enjoyed being in the spotlight, but I did think that my business experience had prepared me well to take on this responsibility and I thought I could do a good job. I talked about how I dealt with people in my job as a manager and that my job frequently required me to conduct meetings. The other candidate said that he also conducted meetings in his job as a systems analyst.

After each of our very brief remarks, we voted and I was chosen, nine-three. Several other jurors would have been fully capable of presiding over the deliberations, but only two were nominated. The other nominee was a very intelligent, non-judgmental person who I felt could be of great help in keeping the proceedings on an unemotional and analytical level, so I asked him to assist. That would prove to be a very wise decision, when things later got very emotional.

The judge was informed that I had been selected as foreman. After lunch, Jerry the bailiff brought in two brown manila envelopes, one containing the verdict forms, the other containing forms for the foreman to communicate with the judge. The blown-up documents and oversized exhibits we had seen during the trial had been placed against the front wall by the blackboard. We were given a list of the exhibits that had been admitted during the trial. Not all of the exhibits that we saw in the courtroom had been admitted. The bailiff also brought us a copy of the judge's instructions.

Someone suggested that we take a preliminary straw vote on each count, but we decided it would be better to study the instructions first.

I'm sure that it is never an easy task to reach a verdict in any case, even a case where there is one defendant and one set of instructions. In this case, there were four defendants, and a set of instructions that covered all of them, as well as some instructions for each one individually. The instructions required that we must decide separately whether each of the defendants was guilty or not guilty.

There were seventy-eight sheets of paper containing the instructions, although some of the pages only had one paragraph typed on them. Although the judge had read them to us in court, our initial perusal left us overwhelmed. We took turns reading aloud. We went over each page to determine what subject matter it covered. If it was in great detail, or if it contained specific instructions about one or more counts, we left it for later interpretation. All of the general instructions covering points of law were read aloud. Before the deliberation was complete, we had read and re-read every page many times.

We found the first page especially significant. It said it was our duty to determine the facts from the evidence that had been presented at trial and not from any other source, and that a "fact" was something proved directly or indirectly by the evidence. It also said that we needed to accept the law as the judge stated it to us, whether or not we agreed with the law.

We examined the verdict sheets, and discussed them. They were passed around to those jurors who wanted to have a closer look. There were twenty-two verdict sheets—one sheet for guilty and one sheet for not guilty for each of the counts against the four defendants.

These were the counts:

Count 1: Violation of Section 245(a)(1) of the Penal Code, Assault by Force Likely to Produce Great Bodily Injury and with a Deadly Weapon. All four defendants were charged with this count.

Count 2: Violation of Section 149 of the Penal Code, Officer Unnecessarily Assaulting or Beating any Person. All four defendants were charged with this count.

On the verdict sheets for the two counts against Powell and Wind, there was a special allegation that if either defendant was found guilty on either count, the determination must be made by the jury as to whether the defendant did personally inflict great bodily injury on Rodney King. These allegations were to be indicated by a True or False entry.

Count 3: Defendant Laurence M. Powell was charged with the Filing of a False Police Report by a Peace Officer.

Count 4: Defendant Stacey C. Koon was charged with the Filing of a False Police Report by a Peace Officer.

Count 5: Defendant Stacey C. Koon was charged with committing the crime of Accessory After the Fact.

For Sergeant Koon, the charges in Counts One and Two were each made in the alternative to that charged in Count Five. If the jury found him guilty in either Counts One or Two, then they must not find him guilty in Count Five. If they found him guilty in Count Five, then they must not find him guilty in Counts One and Two.

So, to summarize, we were being asked to judge:

- Briseno on Counts 1 and 2,
- Wind on Counts 1 and 2 with a special allegation,
- Powell on Counts 1 and 2 with a special allegation and on Count 3, and
- Koon on Counts 1 and 2 (or 5), and on Count 4.

It was not a simple situation. After some discussion and a period of time for familiarization with the counts, we discussed how we would tackle these tasks. It was the consensus that the defendants with the least complicated (or least detailed) counts against them should be looked at first.

We agreed to conduct secret ballots, and to arrive at decisions tentatively at first and vote again later for a final, permanent verdict. Everyone was still a little unsure about the entire procedure, and we did not want to make any irrevocable decisions at that time.

So we decided that we would consider Briseno first, then Wind, then Powell, and lastly, Koon.

That was all we got done on that first day of deliberations.

We left the courthouse, boarded the bus, and were taken to the Travelodge Hotel in Simi Valley, where we convened in a conference room and were given our room numbers and keys. Our bags had been deposited in our separate rooms while we were deliberating.

We were given about an hour to change to go to dinner across the street in a private banquet room at the International House of Pancakes. The county did not let us go hungry. I must say, we did tire of IHOP before it was all over. We were accompanied to dinner by two deputies. We were always accompanied by the deputies wherever we went and during deliberations one of them always sat at the end of the hall.

The jury occupied the entire second floor of the hotel, and the deputies occupied the rooms by the stairs. There was no chance that a juror could slip by them. The deputies were aware of anyone who came up those stairs or went down them.

When we returned from dinner that night, there was a lot of going in and out of rooms. Most of the doors remained open. I was presented a birthday card signed by all the jurors.

One of the jurors, a computer programmer, had been working on a penciled sketch of Judge Weisberg and Mr. Stone that I had admired several times. He gave it to me as a birthday present, and afterward took us all over to inspect his room, which was decorated differently than the others. It had French Provincial furniture and was all lacy and frilly. Very feminine. From that time on we teasingly called him Jury Queen.

The rooms were about the size of most motel rooms, clean, with only one distinction. Most of the rooms had a Jacuzzi bathtub in them, with a small bottle of bubble bath provided. That was a very welcome plus. There was a lot of tension in the deliberation room each day, and it was a physical comfort to be able to relax in the churning water. I wish, however, that I had known before I took my first bath that it was not necessary to use almost the entire bottle of bubbles in one bath. I sat in the tub laughing at all the bubbles that were two feet high. I felt I was being attacked by bubbles.

I had the same problem with the room that I have in most hotel or motel rooms. The lighting was less than adequate for applying makeup. The bed was comfortable but on the first night, I slept very little. That's typical for me the first night in a motel room. Strange bed, strange surroundings, being alone, all combined to make the first night less than satisfactory. The second and succeeding nights were better.

There was some socializing in the conference room and on the walkways outside the individual rooms. Around ten, everything quieted down and everyone apparently went to sleep.

It had been an eventful birthday for me. I had joked with the others earlier in the day, saying, "How many sixty-five-year-old broads get elected jury foreman and sequestered, all on their birthday?"

# Chapter Twenty: Sorting it Out

FRIDAY, APRIL 24, 1992

At the recommendation of one of the other jurors, I had the Swedish pancakes with lingonberry sauce for breakfast at IHOP, and they were delicious. Then we returned to the hotel to board the Ventura County bus to the courthouse.

We were taken up the back stairs through the large jury services room, where we were shown the lunch menu. We wrote our orders on the sheet by our juror number, and proceeded to the deliberation room.

During my period of wakefulness the previous night, I had decided that because of the complexity of the issues, we needed some structure in our approach. First thing upon arrival, I put four numbered steps on the blackboard:

1. Understand the count.
2. Examine the evidence.
3. Apply the judge's instructions and the law.
4. Vote.

I felt we should stick with these steps and know at all times which step we were on, to be sure we considered all necessary information before proceeding to the next step. I asked the jurors if they agreed, and they all did. Someone suggested that we add the word (law) to Step 1, to be sure we understood the law as the judge had communicated it to us. I agreed, so Step 1 now read, "Understand the count (law)."

We had to read and re-read the judge's instructions frequently in order to understand the restrictions under which we operated. We found them tedious, but we were there to judge the facts and apply the law as interpreted for us by the judge, and we were legally and morally obligated to apply the law diligently. To a person accustomed to dealing with the explicit nature of the law, this might seem an easy, simple task. To the jury it was not. We had to consider all the laws and instructions collectively, and not try to apply one isolated law or instruction without the consideration of the others. There was some testimony that was only to apply to one or another of the defendants and not to all of them, and we had to keep all that straight. Some of the exhibits they showed us had been admitted for a limited purpose, so we had to be sure we were only considering it in the context it was intended. It was complicated.

And on Page 37, the instructions said that the defendants were innocent until the contrary was proved, and that it was the burden of the prosecution to prove them guilty beyond a reasonable doubt. Reasonable doubt was defined as "not a mere possible doubt, because everything relating to human affairs, and defending on moral evidence, is open to some possible or imaginary doubt."

The defendants could not be proven guilty if the jurors "cannot say they feel an abiding conviction, to a moral certainty, of the truth of the charge."

Based on those paragraphs concerning the burden of proof and presumption of innocence until proven guilty, we decided that we would consider each defendant innocent on each count until we examined all evidence presented against him or on his behalf during the trial. We would apply the law and then vote. We decided that at any point where a juror voted guilty, they must tell the other jurors the points of evidence that led them to believe the defendant guilty. Sometimes, we digressed from the structure we had defined, particularly when tension ran high, but for the most part, we stuck to this format. It helped to establish a disciplined approach.

I did not dictate this structure. It was suggested by one of the other jurors. We discussed it and all agreed on the format. I was chagrined that an article that appeared in *American Lawyer Magazine* in September 1992 credited me with imposing this rule on the jury. At no time did I impose anything on the jury. Every decision was discussed thoroughly, and if even one juror voiced an objection, it was not adopted.

We pored over the instructions.

We started with Count 1 against Officer Briseno, first reading aloud the judge's instructions on Pages 43, 44, 45, 46 and 47, pertaining to Count 1.

The count accused Officer Briseno of committing assault on the person of another with a deadly weapon or other instrument, with means of force likely to produce great bodily injury. In order to prove the crime, the prosecution needed to have proved that a person was assaulted and that a deadly weapon or instrument capable of producing death or great bodily injury had been used. The instruction said that great bodily injury did not refer to trivial or insignificant or moderate harm. Actual bodily injury was not a necessary element of the crime. What mattered was whether the means used and the manner in which it was used was likely to produce great bodily injury. In order to constitute an assault, there had to have been an unlawful attempt to apply physical force, and the person making the attempt had to have a general criminal intent.

The instructions said, "An attempt to apply physical force is not unlawful when done in lawful defense of another. The people have the burden to prove that the attempt to apply physical force by defendant Briseno was not in defense of another. If you have a reasonable doubt whether the attempt by Briseno was not in lawful defense of another, you must find defendant Briseno not guilty."

If Briseno had reasonable grounds for believing that bodily injury was going to be inflicted on Rodney King, it was lawful for him to protect King from attack.

The instructions also said that if one interpretation of the evidence seemed reasonable and the other seemed unreasonable, we must accept the reasonable interpretation and reject the unreasonable one.

Having assured ourselves that we understood the count against Officer Briseno, we started discussing the evidence. We watched the video several times in slow motion trying to concentrate only on Officer Briseno's actions.

Officer Briseno himself had been Mr. Barnett's first witness. In Officer Briseno's testimony, he said that he put his arm up to stop Officer Powell from using his baton, and the video shows him putting his arm up. But the feeling among the jurors was that we didn't really believe that was his motivation. Most of us felt that there was a reasonable doubt that his action was motivated by any desire to protect Rodney King. So we didn't buy that part of his story.

Officer Briseno had also testified that the reason he put his foot down on Rodney King's back or shoulder was to prevent him from being hit again. We questioned his motivation. We felt that he was actually just trying to keep him from rising again, and that he did not necessarily have Rodney King's best interests at heart.

The former Navy pilot did most of the talking on the issue of

Briseno's motivation, and everyone else seemed to agree with him. Later, we established a routine of going around the table and letting everyone talk in order, but at this point, we were just speaking up.

Everyone seemed to agree that Officer Briseno was not the choirboy that his lawyer wanted us to see him as. We didn't think his motives were as altruistic as he said they were.

We passed his high-top boots around. We were all surprised how lightweight the boots were. They weighed much less than their appearance would suggest.

We had heard a lot of testimony that LAPD policy was to avoid hitting the neck of a suspect. The video did not prove conclusively that the "stomp" or "kick" was directly on the neck.

We concluded, based on the testimony of Dennis Watkins, Gerald Williams and Glen Robert King, that it was unlikely that Officer Briseno's stomp was done to protect Rodney King. On the one hand, we had the prosecution's interpretation that the force applied was not in Mr. King's defense. On the other hand, we had Briseno's testimony that the blow was applied to prevent further baton blows to Mr. King.

Even though we agreed with the prosecution that the blow was not intended to protect Mr. King, the jurors agreed that Officer Briseno's stomp was intended to prevent him from getting to his feet, and in that respect, it could be interpreted as being lawful.

We took our first vote, unanimously deciding to find Officer Briseno not guilty on Count 1, based on the fact that we could not get past the reasonable doubt that the one blow he delivered was unlawful.

It was impossible for me to know conclusively what every juror was thinking. There were those who were aggressive in vocalizing their opinions, and those who were very quiet. I only know the thoughts of those who were willing to vocalize their opinions. But if the subsequent voting was unanimous, the quiet ones must have agreed with the others.

We had heard a lot of testimony about whether or not Officer Briseno had really seen the computer message about the "big time use of force," about whether or not it was still on the computer screen, what time he had been in the station, who had said what to whom, and so on. We felt that it had not been proved one way or the other whether or not he saw the message and that was the reason that he did not report his belief that there had been an excessive use of force. We didn't think it was significant one way or the other whether he thought that Sergeant Koon was taking care of making the report. There had been testimony on both sides as to whether he had seen the message, so we had a reasonable doubt about that. But even if there had been no doubt that he saw the message, we didn't think that was a significant factor.

We talked about the testimony of Officer Watkins and Officer Williams, the retired LAPD officer. They substantiated our basic belief that Officer Briseno's actions were not based on a desire to protect Rodney King, especially the conversation where Briseno told Officer Watkins that they had kicked a little ass that night.

Even though we thought that Officer Briseno was not telling the truth about his motivations, we still didn't think that the one kick or stomp constituted an unlawful assault. Officer Briseno said that he placed his foot on the left shoulder. If his foot was right on the neck, it would have been unlawful, but we could not conclude from watching the video that it was on the neck. The discussion centered mostly around whether Officer Briseno saw the message, whether he was intending to protect King or just keep him from getting up, and what his motivation was when he reached out to prevent Powell from hitting with his baton.

There were seven pages of instructions about Count 2 against Officer Briseno, which accused him of violating the penal code by assaulting or beating a person under color of authority without lawful necessity. To be found guilty, the prosecution needed to prove that Briseno was a police officer, and that someone was assaulted under the color of authority without lawful necessity. If the person being arrested knows that he is being arrested by a peace officer, it is his duty to refrain from resisting the arrest, unless unreasonable or excessive force is being used.

According to the judge's instructions, if the officer is using excessive force, the person being arrested may use reasonable force to protect himself, but the officer may use unreasonable force to prevent escape or overcome resistance.

We did not discuss the evidence again, since we felt we had covered it very well for Count 1 and the same evidence would apply to Count 2. We talked a lot about whether the amount of force used was necessary or reasonable. Briseno's duty as an officer was to make an arrest, to prevent escape and to overcome resistance.

We re-read that passage several times while we were thinking about Count 2. We didn't go over the testimony of individual witnesses, but we talked about the basic premise, that there was reasonable doubt that the blow was unlawful. We talked about the concept of a reasonable officer, and decided that a reasonable officer might very well have used the same force.

We looked at the video again with the idea in mind of trying to see if each of Briseno's actions were without lawful necessity, and if his actions were those of a reasonable law enforcement officer in the same circumstances.

My assistant foreman said it wasn't clear enough on the video to tell, so we had to rely on the movements of Mr. King's body to see where the stomp landed.

The consensus was that we had to find Briseno not guilty on Count 2 as well. We concluded that Elements Number 1 and 2 were present, but there was again reasonable doubt that the one blow delivered by Officer Briseno was "without lawful necessity."

Most of the jurors seemed to feel that the blow was delivered by Officer Briseno to prevent Mr. King from rising to his feet again. No matter what his underlying reason was for preventing him from rising, there was reasonable doubt that it was unlawful.

Applying the "reasonable officer" concept, the jurors who expressed their opinions felt that a reasonable officer might very well have used the same force, given the same set of circumstances, to try to overcome Mr. King's resistance and to effect the arrest.

Having cast our first preliminary vote for Officer Briseno, we turned our attention to the charges against Officer Timothy Wind. First we re-read all of the judge's instructions pertaining to Count 1, to be sure we understood the charge against him. Then we discussed the evidence.

One of the jurors made the comment that it seemed like Officer Wind had kept a low profile during the trial. There just wasn't a lot of testimony about what he did. His own attorney, Mr. DePasquale, had only called three witnesses. We didn't go back and discuss each witness one by one, just what we remembered. Occasionally, someone consulted his or her notes to see what else was said.

Neither of the Singers had much to say about Officer Wind specifically. Melanie Singer didn't see Officer Wind at the scene, only at the hospital.

Sergeant DiStefano testified about Officer Wind's efficiency in the use of the baton, but little else.

Emergency room nurse Carol Edwards had testified that when asked what Mr. King had been hit with, Officer Wind said nothing, but lifted his baton. This testimony seemed to have little or no bearing on Officer Wind's innocence or guilt. The gesture occurred after the fact. If he did or did not commit a crime, it was already over with by the time he gestured with the baton.

We discussed the few references made to Officer Wind's previous police experience. We felt that it was immaterial that he was an LAPD rookie, and did not consider that in our deliberations.

We had little evidence from the prosecution, other than the video, that applied exclusively to Officer Wind. We had to rely on the videotape and the unrefuted testimony of the defense witnesses as to the LAPD policy on use of the baton. There were no prosecution witnesses who disputed the testimony of Sergeant DiStefano, Sergeant Duke or Captain Michael that the baton is used to "break bones," or that LAPD policy is to exert as much force as possible with the baton to effect compliance of a suspect who is resisting arrest.

We felt that Sergeant DiStefano's testimony about Officer Wind's proficiency with the baton at roll call had no meaning regarding his innocence or guilt.

Again, we viewed the video several times, each time concentrating only on Officer Wind's actions. Then, keeping in mind our opinions on the evidence we had examined, we discussed the elements necessary to find a defendant guilty.

The first element constituting the crime was that a person was assaulted. In order to constitute assault, it was necessary that the attempt to apply physical force be unlawful, the person making the attempt had the ability to apply the force, and that there was a criminal intent to apply the force.

It was obvious from the video that there was physical force being applied by Officer Wind. If we determined that it was unlawful, then the other elements must be considered. We concluded that the force applied was not unlawful. The video showed Officer Wind applying force that seemed to be directed toward preventing Mr. King from rising, or ultimately to effect the arrest. There was a lot of undisputed testimony about the escalation and de-escalation of force. The video clearly showed Officer Wind applying force, then stepping back, seemingly evaluating the situation and de-escalating. We felt that Officer Wind seemed to be delivering blows only to try to keep Mr. King from rising. We talked a lot about the concept of levels of command and the principles of escalation and de-escalation.

The same thing appeared to be true of the kicks delivered by Mr. Wind because they were delivered at a time when Mr. King seemed to be trying to rise. My assistant foreman said that Officer Wind only seemed to go in and deliver blows when Mr. King was trying to get up.

We also considered all of the evidence, by prosecution and defense, about the erratic behavior of Mr. King, and his resistance to arrest. We discussed Dr. Burns's testimony about the amount of alcohol it would be necessary to consume for a blood alcohol level of .19. We discussed the size of Mr. King and the testimony that he was "buffed out." We discussed the fact that Mr. King had thrown the officers off his back when they were attempting to handcuff him. All of this evidence, taken as a whole, seemed to indicate that the force used by Officer Wind was justified.

Whenever we talked about the prosecution's expert witness, Commander Bostic, we kept coming back to the fact that the solution he recommended was just too simplistic. Commander Bostic said they should have piled on top of him and held him down, like boys do in a schoolyard. The trouble was, the testimony was clear that this had been tried and it didn't work. They said they tried to swarm him and he threw them off his back. We had the feeling that Commander Bostic had been an administrator so long that he was out of touch with what happened on the street.

Two of the female jurors wanted to look at the video again and specifically study Wind's actions. We watched him deliver blows and step back and assess, and then move in again. Whenever King moved, Officer Wind started delivering blows again. It seemed to us a classic example of how they said escalation and de-escalation should be performed.

There was some discussion of the fact that Wind had not testified, but we also read in the judge's instructions that we were not supposed to hold that against him.

The strongest evidence was the video itself. Even during the last seconds of the video tape, the force he used appeared to be for the sole purpose of keeping Mr. King from rising.

Based on these observations, we felt there was reasonable doubt of his guilt, therefore, we found Officer Wind not guilty on Count 1, and started to deliberate on Count 2.

It was about at this point when I reminded the jury, as I would do several times during the deliberations, of the circumstantial evidence rule.

Again, we read in the judge's instructions the elements necessary to constitute guilt for this crime. Element 1 was true. Officer Wind was a police officer. Element 2 was causing us a little concern because it stated, "A person was assaulted or beaten by a police officer." Someone suggested we write a note to the judge and ask for clarification. In Count 1, "assault" was clearly defined. In Count 2, it could be interpreted that the terms "assault" and "beaten" might be synonymous. I asked the assistant foreman to write the question on one of the forms, and I signed it and handed it to the bailiff to give to the judge.

We again discussed the testimony and viewed the tape with the intent to observe Officer Wind's actions for "unnecessary" use of force. The same observations we had made for Count 1 seemed to apply to Count 2, namely the escalation/de-escalation and the fact that Officer Wind seemed to be delivering blows or kicks to Mr. King only to prevent his rising.

We concluded that a reasonable officer acting under color of authority could have reasonably perceived that Mr. King was actively resisting arrest or trying to escape, given his erratic behavior. We concluded that a reasonable officer could perceive Mr. King a threat, considering the fact that he had thrown the officers off of his back when they tried to handcuff him. We agreed that Mr. Wind could have perceived that Mr. King's lunge toward Officer Powell was a threat.

It came down to the fact that the reason Rodney King was beaten was because he was resisting arrest and threatening the officers' safety. He was also engaging in very bizarre behavior, and we thought that a reasonable officer would think so.

Based on these facts, we could not establish guilt beyond a reasonable doubt. We found Officer Wind not guilty of Count 2. It did not take a long time to reach our verdict for Officer Wind, because there was not as much testimony to consider as there was for Officer Powell and Sergeant Koon.

The juror who had knitted me a scarf, who always kept so busy during the trial, volunteered to be the secretary and record each of our tentative verdicts, to be reviewed later.

We only had one copy of the judge's instructions, and they were so complicated that we felt it would be easier to follow them if we had copies to look at while they were being read aloud. So I asked if we could get three more copies, so that each three people could have one to look at together.

We started to discuss some of the testimony in the charges against Officer Powell, and there was question in the minds of some of the jurors about the comments made by Officer Powell to Mr. King at the hospital. We weren't certain exactly what bearing those comments had on the case. The charges involved what they did to Rodney King at the scene; whether they taunted him at the hospital afterward did not seem to have any direct significance to whether they had used excessive force.

One of the women, the one who had annoyed me earlier by sending the note complaining about Juror Number 10's bizarre behavior and who asked the bailiffs to bring her water when she coughed, said she would like to have that testimony about what was said at the hospital re-read. So just prior to stopping for the day, I wrote a note to the judge asking if we could have the testimony of Emergency Room nurses Lawrence Davis and Carol Edwards re-read to us.

We left the courthouse at 5 p.m. and boarded the bus. Several of us had fully expected to spend extra hours deliberating, particularly if we were making progress. Maybe I have seen too many trials on television where the jury deliberates into the night. Other jurors, however, felt that we should have two breaks a day, take our full lunch hour, and leave promptly at 5 p.m.

We affectionately dubbed one of the jurors "the union representative," because he always wanted to make sure we were not overworked. We had agreed at the outset that even if only one juror needed a break, we would honor that. So we quit every night at 5 p.m. It was probably a very good decision, because the strain was great. We were very tired at the end of the day.

When we arrived at the hotel, we went to the conference room, as instructed by the deputies, and picked a meal from the menu of a Mexican restaurant chain called El Torito. Then we went to our individual rooms and freshened up or changed clothes. We all met in the conference room again and waited for the deputies to bring back the food. This turned out to be a poor plan. El Torito serves good Mexican food but by the time it traveled all the way back to the hotel, it was cold and not very appetizing.

Each night we were sequestered, activities occurred in the conference room. One of the men had brought a putter, a putting receptacle and some golf balls. Some of the jurors had contests to see who could sink the most putts. A little later each night, very carefully selected videos were shown. One night, the bailiff determined that one of the movies that had been chosen had violence in it and therefore would not be appropriate for the jury to view. I did not watch any of them, so it didn't matter to me.

The television sets had been removed from our rooms. You could see where they normally were placed on the dresser tops.

Some of the jurors just gathered on the walkways outside the rooms and talked. There was always a group of jurors leaning on the railing, looking down at the pool and the activities on the first floor. There wasn't much else to do.

# Chapter Twenty-One: Breaking Down in Tears

SATURDAY, APRIL 25, 1992

We were to deliberate during the weekend. The deputies came around and knocked on our doors each morning about 7:30 a.m., just to be sure we were out of bed. After the first morning, we did not get a 6:30 a.m. wake up call. Everyone adjusted, either by getting a call from those jurors who had the foresight to bring an alarm clock, or by their own internal clock. My internal clock always works, but I worried that it might fail me one morning, particularly if I did not sleep well that night. It takes me a lot longer than a half hour to get ready in the morning, so I asked one of the other women, who had an alarm clock, to knock on my door each morning.

Off to breakfast again at IHOP. Then back on the bus that transported us to the courthouse. There were always a few people outside the courthouse each morning when we arrived, and even though it was Saturday, there were onlookers. Most of them appeared to be news media people. We entered the building and proceeded to the jury services room, where we gathered to look at the menu and choose our lunch, then the jurors headed to the deliberation room and the alternates stayed in the jury services rooms.

We started our step-by-step deliberation of Count 1 against Officer Powell. One of the jurors wanted to take an early ballot, just to see where we were. Even though this was out of sequence in our plan, we decided to vote. There were ten not guilty votes, one guilty vote and one question mark. The one guilty vote was a little disturbing because even though we had discussed the evidence against Officer Powell very superficially on Friday evening, I felt we had not yet discussed it sufficiently to warrant a guilty vote at that point, particularly since we had agreed we would all start with not guilty (or a question) and go from there. This vote was probably too premature, but I was trying to be sure every juror's request was granted, insofar as possible.

There were those jurors among us who felt as I did that because we had not yet talked about the evidence or applied the law, a vote for not guilty was, in essence, a question mark, since we were trying to follow the "innocent until proven guilty" path. However, it was sometimes difficult to tell those who were voting not guilty because they had not yet decided, and those who were firm in their opinions.

It seemed to me that there were a couple of jurors who came into the deliberation room with hermetically sealed minds. Most of the jurors, however, were honestly, and without mental reservation, considering all of the evidence and the judge's instructions, applying the law and then coming up with their decision.

There were a very few who were overwhelmed by the task and simply went with their gut feeling. We said many times during the deliberations that gut feeling was an important element, and should certainly be a part of each juror's equation, but we were obligated to put our gut feelings through the test of the law and the instructions. We took an oath that we would follow the judge's instructions. I was not able to read their minds or determine their motivation. These were just my personal observations. After the trial, I discussed these opinions with a couple of the jurors, who agreed with my assessment.

At about mid-morning we were called back into the courtroom. The judge and the attorneys and defendants were present, the attorneys and defendants resplendent in their impeccable business clothes, while the jurors were all dressed very casually. It was Saturday, for heaven's sake!

The judge read the two requests I had sent him on Friday. In answer to the question about the word "beating," he simply answered that it meant hitting repeatedly. While he did not specifically say that it was not synonymous with "assault," we were left with that impression. He then informed us that the jury would convene upstairs for the reading of the testimony of the nurses, which we had requested.

We were escorted upstairs by the deputies, and the regular jurors and the alternates convened in the jury services room. The court reporter came in and said she would communicate only with the foreman, and that she would continue reading until told to stop. She started reading back the testimony of Lawrence Davis. At one point, I felt that she had read enough of the testimony to satisfy our requirements and requested that she go on to Ms. Edwards's testimony. However, one of the jurors stated to me that more was needed, so I requested that she continue, and I did not interrupt her again. She read back the complete testimony of both nurses.

*Moral Uncertainty*

We reconvened in the jury room and continued our deliberation. We re-read the judge's instructions on Pages 43 through 47, the judge's definition of Count 1. Each time we read the instructions, we gathered together by threes, so that not only were we listening to the juror who was reading the instruction aloud, but we were following along on the written copy. The extra copies of the instructions helped us immeasurably. We considered again the three elements constituting assault and the circumstantial evidence rules. We then started around the table with our comments and opinions.

To be sure that everyone understood the counts against Officer Powell, and to prevent the constant re-reading of the judge's instructions, the assistant foreman wrote on the blackboard a condensed version of the elements of each count. On Count 1, it narrowed down to whether assault existed and was it unlawful. On Count 2, it could be summed up by deciding if the beating or assault had lawful necessity. The key word in Count 1 was "unlawful," and in Count 2, the key word was "unnecessary." For the rest of the deliberations on Counts 1 and 2 we simply referred to these words rather than reading the entire definitions.

We had appointed one of the jurors to take charge of playing the video, stopping it when requested, restarting, etc. We played the video many times Saturday and Sunday, each time concentrating only on Officer Powell's actions.

We played the video so many times in slow motion that it began to lose its reality. So periodically, someone would request that it be played in real time so we could be reminded of the timing of the event. We didn't want to be so analytical that we lost sense of reality. Mostly, however, we played the slow motion FBI version. This allowed us to analyze it in greater detail. Sometimes I had to stop and remind myself that a human being was being beaten. I didn't want to lose sight of that.

We discussed the other evidence also. When we discussed Officer Melanie Singer's testimony that she saw Officer Powell strike Mr. King on the left side of his face with a baton, everyone tended to discount that point because the photographs and testimony of medical personnel did not confirm that Mr. King's left cheek had any injuries. The injuries were on the right cheek. Even on the right cheek there was not the elongated injury she described. When she was challenged by the defense about this, she said she "saw what she saw."

Officers Briseno and Solano had testified to head blows by Officer Powell, but in defense cross-examination, said they felt the blows were accidental, deflected blows. The video showed Mr. King's head hitting the ground violently and bouncing back up.

There were two opposing opinions by the medical experts about what caused the facial injuries. Dr. Dallas Long III testified for the defense that the facial injuries were most likely caused by the head hitting a broad, flat surface such as the asphalt, while Dr. Norman Shorr, the prosecution's witness, testified that the injuries could have been caused by a baton blow. Everyone who expressed their opinion concluded that there simply was not enough substantial proof, either from the medical experts or other testimony, that Officer Powell had struck Mr. King in the head. It was a case of adopting the reasonable interpretation of evidence that pointed to innocence.

The one vote in our preliminary ballot for guilty was cast by the woman who had sent the note to the judge about Juror Number 10. So we spent the rest of the day with her trying to present the facts she felt pointed to Officer Powell's guilt. The assistant foreman, who had voted a question mark, presented his arguments also.

Most of what they found compelling was the video itself. There was a lot of simultaneous talking, since both wanted to make their points. But since the female juror was the only one defending the guilty position, it seemed at times as if she was being attacked by everyone. I had the feeling that none of the jurors wanted to attack her; they were simply trying to understand her point of view, but there was a definite lack of patience and the comments became heated.

She was having trouble expressing herself to the other jurors, and on several different occasions, I re-stated what I felt she was trying to say and asked her if it was correct. I tried to keep everyone calm and unemotional but there were strong feelings on both sides. The situation was compounded by a strong personality conflict between this woman and one of the others. The knitting juror became annoyed with me for trying to translate.

We continued, with interruptions for lunch and breaks, until 5 p.m., when we left the courthouse and boarded the bus for the hotel. Just after we turned on to Tapo Canyon Road, the effervescent woman who had brought me a birthday card cried, "Did you see that? We were just mooned."

Everyone looked immediately. A young man in the street mooned us, pulled up his pants and partially lost them again as he went across the street. I was disappointed that I did not see the whole thing, but I did see the young man pulling up his pants as he went from the median strip to the sidewalk. We were clearly in need of some distraction!

Maybe because it was Saturday night or maybe the deputies felt sorry for us, but we were told we were going to dinner at Tony Roma's, not IHOP! We understood how difficult it was for the deputies. They had to maintain a low profile, which was pretty difficult when we drove up to a restaurant in the Ventura County Sheriff's Department bus fitted with cells.

Our restaurant choices were confined to those with a previously negotiated contract with Los Angeles County, and the establishment had to have a somewhat isolated area that we could occupy exclusively. That limited the restaurants considerably. I suspect the allowed food budget had something to do with it, also. I'm sure we stretched that budget to the limit.

The deputies dressed in civilian clothing when we went out to dinner, but they always had their guns with them, sometimes quite cleverly concealed. We speculated about where Mary's gun might be. A petite and very pretty deputy, she wore little, short skirts and heels so high that one juror said the heels and skirt were the same length.

Dinner was good and we were happy for the change of scenery, but many of the jurors were feeling the strain. By this time, the responsibility weighed very heavily upon me and I was not the only one. Each was responding in his own way to the pressure.

About six of the jurors had brought swim suits and went into the pool when we got back to the motel, with one of the deputies accompanying them. Some of them actually did laps, but mostly they sat in the spa area of the pool and talked. The rest of us hung over the second floor railing and watched.

Again, everyone went to bed around ten o'clock. Some of the jurors had expressed a desire to sleep in on Sunday morning, so I asked the bailiff, Jerry, if that was possible, and the answer was a definite negative.

We were offered the opportunity to go to church on Sunday morning if anyone wanted to. Since it was not possible to attend their regular churches, those jurors who had considered going to church declined. So we were up at the regular time, breakfast at IHOP, and off to the courthouse again.

We proceeded to the jury services room to place our lunch order and then convened in the deliberation room. We continued with the examination of the evidence on Count 1 for Officer Powell.

Several points seemed to be the dominating evidence in the minds of the jurors regarding Count 1 against Powell. The following were the most frequently discussed:

- The baton practice at roll call before the officers went on duty.
- Mr. King's refusal to cooperate with the officers who were trying to arrest him.
- Mr. King putting his hand on his buttocks and shaking them at officers with guns drawn.
- Mr. King throwing Officer Powell off his back, causing the officer to land on his buttocks when trying to restrain him.
- The apparent laughter by Officer Powell when calling for a rescue ambulance.
- The video that showed Mr. King rising up and charging toward Officer Powell after having been tased twice.
- The video showing the last few seconds of the blows delivered to Mr. King.
- Mr. King's size, his blood alcohol level and the unsuccessful attempts by the officers to subdue him.
- Officer Powell's *Oops* comment to his friend on the car radio and his subsequent statement that "I haven't beaten anybody that bad in a long time."
- Commander Bostic's testimony about the force being "out of LAPD policy."

We kept referring to the word "unlawful" that we had written on the blackboard. Were the blows unlawful? Also, most of us were trying to keep in mind the reasonable doubt concept and all of the other general instructions and those pertaining to Count 1 as given to us by the judge. Did Officer Powell commit an assault against Mr.

King as defined in the three elements necessary to constitute assault? These were the questions we kept asking ourselves.

One juror said that Rodney King got what he deserved. The one Hispanic juror, a woman who worked as a hospital housekeeper, was upset by that, and said, "No one deserves to be beaten." She was very emotional and kept saying, "Can't you see all those guys hitting that poor man?" She couldn't focus on why they were hitting him.

There was no doubt in anyone's mind that Rodney King was beaten terribly, and if that were the entire criteria, it would have been an easy choice. If we had just looked at the few seconds of the tape, with no further consideration, as the entire country had done, there would have been no doubt of the outcome.

The jurors all agreed that there was too much testimony about LAPD policy regarding force to dismiss it. We all agreed that the use of the baton was within department policy when verbalization did not succeed. This was a case where verbalization was constantly being given, even while the baton was being used.

All twelve of us, as a group, agreed that the baton was not a humane method of subduing a criminal. Several times the jurors expressed that we wished we were trying the LAPD. It would have been a lot easier to judge the methods the officers were trained to use than to determine if the officers had gone beyond policy in the use of the baton.

It was getting close to lunchtime when we called for another vote. We had been deliberating for four days. This time it was unanimous. All the votes were not guilty. The woman who had voted guilty to start with remarked that she would give in on this count but not to expect her to do so on Count 2. This led me to believe that she was just caving in under perceived pressure. I would have addressed this at that time, except that I felt all of our decisions at that point were temporary and could be reconsidered.

The assistant foreman was another story. His gut feeling was that there was some guilt on the part of Officer Powell as far as Count 1 was concerned. I felt certain, however, that he was not giving in to pressure. He simply could not get past the reasonable doubt of Powell's guilt, based on his examination of the evidence and the application of the law as given to us by the judge. He could not persuade himself that the blows inflicted were "likely to cause great bodily injury." He felt instinctively that he was guilty, but he couldn't prove it to himself. He voted not guilty.

It was a very difficult moment. He put his head down on the table and cried. We were all close to tears. Everyone wanted to do the right thing. One of the other women, who had originally voted not guilty, was now sobbing audibly.

When we went out of the room for our break, I talked to her for some time to try to calm her. In the beginning she had felt so strongly about the guilt of the officers, but after all considerations she was not able to say beyond a reasonable doubt that they were guilty. Reconciling this was very difficult for her.

We were all trying very hard to be honest and fair. We were trying to consider all aspects and unemotionally reach a verdict. Not possible! We were all visibly shaken. On the one hand, this was a man's life we were determining, and on the other hand, there was another man who had been severely beaten. It was more of a burden than any of us had realized it would be.

At this point, I still had a nagging feeling that the force used in the last few seconds of the tape was unreasonable, but after considering all of the testimony, I was unable to establish in my mind guilt beyond a reasonable doubt.

We joined the alternate jurors in the jury services room and had our lunch. I doubt that many of us really tasted it. The alternate jurors served a definite purpose that was extremely valuable to me. When we joined them for breaks and lunch, even though we could not talk about the case or our deliberations, they communicated with us and helped us to relax for a few minutes. They were engaged in a lot of little projects, like painting ceramics, jigsaw puzzles, exercises, etc. Mary, the bailiff, brought a set of barbells for the alternate jurors to use for exercise. She assured the female jurors that if they exercised regularly with the barbells they would become as toned as she. Nobody believed it.

Each time we had a break or lunch, we were given an account of the alternates' activities. It was a helpful release. It was a trying time for them, also. The waiting was very difficult for them. This day I was very grateful for their support.

As soon as I had eaten, I was ready to go back to the jury room, but others felt they needed the time away from deliberation, so I more or less fidgeted for the remainder of our lunch hour.

When we returned, we were too emotionally drained to attempt deliberation of Count 2 against Officer Powell, since we knew it was going to be another gut-wrenching session. So we proceeded to Count 3, filing a false police report. We gathered in our groups of three while someone read aloud from Page 42 of the judge's instructions that in Counts 3 and 4, "there must exist a certain mental state in the mind of the perpetrator. Unless such mental state exists, the crime to which it relates is not committed. In the crime of filing a false police report, the necessary mental state is knowledge that the statement was false."

We also read Page 10, which stated: "The (specific intent) (or) (mental state) with which an act is done may be shown by the circumstances surrounding the commission of the act. But you may not find the defendant guilty of the offense charged (in Counts 3, 4, and 5), unless the proved circumstances are not only (1) consistent with the theory that the defendant had the required (specific intent) (or) (mental state) but (2) cannot be reconciled with any other rational conclusion.

Also, if the evidence as to (any) such (specific intent) (or) (mental state) is susceptible of two reasonable interpretations, one of which points to the existence of the (specific intent) (or) (mental state) and the other to the absence of the (specific intent) (or) (mental state), you must adopt that interpretation which points to the absence of the (specific intent) (or) (mental state). If, on the other hand, one interpretation of the evidence as to such (specific intent) (or) (mental state) appears to you to be reasonable and the other interpretation to be unreasonable, you must accept the reasonable interpretation and reject the unreasonable."

The assistant foreman drew on the blackboard a horizontal straight line. At the extreme left of the line was "not guilty." At the extreme right was "guilty." About two-thirds of the way from the left of the line, there was a vertical line labeled "reasonable doubt." This gave us a graphic method of determining where along the line we might be during the deliberations.

It surprised me to hear him say that on Count 1 he had been waffling back and forth across the reasonable doubt mark. I had never completely gone over the line toward guilty, but by the time the last count was taken, I had been a lot closer than I was before we considered all of the evidence.

Next we read the arrest report, Exhibit Number 304 and some of us consulted our own notes. The entries we felt were material were:

- The report indicated that Mr. King had abrasions and contusions, but did not indicate lacerations, even though his face required stitches.
- The report indicated he was possibly under the influence of an unknown drug, but did not specifically say PCP, even though there was testimony by several officers that they believed he was under the influence of PCP.
- The report stated that Mr. King got out of the vehicle then got back in and got out again. The testimony was that he never got out of the car completely, just partially.

We went around the table and each juror was given an opportunity to discuss the report. There was some discussion about the individual entries, but mostly we tended to lump them all together. Then we discussed each of the elements that must be proved to establish guilt. Element 1 was present, Officer Powell was acting as a peace officer. Element 2 was present, he did file a report of the incident.

In considering Elements 3 and 4, in each case there were two reasonable interpretations. One reasonable interpretation of the testimony about the entries was that the inconsistencies in his report were done with the specific intent to falsify and minimize the seriousness of the incident. The other reasonable interpretation was that the report was a reflection of his memory at the time and a condensed documentation. Based on the fact that at the time he wrote the report, he did not know the event had been taped, we felt that could not have been his motivation. The subsequent investigation, if any, would have brought out details he could not have avoided.

We went around the table and each juror expressed his opinion about the charge. According to the law, namely the requirement that we must prove specific intent to falsify, we felt we must adopt the interpretation leading to his innocence.

Then we voted. There were twelve not guilty votes. The juror who was keeping the written tally noted that we had tentatively found Officer Powell not guilty of Count 3.

We turned our attention to Count 1 against Sergeant Koon.

We discussed his testimony and the testimony of several of the other officers present at the scene about the use of the Taser. We concluded that an assault as defined by the law was not committed. Sergeant Koon's sole physical activity during the entire incident was the activating of the Taser. Since the intent of the Taser, according to all testimony, is to stun temporarily, allowing officers to subdue the intended person, we did not consider it a deadly weapon likely to produce death or great bodily injury.

We read Pages 38 and 39 of the judge's instructions pertaining to the aiding and abetting of a crime. The instructions said that those who directly and actively commit a crime, as well as those who aid and abet the commission of a crime are equally guilty. A person aids or abets when he or she with knowledge of the unlawful purpose of the perpetrator, promotes, encourages or instigates the commission of a crime. Mere presence at the scene of a crime, without assisting in committing it, does not amount to aiding and abetting.

Several of the jurors expressed the viewpoint that, since the testimony proved that Sergeant Koon was in charge and directing the actions of the others, he could be considered to be aiding and abetting. According to testimony, he was telling Officers Powell and Wind to "hit him in the legs." I, personally, felt strongly that Officer Powell was being directed by Sergeant Koon to hit Mr. King in the legs with the baton.

However, the wording of the law was such that a crime must have been committed before aiding and abetting can be considered. Therefore, the conclusion was that if we could find Officer Powell guilty of the crime of assault with a deadly weapon, we would be able to consider Sergeant Koon as aiding and abetting.

Since we had not yet found Officer Powell guilty of the crime, we agreed to re-consider the aiding and abetting element of Count 1 against Sergeant Koon after we had completed our deliberations for Officer Powell.

We proceeded to consider Count 2 against Sergeant Koon, referring once more to the blackboard, which condensed Count 2 to the word "unnecessary." Again, we concluded that Sergeant Koon was not a direct participant in the application of force against Mr. King. Most of the jurors felt that if we could establish that Officer

Powell was guilty of Count 2, we could find Sergeant Koon guilty also, of aiding and abetting.

We went on to Count 4 against Sergeant Koon, re-reading Pages 10, 42, 56 and 57 relating to Counts 3 and 4. We read Exhibit 25, Sergeant's Daily Report, prepared by Sergeant Koon. We discussed what we considered to be "material matters" that were being declared by the prosecution as false.

They were:

- Sergeant Koon's report said that "it was immediately obvious that the suspect was under the influence of PCP." In his testimony he said he formed the opinion over time.
- His report said "Taser going entire time." The testimony was that Mr. King was shot with the Taser only twice.
- The report said, "several facial cuts of a minor nature." The prosecution contends that he knew the injuries were not minor.
- His report also said that Mr. King exited the vehicle, got back in and exited again.

Most of the jurors concluded that there simply was not enough evidence to convict Sergeant Koon of filing a false police report. We could not prove to ourselves beyond a reasonable doubt that the mental state existed in Sergeant Koon's mind to intentionally falsify his report. The same two reasonable interpretations that we applied to Officer Powell's report, we applied to Sergeant Koon's. We had to accept the interpretation that led to his innocence.

We tentatively found Sergeant Koon not guilty of Count 4, and our scribe so noted. We went on to Count 5, which charged Sergeant Koon only with the crime of being an accessory to a felony.

The judge's instructions relating to Count 5 read: "Every person who, after a felony has been committed, harbors, conceals or aids a principal in such felony, with the specific intent that said principal may avoid or escape from arrest, trial, conviction or punishment, having knowledge that said principal has committed such felony or has been charged with such felony or convicted thereof, is guilty of the crime of accessory to a felony in violation of Penal Code Section 32."

In order to convict Koon on that charge, the prosecution needed to prove that an assault with a deadly weapon under color of authority was committed, and that Koon harbored, concealed or aided a principal with the specific intent of helping that person avoid or escape arrest, trial, and punishment.

The judge's instructions said that if we found Sergeant Koon guilty in Counts 1 and 2, then we should not find him guilty of Count 5, but if we found him guilty in Count 5, then we should not find him guilty in Counts 1 and 2.

The jury could not get past Element 1. Until or unless we could prove Officer Powell guilty of the felony, there could be no violation of Penal Code Section 32. We agreed that we would re-visit Counts 1 and 2, as well as Count 5 against Sergeant Koon after completing our deliberation for Officer Powell.

We spent the remainder of the day discussing the testimony and evidence pertaining to Count 2 against Officer Powell.

We left the courthouse a few minutes after 5 p.m., as usual, and boarded the bus that took us back to the hotel. I talked on the bus with the knitting juror about the emotional tension in the jury room and told her we were all going to have to be less volatile. She agreed. We went to our rooms for about an hour before meeting the deputies outside their corner rooms to walk across the street to IHOP. Same routine, back to the hotel, meet in the conference room or convene outside someone's room and talk.

I was concerned for the state of mind of the female juror who said she would vote not guilty on Count 1 but wasn't going to give in on Count 2. I went to her room and found her in tears, packing her bags. She had written a note to the judge saying she was not going to continue as a juror. She let me read the note. She felt everybody was against her and I could very well see why she felt that way, but I told her we had sworn to do our duty and that she shouldn't give up just because she was defending an opposing position. I asked for her cooperation and told her that I would come up with a more structured procedure to try to prevent hard feelings. She seemed genuinely willing to try to cooperate. I felt better and I think she did, too.

# Chapter Twenty-Two: Following Instructions

MONDAY, APRIL 27, 1992

We had sweet rolls, muffins, small boxes of cereal, milk and orange juice served in the conference room. Those wishing to go to IHOP could. I chose not to. Back on the bus and back to the courthouse. We got busy immediately.

Because we'd had problems with everyone talking at once and interrupting each other, we changed our format. Those jurors voting guilty would present their arguments on each piece of evidence and then we would go around the table and allow each juror to express his or her opinion on that particular point. Then we would have open discussion, with each juror raising his hand and being recognized by me.

At this time, I was still sitting on the side of the table and one of the men complained that I was looking toward the front of the table most of the time and ignoring those with their hands up at the other end of the table. I traded places with him so I could see everybody with raised hands and ensure everyone got a fair chance to express their views.

This worked very well, with the exception of one time. One of the women interrupted another and she became quite upset. They started airing some of their differences. Another juror said they shouldn't argue and I said, no, maybe they needed to get it out, so I encouraged them to continue. They had been angry over an incident that occurred during the trial when one of them was talking to the bailiff, Jerry, and the other had come up and taken over the conversation completely. Their angry exchange lasted only about two minutes, but I felt it was time well spent if it cleared the air.

After some very brief discussion summarizing where we were in our deliberation of Count 2 for Officer Powell, we took a preliminary vote. The result was two guilty, nine not guilty and one question mark.

The assistant foreman repeated our original plan that we should have the jurors who voted guilty give their specific points of evidence in support of their vote. Another juror asked why we were using this format, and he reminded him that each defendant was considered innocent until proven guilty beyond a reasonable doubt.

Because of the strong feelings on both sides, the arguments became very heated. At times, it was difficult to restore the atmosphere of calm and intelligent deliberation. It took a good deal of arbitrating. Sometimes, we just let the jurors blow off steam and get it off their chest.

I believe that emotions ran high because we viewed the video so many times. It was disturbing. Sometimes we were being so analytical that we stood in danger of not responding to the brutality. I tried very hard to keep this in mind at all times.

We deliberated until lunchtime. The period of time immediately prior to lunch was particularly emotional. When we returned from lunch, two of the women were visibly upset and refused to watch the video again. We convinced them they had to because it was an important piece of evidence and we had taken an oath to "conscientiously consider and weigh the evidence, apply the law, and reach a just verdict regardless of the consequences."

We re-read and discussed the "reasonable officer" concept on Page 52. There was a good deal of discussion about what a "reasonable peace officer in the same or similar circumstances would believe to be necessary to make such arrest, or to prevent escape, or to overcome resistance." We had to consider what Officer Powell's perception of the amount of force necessary to effect arrest might be. All of this, of course, was based on the evidence presented to us during the trial, not just our gut feeling.

The deliberations continued until 5 p.m., when we again boarded the bus to return to the hotel.

It had been an exhausting day. The arguments, the confrontations, the emotions, were all very tiring. I was also experiencing a bit of depression. As foreman it was my duty to do everything possible to facilitate a common verdict, and I certainly was not succeeding. With all of these thoughts in my mind, I elected not to go to dinner. The other jurors went to Reuben's, so I missed out on one of the better dinners. I should have stayed at the motel on an IHOP night instead.

I asked one of the alternates to bring me back some bread and a salad. As it turned out, I got the salad, which was excellent, but not the bread, which was what my stomach really needed.

Same routine. Breakfast at IHOP and back in the bus to be transported to the courthouse. Each day the crowds outside the courthouse in the mornings and the evenings seemed to increase.

We summarized the progress we had made the previous day and took another preliminary vote. This time it was three guilty and nine not guilty. We once more turned to the judge's instructions and read Page 64, which stated that Powell, Wind and Koon were accused of committing the crime of assault by force likely to produce great bodily injury and with a deadly weapon in Count 1, and with the crime of an officer unnecessarily assaulting or beating any person in Count 2. A conviction on either or both counts could be based on more than one act. A defendant could be found guilty if proof shows beyond a reasonable doubt that he committed one or more of such acts.

"However, in order to return a verdict of guilty to Count 1 or 2, all jurors must agree that (he) committed the same (act) (or) (acts). It is not necessary that the particular (act) agreed upon be stated in your verdict," the instructions said.

This seemed very important, because up to this point there did not seem to be a consensus as to exactly what act or acts constituted the guilt.

We agreed that those jurors voting guilty should list on the board the points of evidence that contributed to their decision. The assistant foreman wrote the following items on the blackboard as one of the women jurors listed them.
- Baton training during roll call.
- "Gorillas in the mist" comment.
- Officer Powell being thrown off of Mr. King.
- Laughter on tape of radio transmission.

He added another item of his own:
- The *Oops* message transmitted to Officer Powell's friend.

As we went around the table discussing these points, there were a lot of comments about the "gorillas in the mist" remark.

The woman who was disturbed by it said it proved that Officer Powell was racially biased, therefore his actions were more severe than they would have been against a white person. Most of the other jurors said they did not believe there was racial motivation. This was the only discussion we ever had about race during the entire deliberation.

There was a lot of discussion about the laughter during the radio transmission by Officer Powell when he was ordering an ambulance. Those voting guilty contended that the laugh proved that Officer Powell was considering it light-heartedly and that he was amused by the whole incident. The other jurors felt that there definitely was laughter, not just heavy breathing, as Officer Powell had testified, but that it was probably nervous, exhausted laughter. I remembered the testimony of Sergeant DiStefano that he had seen otherwise stable men laugh, or cry, or wet their pants, or even defecate when faced with the stress of these police situations.

Applying the rule of circumstantial evidence, there were two reasonable interpretations of the laughter. One was that he was laughing because he was callous and insensitive to the situation, the other was that this was simply nervous laughter. I felt I had to adopt the interpretation pointing to his innocence, since they were both reasonable.

There was some feeling that the *Oops* message could be considered evidence that Mr. Powell recognized he had made a mistake or done something wrong. Were we to guess what it was that he felt he had done wrong? Too many options or interpretations to affix to that piece of evidence to come to any definite conclusions. It seemed to be a strong case against him, however. I decided I would come back to that.

We went around the table to each of the jurors and had lengthy discussions about each of the items. Then we turned once more to the video and asked those jurors to point out the specific parts of the video they felt were "unnecessary force."

There were places in the tape where some of the jurors were certain they saw movement that could have been interpreted by the officers as justification for continuing to hit Mr. King with the baton to keep him down. Other jurors could not see the movement. It crossed my mind that if the movement was that undetectable, it probably didn't justify necessary force. They wrote down the frame numbers of the video where they perceived actions that pointed to Officer Powell's guilt. This was to conform to the judge's instructions that we agree on the same act or acts in order to constitute a guilty verdict.

While there were never any specific frames agreed upon, there was a consensus among the jurors voting guilty that the last few seconds of the video, after Officer Briseno's stomp, was the period of time during which they felt the blows were unnecessary. They felt that Mr. King was on the ground at that time, not trying to rise, even though he was rolling around and had not assumed the felony prone position the officers were trying to achieve.

During our lunch break, the bailiff informed us that we could call our homes that evening and make arrangements for clean clothes to be brought to us. We were all reaching the end of our clean clothes. None of us thought the deliberations would last this long. After eating, while I waited to go back into the deliberation room, I made a long list of items I needed from home. We didn't know how much longer we would deliberate.

We returned to the deliberation room and continued discussing the five items listed on the board. We also viewed the video many more times that afternoon, especially the area that was viewed as unnecessary force by the jurors voting guilty. The argument by the jurors voting not guilty was that Mr. King was still resisting, and that the officers could reasonably have perceived that Mr. King might have a concealed weapon he was trying to reach when he put his hands toward his back.

Just before leaving for the day, we took another preliminary vote. The result was four guilty, eight not guilty. One of the men, a telephone technician, suggested that we prepare a statement for the press, to be given out when the trial was over. He drafted it and we all agreed to it:

*We the jury in the case of the* People vs. Powell, *et al, would like to make three things known. First, we would like to thank everyone involved for trying to make this whole experience as easy on us as possible. Second, we would like to ask all members of the media or anyone else who would want to contact us about this case, please do not. If we want to speak about it we will do so in our own time and in our own way. Finally, we would like to say that this experience has been an extremely difficult and stressful one, one over which we have all agonized a great deal. We feel we have done the best job we possibly could have done. Sincerely, The Jury and Alternates.*

*Moral Uncertainty*

That evening, we had hamburgers from Burger King brought in for our dinner, because we were all taking turns talking to our families on the telephone to give them lists of items we needed brought to us.

The process of the telephone calls was frustrating, but necessary. Each juror who wanted to place a call put his or her name and telephone number on a list and the deputies called us, in turn, to the corner room occupied by the bailiff. It was a suite with a sitting room and a bedroom. Each juror, when called, was directed to the bedroom telephone. The deputy placed the call, identified himself to the family member, and said that the call would be monitored. Then the juror picked up the telephone and talked. There wasn't too much I cared to say to my husband while a deputy was listening, so it was a somewhat stilted conversation, but I was able to convey what I needed him to bring to me.

Some of the jurors took their food to their rooms, others ate in the conference room.

It was a restless sleep night for me. I felt that we had spent adequate time in deliberation on Count 2 for Officer Powell. We had rehashed each of the pieces of evidence several times. Even though we seemed to come up with some different aspect or way of looking at the evidence each time we went around the table, I was beginning to feel that we were spinning our wheels. I planned to suggest to the jury the next day that we finalize all of our previously tentative verdicts and ask for guidance from the judge about the remaining count.

WEDNESDAY, APRIL 29, 1992

Jerry the bailiff and the deputies were always very careful what they discussed with us and were always just a little aloof, but this morning there was a definite difference in their manner. They seemed nervous, and everything had a sense of urgency about it. Hard to describe, but the feeling was there.

When we arrived at the courthouse, we were rushed into the jury deliberation room (without choosing our lunch menu) and we were not allowed to visit with the alternates. Later, Jerry came in and asked us to choose what we wanted from the pizza restaurant. It was almost as if they were saying, "All right, you've had enough time. Make your decisions." We all felt the pressure.

When we were all convened, I suggested that we write a note to the judge and ask for guidance. Since we seemed not to be able to reach a unanimous verdict on Officer Powell, maybe we needed the judge to decide if we should continue deliberating. I felt even more strongly about this than I had the previous evening because of the attitude of the deputies. I also suggested that we make final decisions on the verdicts that we had made temporarily. All of the jurors agreed.

I put on the blackboard a matrix with the counts on the top, and each defendant's name on the left. The assistant foreman marked an X in each of the blocks that were not relevant for the defendants.

We started with Officer Briseno. We went around the table and asked each person if they had any more or different thoughts on this charge other than those we had discussed last week. Several of the jurors repeated their opinions, but no one seemed to feel any differently. We had a formal vote which was unanimously for not guilty. We put an "NG" in the square by Officer Briseno's name under Counts 1 and 2.

We then discussed Officer Wind. One of the jurors wanted to see the video once more. We ran the video and we each watched the actions of Officer Wind. Again, we went around the table and allowed each juror a chance to comment. I wanted each juror to have a chance to change their vote, if they had second thoughts or if they felt they had been pressured into making a decision. We did everything possible to avoid that during the deliberation, but I was particularly concerned about the single preliminary vote of not guilty on Count 1 for Officer Powell. After the discussion and the viewing of the video one more time, we took a formal vote and the assistant foreman put an "NG" in the square by Officer Wind's name under Counts 1 and 2.

We went through the same procedure for Officer Powell, and again none of the jurors changed their vote. We had another complete discussion on Count 3 and this time we had one of the jurors read the report aloud, for further consideration. We took the formal vote and put an "NG" in the square by Officer Powell's name under Counts 1 and 3. Count 2 against Officer Powell was left blank.

Since we had not been able to find any of the officers guilty, we very briefly discussed each of the counts against Sergeant Koon and decided we could not find him guilty on Counts 1 and 2 because we had concluded there was not a crime. We then again discussed Count 4 and read aloud Sergeant Koon's report. There was some discussion and then a formal vote was taken. We put an "NG" in the square by Sergeant Koon's name under Counts 1, 2, 4 and 5.

I transferred the verdicts to each of the ten sheets and signed my name at the bottom of each one. Each of the jurors inspected them and then they were passed back to me.

I drafted a note to the judge which said, in essence, "We have reached a verdict on all the counts except Count 2 against Officer Powell. We have deliberated for three days on this count, and would like to request your guidance."

I handed the note to Jerry the bailiff. We still were not allowed to go out and socialize with the alternates. Our pizza arrived, and we were told to eat in one of the two jury deliberation rooms. Jerry asked me if I had prepared the verdict sheets. He told me to keep them with me every minute until we were called by the judge.

I ate my lunch in the jury deliberation room next to the one we were occupying, as did several others of the jurors. I had the feeling from talking to Jerry that the call to the courtroom was imminent. There was still tension in the air and in the actions of the bailiff and the deputies.

# Chapter Twenty-Three: The Verdict

Things happened very quickly. I don't know exactly what time it was when the jury was called into the courtroom, but it must have been after 2:30 p.m. We were all lined up, jurors and alternates alike, by position, and ushered into the courtroom. It was filled with spectators and all of the principals were present.

Judge Weisberg read the note I had sent him and asked several questions about the deliberations on Count 2 for Officer Powell, on which we were deadlocked. He then asked if I thought further deliberation would provide a unanimous verdict.

I told him I felt we would not be able to reach a verdict, but that was my personal opinion and I would like to know how the other jurors felt. He polled each one, and in turn they all gave him the same answer. No, they did not feel we could reach a unanimous verdict.

The judge then asked me if I had the completed verdict sheets and I said I had. He asked me to hand them to the bailiff. I had arranged the verdict sheets so that all of the completed ones were on the top and all of the uncompleted ones were last. He removed them from the envelope and started looking at each sheet, rearranging as he did so.

I will never, never forget the next thing that happened. Just before handing the sheets to the court clerk, the judge's face assumed a very thinly disguised look of disdain.

I was extremely disappointed. Did he think we would ignore his instructions? Did he think we would buckle under political pressure and turn in the popular verdict? Hadn't he said in his instructions, "Both the People and the defendant have a right to expect that you will conscientiously consider and weigh the evidence, apply the law, and reach a just verdict regardless of the consequences." That was what we did.

He then handed the sheets to the court clerk, who read each of the verdicts. As each of them was read, there were increasing sounds emanating from the spectators. The defendants hugged their lawyers, there was scrambling around by everyone, and we were escorted out of the courtroom.

Every juror, including alternates, was crying. We convened in the law library and were taken upstairs to collect our things. We were told that the judge was going to come speak to us, as was customary after such a trial. But he did not come. The publicity people for the county talked to us for a few minutes and asked us if we wanted to talk to the press. We were told that members of the news media were set up in the large auditorium. We reminded them that we had issued our statement and that we did not want to talk to the press. If there was even one among us who was in this for the publicity, I did not detect it. We all declined. We were told that we would be receiving in the mail a copy of all the newspaper articles we had not been allowed to read while the trial was progressing. We were also told that we would receive a tape from CNN of the entire trial.

We were hurried back in to the jury room and directed to gather up all of our personal belongings very quickly. I picked up my small portfolio that I had left in the jury deliberation room, along with my purse and other personal things. As I started out the door, I realized that I had a copy of the judge's instructions inside the portfolio. That was where I always put it when deliberations ended each day. I started to go back, but because we were being rushed, I didn't feel it was important.

We were rushed out the back door and into the bus, which was sitting in its usual fenced-in area just adjacent to the communications trailers and equipment. A lot of people were shouting things I could not understand. We backed out of the area, and encountered an entire parking lot full of people, all shouting and charging toward the bus. Some gave us thumbs down signals and others gave us more obscene gestures. One of the deputies told us to duck if they started throwing things.

The driver parked the bus in the back of the hotel instead of the front as he usually did. When we got out, several reporters shoved microphones in our faces. One reporter said, "What do you have to say to all the millions of people who saw the video on television?" One female reporter followed us up the steps and said, "You need to explain to us what went on in that jury room. There are riots in the streets." We hurried past them as fast as possible.

We were told to convene in the conference room and the deputies waited until we were all present. I asked Mary if there were really riots in the streets. She said not to listen to the reporters, that they were just trying to get to us. After a few minutes, Rhett came in and instructed us to go to our rooms and pack our belongings very quickly. It was evident that they were responsible to protect us at this point and wanted to get rid of us as quickly as possible.

While we were in deliberations that day, our families had delivered the extra clothing and toilet articles we had requested. While I was throwing things into bags, Rhett pounded on the door several times, telling me to hurry. He pounded on all the doors. We somehow got all our luggage down to the corridor just inside the exit. The deputies got our luggage into the bus while we waited in the corridor. Then we ran to the bus and hurried inside, avoiding a couple of reporters waiting for us.

We were preceded and followed by motorcycle escorts onto the freeway and to the East Valley Sheriff's Station where our cars were parked. The reporters were there in force. Some had followed the bus, some were already there when we arrived. The deputies had sealed off the only entrance to the station, so reporters could not get in. Some of them parked their cars on the road, got out and photographed us from the grassy knolls surrounding the parking lot. The deputies made them move their cars off the road.

A lot of the jurors hugged and promised to keep in touch. A few were just happy to be released from the rest of us. When we left the parking lot, several of the jurors and alternates were followed from the entrance to the freeway by some of the reporters who had been waiting there. They were followed home and accosted when they got out of their cars.

The former Navy pilot had experimented with several routes back to Camarillo during the trial and knew some back roads. He had a plan. He would lead in his car, one of the other women and I would follow him in our cars, and one of the male alternate jurors would bring up the rear. I was very grateful to him for the protection.

I arrived home, opened the garage door with the opener, and my husband came out to greet me. Now came the second shock and disappointment of the day. The look on his face said, *How could you have reached this verdict?*

He was as dumbfounded as the rest of America when he heard the verdict on the television news. Everyone had seen the gruesome videotape of that awful beating. It was obvious that the officers were guilty of using excessive force. How could any jury in its right mind acquit them? How could his own wife have voted to acquit them?

Dick didn't say anything as he unloaded my luggage from the trunk of the car.

"You don't agree with the verdict at all, do you?" I asked.

"No, I don't."

I was too tired and shell-shocked even to try to explain.

Silently, Dick helped me carry my bags into the house.

The phone had begun ringing even before I got home. A man who said he was a reporter for the *Los Angeles Times* arrived at the door and asked my husband if he could interview me. Dick said I wasn't interested in talking to news media. A short time later, the fellow reappeared carrying a bucket of Kentucky Fried Chicken. He said he thought we might not have any food in the house. Dick was so surprised that he took the chicken. As soon as he closed the door, he deposited it into the garbage.

We were not hungry. The phone kept ringing. Reporters were calling from all over the world. Our telephone number was listed in the local directory both under Dick's name and my initials. Unfortunately for her, there was also another Dorothy Bailey who lived in Camarillo and her phone was listed too. She got so many calls within the next few days that she had to have her phone disconnected. It didn't take us long to turn on the answering machine to monitor the calls.

A Ventura County sheriff's deputy knocked at the door and said he would be patrolling in our neighborhood around the clock. A Camarillo city police officer stopped by to say he would also be watching out for us. We couldn't imagine that we were going to need any protection, but from the way the phone was ringing, we were beginning to feel apprehensive.

A close friend called and asked Dick if the Dorothy Bailey who was the foreman of the jury was really me. Dick hadn't even known until then that I was the foreman.

Although I was too numb to talk to him or explain anything when I came in the house, Dick automatically took over as my protector. He answered all of the telephone calls, turned people away at the door, and buffered me from the world.

The television set was on and the stations were reporting

mild disturbances and an occasional fire in Los Angeles. The commentators anticipated an angry reaction to the verdict. I could not keep myself from watching. I was pulled toward the television. Between unpacking my bags and sorting the clean from the dirty clothing, I listened to every word. I sat and watched as the rioting spread and it seemed nothing was being done to confine or control it. Palm trees were on fire, roaming gangs of youths were hurling trash cans through the plate glass doors at Los Angeles City Hall, and marauding citizens were breaking into stores and carting off television sets, boxes of disposable diapers and armloads of clothing. Innocent people were being pulled out of their cars and beaten senseless. Television news cameras in helicopters hovering overhead captured the attack on a truck driver pulled from the cab of his truck, bludgeoned repeatedly with rocks and a fire extinguisher and then left lying in a pool of blood on the pavement. No police seemed to be anywhere around. The Los Angeles skyline was orange with firelight. I sat, horrified and sickened, and watched Los Angeles burn, set aflame by angry hordes incited by what I and my fellow jurors had done.

I watched the television reports all night. I cried all night. I agonized over and over to myself, *Did I really cause this?*

By early morning, I was sick. I tried to sleep. I turned off the television and told myself I was not helping myself or anyone else by watching it. But I kept getting up and going back to the television. It hurt me to watch, but somehow I had to. Each scene of looting, fire, and violence tore through me like a knife. I spent my time alternately in bed from weakness, in the bathroom vomiting, and in front of the television because I could not stay away. And I kept crying. Never before in my life had I been the kind of woman who wept. When Dick and I used to have domestic squabbles, I would go in the bathroom so he wouldn't see me bawling. Now I couldn't stop bursting into tears.

The telephone and doorbell did not stop ringing. We learned later that our own local newspaper, the *Ventura Star Free Press*, had printed the names and hometowns of all the jurors in the same edition of the paper that carried the verdict. We couldn't believe that the editors had such little regard for our privacy. We got calls from the news media in Germany, England, France and Australia. A man with an English accent called and said he was from the British Broadcasting Company. Dick said I wasn't going to talk to anyone. A little while later, someone who sounded like the same man called again, but this time he said he was from Australian television.

A man who identified himself as a Beverly Hills resident left a long, angry message on the answering machine. He demanded to know if "Mrs. Bailey" realized what she had done. He said that the city was burning down because of me. He asked how I was going to live with that on my conscience. He went on and on. I was transfixed by his voice, so full of hate, booming out of that box into my house. He must have talked for seven or eight minutes. Then Dick walked into the room and heard what he was saying, and switched off the sound.

My boss called, telling me to stay at home for as long as I needed to. I suspect his offer was two-edged. He is a good human being and had my welfare at heart, and secondly, I believe he did not want any trouble at work. The company was black-owned and there were several black employees working there, including several who reported to me. Ultimately, only one, a man who reported to me, expressed personal anger against me.

My boss passed on a message from the black president of the company that he was proud of me for doing my civic duty. That was not unexpected, because he had told me before that he was proud that an employee of his company was chosen for the jury, and that I should vote my conscience and do my duty as I saw fit. I am sure he disagreed with the verdict, but he harbored no ill will toward me.

Later, I would receive a certificate of appreciation and admiration signed by our company president. I am sure that a certificate is given to all retiring employees, but I do not believe the word "admiration" is included as a matter of course. Whatever the motivation for offering me time off, I appreciated it. I was physically and spiritually ill.

Although all of the jurors had agreed that we didn't want to be interviewed and we wouldn't talk to reporters, on the day after the verdicts, the *Los Angeles Times* printed an interview with one of the jurors who had voted guilty on Count 2, the one on which we deadlocked, against Officer Laurence Powell. Evidently, all of the terrible repercussions from the verdict had frightened her so much that she wanted to explain to the world that she had actually been in favor of convicting on one of the counts. She was afraid for her safety and that of her family. While there were some inaccuracies in the newspaper account, basically it was correct. It is difficult to tell about mistakes in newspaper articles. Has the person being interviewed lost perspective of what really happened or was she misquoted?

One of the judge's instructions was that we needed to render our verdict without regard for the consequences, but who on earth could have foreseen these consequences? Los Angeles was on fire, there was an utter breakdown of law and order in wide-ranging parts of the city and in other urban areas across the country, and the media pounced upon what they called "the Simi Valley jury." The trial was held in Simi Valley, which is a residential community in Ventura County near the Los Angeles County line, but actually only three of the jurors lived in Simi Valley.

The media accused us of racism and ignorance. It was true that there was only one Hispanic woman and one Asian American woman on the jury, and the rest of us were white. Ventura County's population is only 2.2 percent black and there were only six blacks among the prospective jurors called. As far as I was concerned, it was a case about police officers beating a human being. His race was not an issue. I was shocked that the public thought that the verdict was racially motivated.

Even President George Bush decried our decision. According to the news reports, President Bush said that the verdict "left us all with a deep sense of personal frustration and anguish." He called on the Justice Department to begin an investigation "apace" and determine whether any civil rights laws were violated. It is overwhelming for a private citizen who has spent two months doing jury duty to then be excoriated by the President of the United States. I was hurt and stunned.

Los Angeles Mayor Tom Bradley said that the system had failed the public, and Los Angeles District Attorney Ira Reiner said he disagreed with the verdict. California Governor Pete Wilson said he was "stunned" and New Jersey Senator Bill Bradley was quoted as calling the verdict "unjust." The amount of hatred expressed toward us was far beyond anything I had ever imagined that I would experience in my lifetime.

We remained under siege for a week or ten days, constantly beleaguered by the media. Two young women rang the doorbell one morning and told Dick they were from the *CBS Morning Show* and they needed to interview me. Dick said I wasn't giving any interviews, and they slammed the screen door as they left. They got into a car parked in front of our house, but they didn't leave. They just sat there. After twenty minutes, Dick walked out to the car and asked them to please leave.

One of them told him that their boss had instructed them to get an interview and they couldn't leave without one. Dick told them they were wasting their time, and if they didn't leave, he would call the police. Finally they drove off.

On the third day, it occurred to me to get out of bed and rummage around for a copy of the judge's instructions that I had inadvertently stuffed into my briefcase before hurrying out of the jury room. I gave the seventy-eight-page document to Dick to read. He went off and studied it for a while, and then came in and took me in his arms.

"You couldn't have reached any other decision," he assured me.

The succeeding days were all more of the same. Prosecutor Terry White and defense attorney John Barnett were interviewed on NBC's *Today* show by Katie Couric. A retouched version of the blurry part of the video showing Mr. King charging Officer Powell was shown. That was the first time, to my knowledge, that the public was shown the most damaging evidence the jury had seen against Mr. King.

Katie Couric asked Mr. White why he had not put Rodney King on the stand. She said that he seemed such a mild-mannered person when she had seen him on television. Mr. White replied that Rodney King was not a witness in the trial because he brought "a lot of liabilities" to the case. Mr. King was a felon on parole, driving eighty to ninety miles per hour, who had failed to stop when the California Highway Patrol was chasing him. He cited Mr. King's erratic behavior, such as placing his hands on his buttocks and shaking them at policemen who had their guns drawn. He said that Rodney King was now saying that officers used racial epithets during the incident, and insisted that he complied with requests of officers—facts he had not mentioned to the grand jury when he testified before them.

The juror who had given the newspaper interview also appeared on the *Today* show. The entire interview centered around the deliberation on Count 2 against Officer Powell, which caused the jury to be hung.

About a week after the verdict, there was a boxed article on the front page of the *Ventura Star Free Press*, apologizing for printing the names and hometowns of the jurors. The editor, John Bowman, said that if he could turn back the clock he would not have published the names.

Although the article did not mention it, I had heard from a friend that many people had canceled their subscriptions because the names had been printed.

The next day, there was another newspaper article quoting an anonymous juror that had some degree of accuracy to it. I could tell which juror the reporter had talked to, although he had asked that his name not be used. That article was accompanied by a huge nine-by-six-inch photograph of the woman who had gone on the *Today* show, who was the only juror who had been willing to be photographed.

One of the alternates became the subject of an article in *Los Angeles Magazine* entitled, "The Last Angry Woman." The trial, and specifically the negative reaction to the verdicts, affected her very adversely even though she was not involved in the deliberation process. She was still hounded by the media and received threatening and negative telephone calls. She lobbied heavily for the passage of California Senate Bill 1299, which would make it a crime to publish information that could lead to the location of a juror. The bill subsequently passed and was signed into law by the Governor of California.

Two jurors who lived in Simi received death threats, but as far as I know, there weren't any threats made against those of us who lived in Camarillo. As a precaution, Dick removed our name from the mailbox in front of the house. One of the women jurors moved out of her Simi Valley house, and a male juror moved somewhere and none of the rest of us ever heard from him again.

We were worried that the media assault and the anger directed at the jury was going to interfere with the sale of our house. We had been living in California for eight years because of my work, but I was ready to retire from my job and we planned to move back home to Utah. We'd had our house up for sale for two years, and during the trial, we had finally gotten a cash offer on it from a seventy-nine-year-old widow. When other jurors started receiving death threats, and there was so much notoriety about us, our prospective buyer became skittish. One day she wanted to go through with the deal, and the next day she didn't.

When I thought the house had sold, I told my boss I would take my retirement, and not come back to work. When our buyer got cold feet, I called to say that I might not have sold my house, and I wondered what my options were. My boss said my options were whatever I wanted them to be; I could come back to work if I wanted to. That made me cry. I was so emotionally fragile that just about anything could make me weep.

Finally we determined that what worried our buyer most was who would pay for any damage to the house if it were firebombed or vandalized. She had insurance, so we suggested that if anything happened, that we would pay the $250 deductible. In fact, we just wrote her a check for $250. That satisfied her, and we were able to go ahead with the sale.

We had reached the verdict on April 29, and just two weeks later, on May 15, Dick and I and the dog left California to return to the home we had built seventeen years earlier in the foothills overlooking the Great Salt Lake.

It was a relief to leave the tension and fear in California, and to be in a place where no one suspected that I was one of the King jurors. Dick said he was so proud of me that he wanted to shout out to other patrons in restaurants that his wife was on the jury, but fortunately, he didn't.

I never have enjoyed the limelight, and I really hate making public appearances. But I finally decided I needed to explain to people how we had reached our decision. In the spring of 1993, when the federal jury began hearing the second Rodney King trial, the federal civil rights case against the four police officers, I began accepting invitations to appear on national television programs.

I had never been to Washington, D.C., before ABC flew me there to appear on *Nightline* with Ted Koppel. When we first started talking, I could tell that Mr. Koppel was as skeptical as everyone else seemed to be, certain that the jury was ignorant, racist, and had simply erred. As we spoke, he appeared to change his mind and to realize that I actually made sense, that the jurors had reached the only conclusion possible based on the judge's instructions.

"There was undisputed, unrefuted testimony by some of the experts—unrefuted by the prosecution—that batons are used to break bones, to immobilize. It was extremely shocking for us to hear that," I told Koppel. "We could not prove to ourselves . . . beyond a reasonable doubt . . . based on testimony and looking at the video, that there were head shots."

If I had seen a head shot, I would have thought that they were guilty, because we were told that police officers are not to strike a suspect in the head.

"In all that time in the deliberation room, I had a vague, nagging feeling that for at least the last ten or eleven seconds of that tape, there was guilt. But, Ted, you cannot convict a man on a vague, nagging feeling. You must have an abiding conviction, to a moral certainty. It would have been easy to go in and say, I have a gut feeling, and find him guilty. But we couldn't do that."

A still photo of Rodney King being beaten by police officers from the March 3, 1991 video taken by George Holliday.

Next page: A photo of Rodney King taken three days after his beating was one of three introduced into evidence by the prosecution in the criminal trial.

Mug shots of the defendants: Sergeant Stacey Koon and Officers Theodore Briseno, Timothy Wind and Laurence Powell.

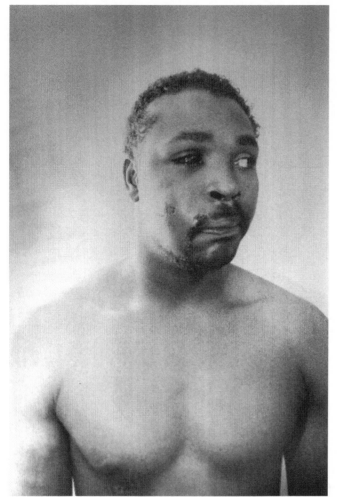

AP Photo (2)

KOON  BRISENO  WIND  POWELL

## PART TWO

# Chapter Twenty-Four: Bob Almond's Story

When I got the summons for jury duty, I was sure I was going to be picked for the federal Rodney King civil rights trial.

My wife was a skeptic. She kept saying, "Sure, Bob, sure. You're still sitting in the audience."

But I'm a real optimist. I believe these things will happen. I'm a big talk kind of guy.

So it came as a shock to her when I came home and said, "Guess what? I'm on the jury." She knew I had been going downtown to jury selection for a whole week, but when I came home and told her it was all settled and the jury was picked, she was taken aback.

"What does it mean?" she asked. "You mean you're really going to be away for the whole trial?"

We had been married twenty-five years and the only time we had been apart was when I went to Vietnam. There were a couple of other times when we were separated for a night or two. I'd gone on camping trips with the guys, or to Las Vegas, but we'd never been away from one another for months at a time. She was really upset.

She had been on jury duty herself the year before, and had come home every evening telling me how interesting it was. She listened to a breach of contract case involving an earth-moving company.

It is always exciting to be part of the system, but the idea of being on the Rodney King jury was exhilarating. This trial promised to be not only newsworthy, but even historic.

When I got the jury questionnaire in September or October, it asked if I would have a problem being on a sequestered jury. So I guessed it was the Rodney King case. I hadn't heard of any other federal case where they were talking about sequestering. I really wanted to get on that jury.

It was a fascinating case, one that everybody had heard about. People had rioted after the first trial, the one they called the Simi Valley trial. It had been the worst civil insurrection in U.S. history. Fifty-four people had been killed. The widespread public perception was that the criminal justice system hadn't worked, that there was no justice for poor people, or for black people, or for minorities. People were calling the Simi Valley jury a bunch of bigoted, pro-police white racists. There was so much public sentiment that the jury had made the wrong decision, that even President George Bush had called for a new trial.

The Justice Department had gotten in gear less than an hour after the Simi Valley jury acquitted Stacey Koon, Theodore Briseno and Timothy Wind on all charges, and acquitted Laurence Powell on all but one charge, on which they could not agree. The Civil Rights Division, it was announced, would review the incident to determine what action could be taken under federal laws.

One week later, a Los Angeles federal grand jury began three months of hearings on the King beating. On August 4, 1992, indictments were handed down against all four officers, charging them with violating Rodney King's civil rights.

Like everyone else in America, I was familiar with the videotape of King's beating. I had seen it on the first day it was on television. I was sitting in my den watching the news, and I yelled at my daughter to come watch. A group of police officers were standing around in a circle, beating a black guy for some reason that was not apparent to me. Even when he was on the ground, they were still whacking him with their billy clubs. I didn't see anything in the video that made me think that King was being at all aggressive. It was as though we were back in the 1960s, beating people up just because they aren't doing what police officers want them to do.

The day the verdict came in, I was driving north on the Harbor Freeway on my way to attend a college fair in Pasadena. My daughter, Kelly, was a junior in high school, and I wanted to get some information about scholarships and financing, since I had not a small stake in the matter. There was a lot of traffic on the Harbor Freeway, and I had gotten exactly to Florence Avenue, in the fast lane going north, when I ran into a major jam-up. The newscaster on KFWB radio was saying that people were being yanked out of their cars by crowds at Vermont and Torrance, and then I realized that what he was saying was Vermont and Florence, and that was precisely where I was.

Holy moly! I felt as if it were the beginning of a revolution. I got through the area where the turmoil was, and I went to the college fair, but I left early. I worried about how I was going to get to my house in San Pedro, because I didn't want to go back down the Harbor Freeway, and taking the 405 through Inglewood didn't seem like such a good idea, either. I finally took the Pasadena Freeway downtown, then took the Santa Ana Freeway and the 710 south. I was probably going eighty-five miles per hour and I must have been the slowest driver on the road. I could see palm trees on fire. I got home pretty quickly and started watching television.

The rioting was widespread. Stores were being looted and burned, and people were being pulled out of vehicles and beaten by angry mobs. I felt so sorry for the people who lived in those neighborhoods. People were getting hurt, and a poor area doesn't need to have all its grocery stores and service stations burned down. That happened twenty-five years earlier during the Watts riots, and South Central Los Angeles had never really recovered. It was too bad that poor people have to pay the price. Poor people are the ones who are most likely to get arrested to start with. I thought a lot of the rioters were opportunists, just taking advantage of the situation to break the law.

I was mad at the newscasters too. I felt like the television media were egging the rioters on, telling them, "Please come on down. There's nobody guarding this 7-Eleven." Then the National Guard showed up without bullets. The whole thing was a total screw-up, in my opinion.

In the next couple of days, the names and addresses of the Simi Valley jurors were published in the newspaper. I was shocked. That was a terrible thing to do. Those guys had done a job they had to do and now their privacy was destroyed. They were being blamed for the rioting, and some of them received death threats. I thought that was awful. The riots weren't the jury's fault. They just did what they had to do.

I had been horrified by the beating itself, because I thought there was no question that the police were wrong, but apparently, that was not proved to twelve jurors, and that was good enough for me. I understand that the black community felt stabbed in the back, because blacks get beaten by the police the most, but I felt like, keep the faith, baby, the system works.

When the officers were indicted on federal charges during the summer, I read an article in the *Los Angeles Times* about double jeopardy. It seemed to me that the Los Angeles County prosecutors in Simi Valley trial had done the best they could, and the jury found the officers not guilty, so I didn't see any need to prosecute them again. It was a case of double jeopardy, as far as I was concerned. But of course, it wasn't my call. The federal government had come up with these civil rights laws during the Civil Rights Movement because people, primarily in the South, weren't being protected under state laws. Back then, the good old boys would not prosecute each other.

When I got the notice to appear for jury duty, I just knew it was going to be for this history-making case. To be on this jury would be much more exciting than any I could remember. It was an opportunity to be part of a news event, and I was thrilled.

I was instructed to appear at the old federal courthouse in downtown Los Angeles at 8:30 on the morning of Wednesday February 3, 1993, and I showed up real early. I got there at 7:30 to beat the traffic and get a good parking place. Another prospective juror was there early, too, a black gentleman named George, and he and I sat outside talking. George was in his sixties, with white hair and a white beard. He sold tires at Sears. It was pretty obvious to both of us that the case we were being considered for was the Rodney King trial, and he didn't like the idea.

There were television cameras and news crews milling around, and we sat and watched the commotion. We saw one of the defense attorneys, Michael Stone, arrive. This guy had a way about him, an air of authority, and the reporters and cameramen surged up to him.

George and I went inside and checked in. They gave us a lot of paperwork to fill out. There were hundreds of people, most of them apparently not very happy to be there. My point of view, being pleased to be considered for a highly publicized case, did not seem to be shared by very many. There were only twenty-five or thirty black people in the room. There were maybe ten Asian Americans. I was Number 483 out of 750.

We filed into an auditorium, and I sat down in the front row. Every seat was taken and there were people standing. A man wearing a nice suit got up and introduced himself as U.S. District Court Judge John G. Davies. He told us we were going to be given a fifty-one-page questionnaire and we were to tell the truth and do the best we could, to be as complete as we could be.

One guy called out, "Hey, man, what are you going to do to keep us safe?" He said he was afraid for his family.

Judge Davies seemed shocked. "Sir, if you have that much fear, you're excused." Anyone who was afraid, he said, was free to leave. Anyone who wanted to be excused should report to window 4. He wanted to make it perfectly clear if anyone feared for their safety, they could get off the case. So I could have left right then. Some people did.

The rest of us spent the next two or three hours filling out the questionnaire. It asked where we were born, where we went to school, the name of the last movie we saw, how often we went to movies and sports events. What do you know about the first trial. What do you know about Rodney King? How do you feel about race riots? I was amazed that it was so complete.

I answered everything completely honestly. I hadn't followed the first trial very closely. I remember hearing that Officer Powell was a weak hitter, that if he had hit as hard as he should have, Rodney King would have been dead. And my first thoughts when I saw the videotape on television had been to assume that those officers were going to be in deep trouble. But I knew you can't decide a court case on anything besides the evidence you hear in court and I was sure I could set aside any of my prior opinions and just listen to the evidence.

A week later I got a letter saying to report on February 16. Seventy-five people were there that Tuesday morning, only ten percent of the number who had been there the first day. I figured I must have done a good job filling that thing out.

I did have a few underlying fears. After all, the first trial ended in riots and those jurors had received death threats. I had to think about the safety of my family. I could wind up having to sell my house and quit my job. But I had made up my mind I wanted to be on this jury.

In my not-so-humble opinion, I was the ideal juror. Born in 1945, I grew up in Eagle Rock, California, which is not exactly a suburb of Los Angeles, but a pleasant, middle-class residential area within the urban sprawl, north of downtown Los Angeles, between

Glendale and Pasadena.

I served on jury duty once before, in the late 1970s, in a case of grand theft of firearms. The defendant was accused of stealing firearms from his brother, but all the witnesses were full of double-talk, and there was no evidence that there ever were any guns at all. The guy probably did steal the guns, but we had to let him off because the prosecution didn't prove it to us.

I was in a traffic accident when I was a teenager and the other driver sued my parents in Small Claims Court. He was swearing and calling me names. The guy was still yelling when we left the courthouse. The judge later sent his decision, which was that we were both at fault, so we were both responsible for repairing our own cars.

I also got a ticket once when I had just started driving and I had to go to court with my parents. I didn't think I deserved that ticket, and it sort of soured me on the justice system. I thought all these people must have something better to do with their time. I'm still mad about that speeding ticket.

So those had been my three encounters with the judicial system before I got my jury questionnaire in this case.

The seventy-five jurors who reported on February 16 were bused over to the Roybal Federal Courthouse, a brand new building with a large underground parking garage. We were taken up to the eighth floor to be questioned by the lawyers for both sides. I was pleased to see that my friend George was still in the pool of prospective jurors, and he and I took seats together in Courtroom 890.

It was the first time I had seen the defendants in person. They looked scared. The defense lawyers all looked upbeat, kind of like, *Hey, this is what I do for a living. I'm ready for a fight.* The prosecutors seemed tense. They were a much more uptight, close-to-the-vest group than the defense lawyers.

The clerk called the numbers of twelve prospective jurors and had them sit in the jury box. Out of that first twelve, five eventually wound up on the final jury. They were Maria, a black postal worker; Norman, an electrical engineer; Gary, a twenty-one-year-old former security guard who worked for his father's soil engineering company; Eric, a welder for a large chemical company, who had been on six juries before; and Fred, a long-haired, bushy-bearded unemployed jeweler.

The prospective panelists were asked what they knew about the first trial, and questions like, "Do you think police officers lie?" and "Can you promise you will give these defendants a fair trial?"

One man was excused because he had a medical problem, and another because he said he was afraid to be on the jury. I don't know why he didn't leave that first day when Judge Davies said people who were scared were excused. One lady said she was going to write a book and keep a journal every night. They let her go.

The questionnaire had asked some basic questions like, "Do you agree that a suspect is innocent until proven guilty?" Some people had gotten that mixed up and answered backwards. They had answered "no." So the lawyers would ask them what they meant by their answer.

I was just watching. I didn't really feel like I was part of this process. It went on all day Tuesday, Wednesday, Thursday and Friday. They kept us cooped up in the jury room, and the only time we saw the public was during the lunch hour. The marshals wouldn't let us go out, not even for a cigarette.

The only thing different about the period while they were questioning us and afterwards, was that we still had to pay for our own lunches. We were not yet guests of the federal government. George and I sat together every day in the courthouse cafeteria. We weren't supposed to talk about the other jurors, but we did. We predicted that one black guy wasn't going to make it because he was too jive, and another fellow was too much of a cowboy.

I thought all along that George was going to get on, if they ever called his number, because he was black. I figured they would want some black jurors, and there were only a few among the prospective jurors. Since this was a federal panel, prospective jurors had been summoned from all over the Central District, so many of them weren't from Los Angeles at all. In fact, some of them were from Ventura County, and even from Simi Valley, the site of the state trial.

Both the prosecution and the defense had photocopies of the questionnaires and the defendants and their lawyers were studying them. What happens if we send these guys to jail, I wondered. They would know who I am and where I live. The judge made a big deal about how our identities would be kept secret, but the only people

I was worried about knowing my identity would be people I found guilty. I wouldn't feel threatened by my fellow jurors or by the press.

I was beginning to experience some anxiety about whether I was going to make it. At first, I kept thinking that at any minute they were going to call me, but I went home Friday night and they still hadn't picked me. There weren't many left who hadn't been questioned.

During that first week, sitting all day long every day watching the jury selection, I also started getting very anxious about how I was going to get my income taxes done. It was only the third week of February, but if I was on the jury, I was going to be locked up for a while, maybe even past April 15. Every day I stopped off at the post office, the bank, the library. I couldn't find all the right forms that I needed. It was so ridiculous. I was spending the whole day in the federal courthouse just a couple of hundred feet away from the Internal Revenue Service office, but I could never get over there to pick up the form, because the marshals never let us out of their grasp.

Finally on Friday, I made up my mind that on Monday I would break loose during the lunch hour and get over there and pick up Form 8483, the non-cash contributions form.

By Monday, the marshals were sick and tired of hearing the smokers complain, so they let them go outside. So while everyone was complaining, I just left and went to the IRS. Nobody saw me go.

There was this big semicircle where the press had set up the cameras just outside the windows in the big lobby. We were separated only by glass. I walked along the semicircle, actually kind of impressed to be out among them, and went across the veranda into the other federal building. I walked down the hall to the IRS, asked for two forms—no, make that three—and walked out. My exit was blocked by a major dog. A German shepherd. A real big dog. Rin Tin Tin. Right behind it was the LAPD bomb squad, wearing headgear. Oh, great. I sneak out and five minutes later the whole world explodes. But I managed to make it back and slip into line with the other jurors. Nobody noticed I was gone. So security was tight, but not that tight.

When we went back into court for the afternoon session, they called Number 483 to the jury box. At last, I was where I wanted to be. And after that, they called George, Number 263. George lived in Torrance, but he said he lived in Watts and had lived there for twenty-five years. He had written in his questionnaire that he was disappointed by the officers' acquittals in the state trial, but during questioning he said he really hadn't paid much attention to the verdict because he was too busy working. I got the impression neither side liked him very much, but they didn't excuse him.

All during the selection process, the defense had a jury expert there watching us. We were all aware of her. We thought she was a psychologist. She sat right behind Officer Ted Briseno, really concentrating. Until they put me in the jury box, I had been sitting right behind her. The lawyers had our fifty-one-page questionnaires, and they conferred with her about them. It seemed to me that they had decided in advance which jurors were pluses to them and which ones were minuses.

I think that I was one of their pluses. It was pretty obvious they wanted me on the jury. The prosecution asked me four questions. I had mentioned on my form that I belonged to an organization called the International Right-of-Way Association. One of the prosecutors asked about it obliquely, to avoid saying anything that would identify me to the press. He said, "It says on page thirty-seven of your questionnaire that you belong to an organization?"

I answered that it was a group of real estate experts that I belonged to because of my work. The reporters in the courtroom jumped to the conclusion that I was in the real estate business, and in the short profiles published in the newspapers about the jury, Juror Number 5 was always described as being in the real estate business. My friends couldn't figure out which juror was me, since there were no engineers listed.

The defense didn't ask me any questions at all. I felt that they were happy with me. It surprised me, because my understanding of lawyers was that they would want an emotional person for a jury, most of the time, not an analytical person. An engineer ought to be the furthest thing from what they want. An engineer will base most of his decision on facts, and lawyers usually want an emotional decision. I think both sides want to play on your emotions.

I was also astonished that they kept a woman named Anne,

because she must have argued with the lawyers for fifteen minutes. Finally, Judge Davies told her not to debate the lawyers. Marty, a Hispanic man, said he wasn't familiar with the concept about being innocent until proven guilty, and he had never seen the videotape. He didn't even know there had been one. In fact, it was news to him that there had been a previous trial, and he had asked friends why people were rioting. Maybe he had no prior opinions, but he just seemed so unaware that I was amazed they would want him as a juror.

But at three o'clock in the afternoon, the lawyers on both sides said, "We accept the jury."

They put us in this little room and everybody realized, "Hey, can you believe we're on this jury?" We were not high-fiving, but pretty close. This was exciting. The mood in the room was pretty happy.

Right from the start, I took charge. I sat down at the far end of the table. To be the guy in charge is real important. I'm the kind of guy, if I'm on the committee, I want to be chairman. If I was going to be involved, I wanted to do the most and be the best. If you are going to do it, do it. Be the foreman. How am I going to do it? Sit in the power seat.

Gary, a young kid about twenty-one, sat at the other end, He wasn't trying to be the leader; he just plopped down in the closest available chair. From the first time we sat down in those seats that first day, nobody changed places. Those were our places for the rest of the trial and all during the deliberations.

From an engineer's point of view, the jury room was really weird. It wasn't rectangular. It was a triangular-shaped room, with a big window on one wall. It was a brand new building, real stark, and as you walked in the door, on the right and left were two bathrooms, strictly government issue. Then there was a long conference table and behind it a window five feet wide and six feet tall, with a plastic coating so you couldn't see out at all. It didn't block out the light, but all vision. You could see color through it. You could see daylight out there. The shading stopped before it got to the top of the window, so we could see the sky and sometimes airplanes flying overhead.

The taller jurors could perch on the windowsill and peer out the clear part of the window, but whenever anyone was doing that, everyone else stepped back, for fear the peeper was going to lose his balance and topple off.

On that first day, one of the jurors took a key and scraped the plastic stuff off an area about an inch wide. We could put our eyes up to the scraped-off patch and look down and see all the television cameras and watch the lawyers being interviewed.

Fred sat to my right, then Norm, Cathy, Ruth, Daryl, Maria with Gary at the other end, Anne, Marty, Jim, Eric, George, Stanley and Mike almost right behind me. There really wasn't room enough at the table for more than thirteen to sit comfortably, and with the alternates, there were fifteen of us. So Stanley and Mike didn't sit at the table. They sat just behind me and when we had lunch, they ate on trays.

Gathered there for the first time in the jury room, we were full of question marks. Where are we going to stay? I hope they feed us good. Things like that.

I had read an article in the *Los Angeles Times* about what happens when a jury is sequestered, but I seemed to be the only one who had any idea what it meant. Everyone else was very nervous about where we were going to stay. The women especially were very concerned about the quality of the hotel accommodations. I wasn't worried.

I said that I had been talking to the marshals and they told me we were going to have to share, three to a room. Since there were four women on the jury, there was going to be one extra woman. "Who wants to share a room with me?"

To my astonishment, all four registered fear on their faces. They actually thought I was serious.

"Listen, I'm just kidding," I said. "We will all get separate rooms in a nice hotel."

Mark Neuberg came in. He was the federal marshal who had been working since November to make all the hotel and security arrangements for the jury. He announced that we were to meet on Wednesday morning at an undisclosed place and undisclosed time. He really said that. Even though we were the people who were supposed to meet him.

It was strange. There were fifteen of us now, and the selection process had been going on for a week already, so we kind of knew each other. I could have picked any of them out of a crowd. It was like I was joining a club, and they were all joining at the same time.

We were like compatriots. There was a feeling of camaraderie, a sense of *Well, here's the team. We're going to do this thing right. We're going to get this job done.*

I was impressed by the cross-section of people they got.

Anne, the one who had debated the lawyers, looked like money. I figured her husband probably made a lot. She was an executive with an insurance company herself, in charge of West Coast marketing. She looked rich. It wasn't just the way she dressed, but the way she acted.

Fred wore tank tops every day to show off his tattoos. That's just his kind of clothing. I would never wear a tank top myself. Fred had broad shoulders, with some meat on them. He was a jeweler, but he was unemployed, and he needed the forty dollars a day they paid us.

We got the forty dollars a day on Saturdays and Sundays, too. I had to give my weekday pay back to the city, because they were paying my salary, but I got to keep the forty dollars a day for weekends. After the trial ended, the judge paid us for the Monday, Tuesday and Wednesday of the next week, so it was like we got a three-day paid vacation.

There were two black people on the jury, George and Maria, and one black alternate, Daryl, a young man who had taken some time off from college. Marty, the Hispanic man who had never seen the tape, was the manager of a grocery store in Riverside and lived with his married sister.

There were four women—Maria, Anne, Ruth and Cathy—and eight men, plus the three male alternates. We ranged in age from Daryl and Gary, who were twenty-one, to George and Stanley, both in their sixties. We were quite a cross section, and now we were a team.

Mark Neuberg sent us home with instructions to report on Wednesday, and then we got a phone call saying we didn't have to come in until Thursday. We were told to be in the parking lot at the Terminal Annex Post Office at 8:30 a.m. So I had an extra day in my life to get ready. I went out to lunch, packed up my Levi's and cotton shirts, and kissed my wife good-bye a couple more times.

Clairene had to take off from work to drive me to court. There was no sense having my car parked downtown for a couple of months, and besides, I shared my car with my teenaged daughter, Kelly. My wife is chronically late, no matter where we go. We are always in a panic. So I was the second to last person to show up. Gary was a half hour later than I was, because he had to get his brother to drive him.

As we drove up, I was pointing out the other jurors to my wife, and asking her stuff like, "How old do you think that woman over there is?" I kissed her good-bye, she drove off, and a federal marshal grabbed my bag.

"What's your number?" he asked.

"483," I replied. From then on, I was 483. All of us jurors knew each other's numbers. George was 263, Eric was 362, Cathy was 382, Anne was 383. When our lunch orders would come, we'd call them out by number.

From the moment we were picked, it looked like they were really trying to keep our identities secret. They told us not to take along anything with our name on it, so nobody would be able to find out who we were.

The marshals fostered a certain amount of fear, in the way they acted around us. I showed up for jury with absolutely nothing with my name on it, except the indelible laundry mark on the tail of some of my shirts. I usually keep my shirts tucked in, but it actually crossed my mind that the hotel maids might be able to figure out who I was.

For most of the trial, we only knew each other by our first names, except for Anne. She talked about herself so much that her last name slipped out repeatedly without her realizing she had said it. "And then he said to me, Mrs. _____," and there it was. She'd told us her last name.

I use my last name a lot in casual conversation too, like I'll say, "This is the way Almonds do it," but I have such an odd last name that people don't always know that's what I'm talking about. On the last night, after we had already reached a verdict, I showed some of the other jurors photographs of me when I was in the military. I had talked about being a Vietnam vet, and they wanted to see what I looked like when I was a 130-pound, six-foot American fighting man. In the pictures, you could read my name on the front of my uniform shirt, so most of them found out then what my last name was. But at the beginning, I was so paranoid about being anonymous, I didn't even take my driver's license with me.

# Chapter Twenty-Five: Trial Number Two

THURSDAY, FEBRUARY 25, 1993

The marshals took our bags to the hotel, and we proceeded to Courtroom 890 in the Edward Roybal Federal Courthouse for the trial to begin. At about 10:45, Judge Davies turned to us, and said, "Ladies and gentlemen, you are now the jury in this case."

First came the opening statements. Assistant U.S. Attorney Steven D. Clymer, a barrel-chested man who reminded me of a pit bull, spent about an hour describing the prosecution's version of what happened to Rodney King that night nearly two years before. He said King was an ex-con on parole and that he was drunk when the California Highway Patrol started chasing him. For miles, he sped along on the freeway, failing to pull over, and then when he did stop, he tried to get away from the officers.

Clymer said that King would testify in this case, along with a few other witnesses who did not testify during the first trial. He emphasized that we were trying the officers, not King. "The issue of whether he was guilty or innocent that night is not on trial." He said that King's memory of the incident had been impaired because of his head injuries, which included facial fractures and a shattered eye socket.

Clymer played the videotape for us at the regular speed and in slow motion, and said that medical testimony would show that King was hit in the head with a baton. He said that the officers would deny that. He also said that we were going to hear evidence that the officers had lied to protect themselves.

"When they filled out their reports, they didn't know that there was a impartial, neutral record of exactly what they had done that night during the time that the video camera was recording," Clymer said. "They left out critical details that they had a duty to report."

His theory was that if the officers thought they had nothing to hide, they wouldn't have needed to lie on their reports. They must have known that what they did was wrong.

Clymer said that instead of taking King directly to the jail ward at Los Angeles County-USC Medical Center, that Officer Laurence Powell took him back to the Foothill Division police station and showed him off to other officers. "He sent police officers out to look at Rodney King while Rodney King was in the backseat, waiting for medical attention."

He said that to cover up the two-hour detour to the station, Powell and Wind falsified their police report to indicate they left Pacifica Hospital at 4:45 a.m. instead of at 3:30 a.m., when they actually left. "They omit completely on that log they ever went to Foothill Station."

Clymer said that while police are allowed to use force, in this case, they exceeded their authority. He said that the Los Angeles Police Department trains its officers that they can't strike a suspect in the head or face unless they believe that their own lives are in danger.

"This case involves police brutality," he said.

Next the lawyers for three of the defendants made opening statements. There was no opening statement for Timothy Wind. The defense attorneys denied that King was hit in the head, that the officers falsified reports, or that they did anything inappropriate. They said that they had medical experts who would testify that King's head injuries occurred when he fell and smashed his face on the pavement.

Ira Salzman, the lawyer for Sergeant Stacey Koon, called the incident "Eighty-two seconds that shook our society." He said that nothing Koon did was illegal or inappropriate. In fact, he called Koon's behavior beyond reproach. He said that Koon did not file a false police report and did his best to report everything that happened accurately.

Powell's lawyer, Michael P. Stone, spoke for two hours. He laid out the defense case in a methodical fashion, and showed us an enhanced version of the tape. "This incident, far from being an out-of-control beating of a motorist, was a controlled use of force. In a sense, it was the suspect who was in control."

Stone said that when the officers left Pacifica Hospital to drive King to Los Angeles County-USC Medical Center, they didn't know that he was seriously hurt. The doctor who treated King at Pacifica Hospital had released him to the police and his report just said that King had been treated for a PCP overdose and superficial lacerations. He said Powell and Wind took King to the Foothill Station to facilitate the booking process, not to show him off.

Stone said that King's head injuries were caused by falling on the ground face first.

Harland W. Braun, the lawyer representing Officer Ted Briseno, who was the turncoat in the first trial, did not argue this time that Briseno tried to stop the brutality. He just said that the four officers had different perspectives on what happened during a period of "rising violence against police officers."

By the end of the day, we had seen that videotape at least half a dozen times.

After court, we boarded the vans to be taken to the hotel. I didn't know what hotel they might be taking us to, and as we drove along, I realized that it was going to be the Los Angeles Hilton. We pulled up beside a white canvas tent on Seventh Street just west of Figueroa Street. They had erected a twelve-foot canopy in front of the security entrance to the hotel. We got out of the van and went directly into the tent. Three or four marshals accompanied us, past the barber shop and up to locked elevators. We were taken up to the tenth floor where we convened in a suite which was to be our television room, and were given our room assignments. Three of us—Ruth, Eric and me—had ordinary hotel rooms, but everyone else had a suite with two bathrooms. Some of the women used their extra bathrooms to launder their underwear and hang it up to dry.

Mark Neuberg explained the rules about no use of the telephone except while monitored by a marshal, and that we weren't allowed to go in each other's rooms. Then we went to our rooms to unpack.

Dinner was in the Gazebo Room downstairs at the hotel. It is a lunch place, and nobody but us was there during the evening. We ordered from the menu, and it took more than two hours to eat. From then on, we ordered upstairs at 5:30 p.m., and went down to the dining room at 6:30 p.m.

There was a party atmosphere at dinner that night as we all got better acquainted. We knew we were supposed to keep our identities secret, but it seemed ridiculous not to divulge our first names, so we exchanged those, and started to get to know one another.

FRIDAY, FEBRUARY 26, 1993

The prosecution's first witness was Captain John Mutz, the watch

*Moral Uncertainty*

commander who was the boss of these guys. He talked about the time cards and where they checked out their Taser guns. He pointed out on a drawing of the police station where things were.

My impression of Mutz was that he had gotten to be a captain in the Los Angeles Police Department by being very gifted at staying out of trouble. He was a real cover-your-ass kind of a guy. He struck me as just the opposite of Koon, who was the type of guy who said, "I was in charge and I take full responsibility."

I personally didn't see anything important in what he had to say. I guess they were just laying the groundwork for future testimony from other witnesses.

Next up was Delia Ascrio, the California Highway Patrol dispatcher. She identified a log of the radio calls starting when the CHP radioed that the LAPD was behind them. Clymer led her through the whole tape. I don't know why any of this was important, but the tape did parallel the chase.

The third witness was John Halterman, the California Highway Patrol radio man, who telephoned the LAPD. We heard the tape of that call. It wasn't earthshaking, as far as I could see. This was all background stuff, although it was interesting to see the map of the police station and to see the videotape in slow motion. We were to see it another fifty million times, of course, but for now, it was still a novelty.

The fourth witness was Leshon Frierson, a police service representative. Nothing he said seemed important enough to me to write down in my notes.

The fifth witness was Dorothy Gibson, a middle-aged black woman who lives downstairs from George Holliday, the man who shot the homemade videotape of the beating. She was awakened by the sound of a police helicopter. She had watched the whole thing and she was mad. She thought it had been disgusting. "An officer hit him with a black stick. The other officers were hitting him with a stick. They were hitting him all over. He didn't do anything. He kind of dodged the blows. It sounded like I heard him scream out, 'Please stop.' "

She got down from the witness stand and demonstrated how the kick looked. She said the baton sounded like chopping wood. "I saw them kick him with their feet on both sides, all over . . . any way they could get a lick in."

One of the prosecutors, Barry F. Kowalski, asked her what the officers were doing after they got King under control. Once King was hog-tied and lying with his face in the dirt, she said, "They were talking and they were laughing. I didn't want to see it anymore." Her voice cracked.

Stone asked her on cross-examination if she was positive it was King who said, "Please stop."

"You don't know who it was who said it, do you?" Stone asked.

"No, I don't know," she said.

Wind's attorney, Paul DePasquale, pointed out inconsistencies between what she told us and what she told the grand jury and an investigator from the Los Angeles County district attorney's office. In one of the previous accounts, she apparently said there were five officers beating King.

She insisted that what she was telling us now was true, and there must have been mistakes in the transcripts of the earlier proceedings.

The sixth witness was Robert Hill, a young county probation worker who lived in the same apartment complex. He was on his way home when he saw all the police officers, and he watched the beating from behind a wrought iron gate about thirty yards away.

He demonstrated the position that King was in while they were hitting him. He said King yelled and screamed and that King was squirming on the ground. He said the officers were laughing and talking, and he said there were blows to King's upper torso.

The defense asked him to point out on the videotape the hits he saw firsthand. Stone tried to get him to say that the officers only hit King while he was moving, which I guess he wanted us to think meant that he was trying to get away. But Hill said King was moving when he was hit because he was reacting to the blows. I'd squirm around if somebody was beating me with a stick, too.

Court adjourned for the afternoon and for the week.

We had to spend the weekend at the Hilton, and the government tried to keep us entertained with a field trip. Where we were going was a secret, because they didn't want anybody meeting us anywhere. We went to the Rose Bowl, and were allowed to walk wherever we wanted. A lot of the jurors headed straight into the bar at the golf course where they could buy their own drinks without being restricted to two, as we were at dinner every night.

It occurred to me that they had pay phones there, so I called my wife and my sister. We weren't allowed to make unmonitored phone calls from the hotel, so I took advantage of the chance to talk privately.

After I got off the phone, George and I strolled around the golf course. When we got back, Mark had gone to the bar to round up the drinkers.

After that, they never let us go anywhere by ourselves, because it was obvious we couldn't be trusted. On Sunday, we could have our families come visit us for an hour, but we had to stay in the communal areas, and had no privacy.

MONDAY, MARCH 1, 1993

The first witness of the second week was George Holliday, who testified that he was sleeping when the commotion woke him up just after midnight, March 3, 1991. "I saw a white car that had been stopped by several police cars. I saw a black man who was spread-eagled on the car."

He said he ran to get his brand-new video camera.

The defense made a big deal about asking him what the weather was like. He said it was cold. They asked him if anybody was sweating. Now, he was eighty to ninety feet away. It was cold, and no one could be sweating from the temperature, but he wasn't close up enough to see whether King was sweating.

Maybe the fact that King was sweating meant that he was on PCP. Probably they were trying to make the point that if it was too cold out for anyone to sweat, but King was perspiring, then a reasonable officer would conclude that he was on drugs and that they were going to have to hit him to subdue him.

From what I found out later, they were doing it wrong. The trouble is, if a guy is on PCP, you don't do what they did. If they really thought he was on PCP, they should have tried to keep him calm, not shine bright lights on him. They should have tried to talk to him in a calm voice. Instead, they went in shouting and aggressive. If they really thought he was on PCP, they were going against policy.

I think the point that Clymer was making with these witnesses was that it didn't happen the way the defendants said it did. I was always trying to figure out why they were telling us this. There was all this discussion of whether or not he was sweating. Whether or not the police were afraid of him doesn't affect whether or not their actions violated Rodney King's civil rights. That the police were afraid wasn't relevant to me.

The next witness was George Skaluba, an FBI video support technician. He was the one who enhanced the videotape so that the whole thing lasted nine minutes. He also put a tape together dubbing the radio calls in at the appropriate time on the videotape. What he did was real technical.

Next was Sergeant Robert Ontiveros, who had been with the LAPD for twenty-five years and was the day watch commander. He pointed out who was who in the video.

Dr. Majid Rabbani, who works for Kodak, testified that he worked on the videotape with the FBI. The enhancement didn't really help that much, as far as I could tell.

The eleventh witness for the prosecution was Officer Rolando Solano, Ted Briseno's partner. They weren't part of the pursuit. By the time they got there, there were already several officers on the scene, and Rodney King had his hands up, his palms forward. The officers told him to get down on his knees.

Solano said that Rodney King looked hostile. He was down on all fours, with Koon ten feet from him, saying, "Do as you're told or I'll tase you." The CHP had approached King with their guns drawn.

Solano said that someone forgot to turn off their siren, and it was screaming, adding to the confusion. After Koon started yelling, King went down, but he wasn't in the perfect felony prone position, because he had his head up. There was some discussion of the swarm technique versus the team takedown.

Solano said police officers were taught not to "tie up" with a suspect, to avoid wrestling with them. He said they used to get around this problem with the chokehold, but when people starting dying from chokeholds, they changed their policing procedures. Now they use batons, because if they are going to use the chokehold, they might as well just shoot them. Now, if a police officer is in a fight for his life, he is allowed to just go ahead and kill them, because he is allowed to shoot or to hit him in the head with the baton.

I never understood what Koon said to Solano, Powell, Briseno and Wind, but they went in to try to swarm King, to jump on him. King was on his belly with his hands on his butt and Powell approached him from the rear and dropped to his knees in the middle of King's back, according to Solano. Solano grabbed hold of the left leg.

My impression was that the police officers were really afraid of King. Solano described him as a giant of a man, and when Powell jumped him, with his knees in his back, that should have hurt. But he threw them off. Everybody jumped back. When Rodney King got up, Koon fired the Taser, Solano said.

Solano had considered it a high-risk situation and had drawn his own gun. He said something about having testified at a Skelly hearing. I knew because I worked for the city that when a public employee is fired or suspended from his job, he has a right of due process, and the hearing he is entitled to is called a Skelly hearing after a case called *Skelly v. California*. My impression was that it was Solano's own Skelly hearing, and that he was punished for not notifying the LAPD about the excessive beating, that he failed to file a report. Apparently he was suspended from the LAPD for twenty-two days because of the beating.

He repeated several times that he didn't think any officer did anything wrong.

Solano said that King charged Koon first, that he was down on his stomach and threw the officers off, and jumped up to his feet. There wasn't any video of that. He said Rodney King started to get up and Koon fired the Taser and hit him in the back, and Koon continued to try to get up, and Koon fired the Taser again.

Solano said he did not see any blows to King while King was on the ground. Solano was ready, he was crouched and doing his job, and he didn't see King hit by a baton while he was down. Solano said Briseno said to him later that the "sergeant should have handled it better."

The defense lawyers objected and asked that Solano's remark be stricken from the record. The judge ruled that we were only allowed to consider that remark as evidence against Briseno, not against Koon.

Solano reported that he saw Powell at the police station, where Powell told him Rodney King needed stitches in his mouth. Clymer had told us that intent to harm Rodney King could be demonstrated through the lack of concern the officers showed for looking after his medical needs afterwards. Here they had a guy they supposedly thought was high on PCP, with a broken head and his face bashed in, and Powell left him sitting in the car while he went into the station and told war stories. The prosecution was trying to show us that those actions showed Powell's lack of concern.

TUESDAY, MARCH 2, 1993

Solano was back on the stand. He said the police usually don't use the swarm on anyone who might be armed. He said they would use it on a PCP suspect who was naked, or who had already been double-cuffed. He said because he thought King was on PCP, he didn't think there was anything unusual about how the police handled the situation.

When the defense cross-examined Solano, he told basically the same story, that everyone was yelling at King to get in the felony prone position. I wonder if King knew what that was? If I were arrested, I wouldn't know what the felony prone position was. Maybe King would know because he had been in prison.

Solano demonstrated how to use the PR-24 baton for a power stroke, and he talked about the continuum of force, escalating and de-escalating.

The defense asked about the chokehold, and he talked about the baton being the last step before using lethal force.

Under cross-examination, Solano said that some of Powell's blows hit King on the head, but he thought that Powell was aiming at the shoulders and arms and only hit the head by accident.

"Did you observe any misconduct?" Salzman asked.

"No," Solano said.

"Did you see any officer do anything improper?"

"No," he replied.

Solano said he had testified before the federal grand jury and that Clymer had threatened to charge him with perjury because he didn't believe what he was saying.

On redirect examination, Clymer pointed out that Solano's version doesn't square with the video, and Solano conceded that it didn't. He said he couldn't see everything that was going on around him, and was under a lot of stress while it was happening. He had "tunnel vision."

The next witness, Number 12, was LAPD Sergeant Glenn Hess, who knew everything anybody would ever want to know about Tasers. They have fifty thousand volts, and low amps of power. It can't kill you, but it tightens your muscles. This thing had a lot of voltage. We saw two or three videos of people getting zapped with the Taser. They all fall down when they get zapped. Everybody at the LAPD gets tased, to see what it feels like, Hess said.

The thirteenth witness was Benjamin Avila. He was riding a bus that went by while Rodney King was being beaten. He didn't speak English, and they had to bring in an interpreter. He said he was on his way back to Sacramento with a musical group called Banda El Rincon, and the bus stopped right by the scene. Most people on the bus were asleep, he said. He saw the police hitting King's body and he said that King wasn't fighting back.

I thought this was damaging testimony, because he testified that all four cops were hitting him and he wasn't resisting them. The videotape showed only Wind and Powell hitting King.

Felipe Lopez was another passenger on the bus. He thought he saw eight kicks. That was pretty close. There were seven. He also thought all four policemen were hitting him.

"I don't think he was trying to flee or whatever," Lopez said. "I think that his instinct to protect himself made him flee from the blows."

Lopez said King "looked bad . . . I don't know whether it was pain or desperation or what."

There were some comments from the defense lawyers about the inaccuracy of the memories of the two bus riders. Neither of them spoke English and they had their facts mixed up. They were watching from across the street, of course, but they just didn't have a lot of the details straight. Salzman implied they had been influenced by watching the tape.

I figured that the band members probably all had a few too many drinks before they got on that bus, and the reason that the others didn't testify was that they were too zonked to wake up while the beating was going on. The two who testified had so many details mixed up that I couldn't rely on their testimony at all for its credibility, but I did take into account how emotional they were. They were like the neighbors who had witnessed the beating; everyone who saw it first hand was very shocked and disgusted. I thought that part was significant, although I knew I couldn't count on the details to be accurate from these witnesses.

# Chapter Twenty-Six: Use of Force Expert

This was the two-year anniversary of the Rodney King beating.

The only witness was Sergeant Mark Conta, a use of force expert working for the prosecution. He said that police are supposed to use the minimum force necessary to get the situation under control.

Conta went over every frame of the tape with us, and told us whether or not the officers were within the LAPD policy. He would say okay, he's being combative here, now boom, right here, everything from here on is out of policy.

He said Powell was justified in hitting King early in the incident. During the first thirty-two seconds of the tape, everything the police did was fine, because King was standing or trying to stand and posing a threat. But after the first thirty-two seconds, every baton blow and kick was against the rules, Conta said.

My word, can you really break it down like that?

Conta was like an old lady. Yes, boom, right there is when everything was suddenly outside of policy. Overall, there was a point where everything just fell apart. They should have stopped, but they continued.

In the part of the tape where the sergeant was yelling at them to hit him in the bony parts—to break his bones—we could see him yelling on the videotape, and it was believable that was what he was saying. And the policy calls for them to try to control the suspect by verbalizing, and then to use compliance techniques like the wrist lock, and then to go to intermediate force, the kick, then the Taser and the sap or chemical sprays. Then after that they escalate to deadly force, to hitting them in the head with the baton or shooting them.

The prosecution introduced as Exhibit 28B the LAPD procedure manual that said the baton was not to be used to force compliance to commands; they weren't allowed to use it to knock the guy down. In other words, they can't whack the guy just because he's not doing what he's told to do.

Conta said you can't hit the head, the neck, the throat or the spine. Wind hit close to the spine, but I think he missed. He was so accurate with the rest of his strokes. With the number of blows he hit, to have one off was not bad. In baseball, it would be a good average.

Conta had a kick chart of the kinds of kicks to avoid tying up with a suspect, or to keep them at a distance.

When Powell hit King on the chest, there was no aggressive behavior by King, Conta said. So he was saying the violation of the use of force policies occurred when Powell hit King in the chest.

Wind struck King while King was on the ground, and kicked him while he was on the ground. But Wind was still being given orders to do it.

Conta was a little guy. He was up there kind of trying to say that it's easy when you're not in a fight to criticize the guy who is in the fight. That's really the whole thing.

He also thought Briseno's stomp was a violation of policy. I do too, but what was Briseno's intent? I think he may have been confused, and he may have used excessive force, but I don't think he had any intent to harm King.

Let's just talk about intent to violate King's constitutional rights. No intent had been proven, as far as I was concerned. The act itself can show intent. Is it possible that Briseno was trying to help King, to get the guy on the ground so they'll stop beating on him?

Conta's opinion was that Koon violated LAPD policy because he should have intervened. He failed to stop the excessive use of force. Conta was asked, if the guy was on PCP, would that change your opinion? And he replied, no, not at all.

I wasn't really impressed with Conta. I thought he was a big joke. He just wasn't credible to me. He was too perfect. Oh, come on, guy. Give me a break.

If Rodney King was on PCP, how come the smallest guy there, Officer Ted Briseno, finally threw him down and put the handcuffs on him? Conta said that when King was being combative, nobody could control him, but when he was beaten into submission, the littlest man there could control him. Every time I saw the tape, I was convinced that King was being cooperative, and that anybody could have gotten the cuffs on him at that point.

Conta said he had spent thirty hours with the feds reviewing the tape and studying the records. When he was contacted by the defense, he refused to talk to them.

We spent the whole day today listening to cross-examination of Mark Conta, who seemed to be the prosecution's key witness. Stone did most of the questioning for the defense all day.

Conta testified that he had not read the Christopher Commission report. He said it wasn't his job. I thought that was odd. It bothered me that he hadn't read it. I thought this guy would have read that report.

Stone asked Conta if they could have controlled King if they had been able to use the chokehold. Back to that refrain. Conta had testified that the officers should have used the swarm technique, but he told Stone he didn't know if they had been trained in that method at the police academy. Conta also conceded that an officer had the right to strike a suspect with a baton if he thought the suspect was going to hit him.

Stone suggested that Conta had no way of knowing what was going through Powell's mind, and that officers had to make decisions in a split second. But Conta insisted that it didn't matter whether or not Powell was afraid of King; he should have stopped hitting him at a certain point. He said Powell should have stopped hitting King when he thought he was no further threat, even if Koon ordered him to keep it up.

FRIDAY, MARCH 5, 1993

Conta was starting to really bug me. He wore his uniform to court, and was just so sure of himself. He was willing to give the benefit of the doubt to everyone but Wind. He couldn't figure out what Wind was thinking about. He thought everyone used excessive force, but didn't know what Wind was doing out there. Going through the tape frame by frame, it looked to Conta like Wind was stepping back and evaluating.

Conta was asked if he would disobey his supervisor. Would he have not hit King if his superior officer was ordering him to do it? Conta said he wouldn't follow an illegal order. That's easy to say, but in reality, that's pretty tough to do.

Conta was asked if he would use the chokehold if he thought it was necessary. He said he would disobey his superior officer, but never the police commission, which banned the chokehold.

My kind of guy.

Harland Braun, who represented Briseno, confronted Conta with the tape of an interview he had given in 1991 when he said Briseno's stomp helped control King so he could be handcuffed. Conta agreed he had said that, but it was a violation of LAPD policy anyway.

Conta got a little testy, but he didn't back down much.

At last they were finished with Conta. The next witness up, the sixteenth for the prosecution, was Glenda Jean Tosti, an LAPD computer expert. She told us all about the various codes, and about the Mobile Display Terminals in the cars. She talked about Koon's message that said, *You just had a big time use of force* and Powell's *Oops, I haven't beat anybody this bad in a long time.*

You could say that these messages showed intent. Powell sent that callous message and didn't really do anything to help King. Koon's message just seemed like a logical report for him to be making to his superior officer.

Next we heard from Corina Smith, an LAPD officer who apparently used to be Powell's girlfriend. She testified about Powell's messages to her. We heard the audio of the radio call.


MONDAY, MARCH 8, 1993

The eighteenth witness was Clifford Bernard, an apartment building manager who had a video camera of his own, and after Rodney King was already handcuffed, he started taping for about fifteen minutes. He had a lot of tape of the CHP officers. The two other guys in Rodney King's car weren't even arrested. They were just detained by the CHP. One of them walked and got in the back of the police car. The other just got left there at the scene.

Bernard had tape of the ambulance arriving. It was pretty boring. It was all after the fact. He had pictures of King sitting there on the ground.

The next witness was Carol Denise Edwards, an emergency room nurse at Pacifica Hospital. She said that Rodney King was cooperative. She said when she asked Powell how King got his injuries, he patted his baton and Wind held his baton up.

Big evidence. The whole world knows what they hit him with.

The nurse testified that Powell asked King what kind of work he did at Dodger Stadium and King said he was an usher. Powell said he wanted to be sure he didn't sit in his section.

She said Powell had bragged that the officers had been playing hard ball with King, that he had lost and they had won. She was sure Powell was the one who made the remarks because he was standing right behind her. Powell claimed he never said it.

I didn't really put a lot of credence in this stuff. It just didn't matter. The officers could have done their jobs and done nothing inappropriate and still talked like that. What they said to King afterwards had nothing to do with whether or not they used excessive force when they were arresting him. If Powell did everything right, and he stopped hitting him when he should have, he still could have been insulting to King at the hospital, and he wouldn't be guilty of using excessive force.

It might even have just been his idea of humor. Gallows humor.

The nurse said there were no Taser darts stuck in King's skin. She said that Powell and Wind told her that they didn't have to be in the skin to have worked. She said there were no electrical burns on his skin that would have indicated that it affected him.

I think the Taser did work, because King went down.

Edwards said that she had written in the report that he allegedly was on PCP, and that his vital signs were normal, but he had rapid eye movement. She said they didn't take any blood tests for drugs. She said the pictures they showed her of King's wounds made them look worse than she remembered them being.

She talked about "tattooing," which is road dirt from being scraped on the ground. She said he would have had tattooing on his face if he fell.

She said she had a hard time getting the IV in King's arm, because she couldn't find his veins. He was sitting there calmly.

The next witness was Dr. Antonio Mancia. He said that Rodney King didn't answer questions for his history. Mancia testified he had no clue that King might be on PCP. If he had thought King was on PCP, he wouldn't have stuck his hand in his mouth.

Both Mancia and the nurse testified that King's blood pressure was normal.

Mancia seemed to disagree with the nurse. She said King was cooperative. She knew that his head was injured badly. Mancia said that from the bruises on King's chest, he was more concerned about a collapsed lung than the head wounds.

The next witness was Richard Jackson, an LAPD officer in the major crimes division. What a job this guy has. He and three cohorts collected the evidence against their fellow officers. They went through the lockers and got the batons and the Taser. They got the weapons from all the officers involved. They got Powell's baton, Wind's baton and Koon's Taser.

Braun asked them if they had gotten Ted Briseno's shoes. He was making light of the whole testimony. Braun was kind of a mind-game lawyer.

TUESDAY, MARCH 9, 1993

My daughter's eighteenth birthday. My wife was unhappy that I missed the occasion, because all birthdays and holidays are big deals to her. And the eighteenth birthday seemed like a special one, because it signaled the fact that our little girl was grown up. I talked to Kelly on the phone and wished her a happy day and asked her what her mother had bought for her.

Back in court, the next witness was Dr. Charles Aronberg, another doctor at USC Medical Center, who testified that at 6:45 a.m., King's blood alcohol was .094. So six hours after the incident, King was still legally drunk.

He said the urine sample was positive for marijuana. That was the only mention we had of marijuana.

They showed us pictures of King's face, and he said King had a broken cheekbone and eye socket and a damaged sinus. "There were innumerable small fractures," Aronberg said. "In some areas, the bones were reduced to a very fine powder, like sand."

Under cross-examination by Harland Braun, Aronberg insisted that the injuries came from baton blows, not from hitting what he called the tarmac. "I know that someone suggested that they were the result of falls to the pavement, and that's out of the question," Aronberg said. "I think that the injuries were caused by blows to the face and head by batons."

The next witness was Dr. Stanley Cohen, a neurologist who examined King eight days after the beating. He said that King had memory loss. I didn't take any notes on what Cohen said. I don't usually drink a lot of coffee, but the testimony was getting so boring and repetitive that I could hardly stay awake. I had started ordering a pot of cappuccino with breakfast so I could stay awake. Why are they doing this to me?

Everybody has a right to their day in court.

# Chapter Twenty-Seven: Rodney King Testifies

Federal Prosecutor Barry Kowalski stood up and said, "The United States calls Rodney King."

This was the one we had been waiting to hear. He didn't testify at the Simi Valley trial, and we had heard so much about what a monster he was. Wow. I was amazed at how well he looked. He was really well dressed. He had a mustache and a goatee. He was wearing a charcoal gray pin-striped double-breasted suit and lavender-and-black tie, and it looked good on him. He walked in, standing straight and tall, like a real trouper. Sure, he seemed nervous, but he looked like a million dollars.

He was also a lot smaller than I thought he would be. After all the testimony about him being this big guy, this superhuman hulk, this buffed-out prison inmate who worked out, I was expecting a giant. Maybe he had lost a lot of weight, but he didn't look that tall to me, or that big. I was quite shocked at his lack of size.

I was impressed with him before he opened his mouth.

He claimed that the police officers taunted him with racial slurs. He imitated them, talking in this high squeaky voice: "We're going to kill you, nigger. You'd better run, nigger."

Some people in the audience gasped. King had apparently never said this before.

He said they called him "Killer."

"Hey, Killer."

Was he trying to convince me that Powell or Wind talked in that high, squeaky little voice? Briseno is a small guy, but Wind and Powell are big. I couldn't imagine them using that tone. I didn't believe they made those racial slurs or used that tone of voice. Killer? Why would they call him Killer?

Kowalski asked King why he didn't say this to the grand jury, and he said that his mother had advised him not to make it a racial issue. King also said his memory wasn't very good, and admitted some of the things he said in the past were lies.

"Mr. King," Kowalski asked, "do you remember whether the word that was being used was killer or nigger?"

"I'm not sure," King said. "I'm not absolutely sure which word it was, if it was killer or nigger. I'm not sure."

Harland Braun objected. He said the prosecution was trying to inflame the jury with the racial slur even though the evidence didn't support the claim. He asked the judge to tell us to disregard the comment.

Judge Davies refused. It didn't matter, because I didn't believe it anyway.

King recounted how he met the two others at seven o'clock at Bryant Allen's house and had bought a quart of malt liquor which he drank. He downed another quart in the car, he said. They went back to Allen's, where they watched a basketball game, and King finished off one more quart. He said he consumed a total of four quarts during the evening.

He said he was driving to Hansen Dam because he had been there before, fishing with his dad when he was a little kid.

He was asked why he didn't get off on Osborne if he was going to Hansen Dam, and he said he was planning to stop at a liquor store on Paxton. He said he didn't realize the CHP was chasing him. He just got off the freeway to buy more beer. He admitted he was going seventy-five to eighty miles per hour and said Allen told him to slow down. Allen told him the police were chasing him.

"So you knew the police were behind you?" Clymer asked. "Why didn't you stop?

"I thought they would just go away," King said, all meek and mild.

He said when he started to get out of the car, his seatbelt was still on and it prevented him from getting right out. He said he was trying to do what they asked him to do. "It was very confusing. They said, 'Put your hands on the top of the car,' and then, 'No, no, no, no, no. Put your hands on the hood of the car.' "

King said he lay down on the pavement. A female CHP officer approached him with a drawn gun. "I didn't want to watch her shoot me so I turned my head face down," King testified. "I received a blow with a hard object to the right side of my face."

What was he talking about? He didn't get hit in the face while Melanie Singer still had her gun out, did he?

He said one of the officers grabbed his arm and twisted it behind his back "like he was trying to snap my wrist." He said he yelped in pain, and he demonstrated the yelp.

When the Taser hit him, "It just felt like my blood was boiling inside me. I just kind of laid down and took it. I was hoping it would go away shortly."

He said one of the officers said, "We're going to kill you, nigger, run."

So he jumped up then and tried to run.

An officer, which had to have been Timothy Wind, rode with him to the hospital. King said he "kept snatching me by the back collar of my shirt and saying, 'Stay with me, stay with me now.' It was real painful for me to try and sit up straight because of the injuries all over my body."

In the hospital the next day, he had trouble remembering what had happened. "But I knew for sure I had been attacked by police officers. I just was wondering what did I do to deserve that type of pain."

He said he had watched the video about ten times, and that he still had bad dreams of the police chasing him. He said he had nightmares about being tased. "I would have nightmares about being struck with a hard object. I just couldn't seem to get away from it in my sleep. Just, you know, real horrible nightmares over and over."

He said he couldn't bear to watch the video anymore. "It's sickening to see it. It makes me sick to my stomach to watch it," he said.

"I was just trying to stay alive, sir, trying to stay alive," King told Kowalski. "They never gave me a chance to stay still, never gave me a chance to stay still."

In the afternoon, the defense attorneys began cross-examining King.

"Did you know you were committing a crime that night?" Salzman asked.

"Yes, sir, " King said.

"And you did it anyway?"

"Yes, sir."

King seemed a little befuddled by some of the questions, but he stayed calm. Sometimes, he stopped and gazed at the ceiling for a while before he answered.

Salzman asked him how he knew it was a baton that hit him in the face. "Who told you it was a baton? Was it your lawyer?"

"Nobody had to tell me that, I felt it," King said.

He said that after the beating, "I was coughing and laughing blood out of my mouth. I didn't want them to get the satisfaction of what they were doing to me."

The defense lawyers gave King transcripts to read, but he asked them to read it to him so he could understand. Judge Davies told a defense lawyer not to read it to him, and King said, "I can't read it."

Stone seemed to be using big words just to confuse the guy. He went out of his way to embarrass and demean King. He was blatant about it. That really disturbed me. The racial slur that King talked about came across as a lie. It just wasn't believable at all. But they didn't have to make him look like an idiot.

He said he was searching for the park where he had gone fishing. That made sense to me. He pulled into the entrance to the park, and there was a cable across the road, so he was boxed in.

King said they burned all of his clothes at USC County Hospital, so when he left, he didn't have any clothes, just his shoes.

DePasquale got him to say he couldn't really remember anything, but he did remember the liquor store on Paxton, although he hadn't been there for sixteen years.

King told DePasquale his mother visited him at the hospital. "She said, 'We all know what went on. You don't need to make this a race issue; you don't have to have it a bigger issue than it already is.' So I decided to keep my mouth hush."

Stone asked King if he expected to make money from a lawsuit against the city. He said he expected to make a lot.

"What's a lot of money, sir?" Stone asked.

"More than what I have now," King said.

He said he didn't remember telling the police that he had been beaten while he was handcuffed and hog-tied. "Sometimes I forget things that happen and sometimes I remember some things."

Braun was the last attorney to question King and the most aggressive. "You can't say for sure that any officer used the word, 'nigger,' that night?"

"I can't say it for sure. I can't say it for sure, no," King replied.

Braun asked him why he hadn't told the grand jury about the taunts. He said he had forgotten.

"As an African American who was admittedly beaten, you would forget if police officers called you nigger?" Braun asked incredulously. "Is that the type of thing you forget from time to time?"

He wasn't really a very credible witness. Perhaps he was just confused. He was beaten and fighting for his life, and he really didn't remember the sequence correctly at all. He might have been lying. There were so many contradictions in what he said.

But he got to me emotionally. To hear about him being hit in the head and being so scared and in so much pain made me feel a lot of sympathy for him. I thought he was lucky to be alive. I couldn't believe he was alive, as a matter of fact.

Although I felt sorry for the guy, I didn't buy his version of the story. Some things I thought he was lying about, and some things I think he just didn't remember accurately.

A lot of what he said was just unbelievable. He said he hadn't been to the park in sixteen years, but he knew there was a liquor store on Paxton. The guy didn't have such a great memory, and not a lot of intelligence. It was just too much to believe he would remember where the liquor store was.

Just at the end of the day, the prosecution put Dr. Harry Smith, an expert in biomechanics from San Antonio, Texas, on the stand. He had a degree in civil engineering, a master's in civil engineering and a Ph.D. in civil engineering from Texas A&M. And then he went into medicine, and got his M.D. in 1978. He had been an emergency room physician and a radiologist. He said that biomechanics is the study of how injuries are caused.

Smith presented a list of Rodney King's injuries, and talked about the MRIs and CAT scans that had been done on him. He was a very believable witness.

He showed us a plastic skull and pointed out King's fractures. He said his right sinus was "pulverized."

# Chapter Twenty-Eight: More of the Prosecution's Case

Dr. Smith testified that King had a lot of cracked teeth, on both the top and bottom of his mouth. He told us which teeth exactly were cracked.

He was very articulate and polished, and said that the officers' explanation for King's fifteen facial injuries—that he hit his face on the ground—wasn't supported by the medical evidence. He said it had to be baton injuries. "The patterns and associated injuries I have talked about today are not caused or causable by a fall. These are baton injuries."

I still believed his cheek hit the ground.

Smith thought the injuries were from a baton blow. He said the first blow was horizontal and caught King under the nose.

He showed us CAT scans and X-rays. He was very believable at the time. He said if the injuries were caused by hitting the ground, how come there was no tattooing. There should have been gravel under his skin from when he hit the ground.

He said in the blurry section of the videotape he saw eight to ten head blows.

Smith spent most of the day standing in front of huge blow-up photos of King's face and using models of a skull to point out injuries.

Salzman had fallen asleep. His head was nodding.

There were other times during the trial when Braun fell asleep, or when he looked around the courtroom like he wasn't interested.

FRIDAY, MARCH 12, 1993

The twenty-sixth witness was Yolanda Franke, the registrar at Pacifica Hospital. She had the hospital log, and had deleted all the other names to show us what time Rodney King was brought in.

Next was Frank Torres, a sheriff's deputy who did the booking at the jail ward at USC County Medical Center. He didn't see any symptoms of PCP in Rodney King. He was asked if it was true that the symptoms of PCP wax and wane, but he didn't see any sign of that, either.

He said an officer said that King was "dusted," and King said, "I'm not dusted."

Next was an FBI agent named Sheri Thomas. Her job was to measure the distance and the time it took to get from Pacifica Hospital to the Foothill Division police station to the USC Medical Center. From Foothill to USC was 19.7 miles and it took her twenty-seven minutes, she said, going sixty-five miles per hour.

Now, the officers taking Rodney King left Pacifica at 3:31 in the morning and got to USC at 5:35, so it took them two hours and four minutes, and it took her less than half an hour.

But since the speed limit on the freeway is fifty-five miles per hour, I still didn't know how long it should actually take, since Sheri said she went sixty-five miles per hour, and nobody ever questioned her about that. She was very good-looking, so a worthwhile witness from that standpoint, but I didn't gain much useful information from her testimony.

The next witness was Daniel Gonzalez, an LAPD police officer who said he heard a Code 6, which meant that a chase had stopped. Gonzalez's partner, Martin Garcia, was a rookie who wanted to see a little action, so they drove over, and Gonzalez pulled up and spoke to Officer Susan Clemmer, who said everything was under control. They saw Tim Blake, Clemmer's partner, and later he saw Powell at the station. He said he saw Powell talking to other officers, telling war stories. Seven or eight officers, for thirty or forty minutes.

The prosecutors were trying to get out that Powell was smiling and happy, but Gonzalez said they didn't seem particularly happy or sad. Gonzalez asked Powell if he could see King. He said he wanted to see the face of a suspect "who tried to hurt another officer so that if I ever ran into him, I could beware."

He flashed a light in King's eyes. Wind asked Garcia and Gonzalez to please leave and they did. They were there two minutes and Wind complained four times. Wind told him to calm down and said to leave the guy alone. Wind, he said, "made it very clear that I was making Mr. King upset and I should just get the heck out of there."

On cross-examination, Gonzalez said that Powell was not

boasting, bragging or laughing.

The next witness was Sergeant Michael Schadel, who worked in the LAPD jail division. He was there to explain to us the proper way to book a suspect. We had heard all this baloney about going to Foothill Station to do the booking. That was just a big waste of time. They could have gone straight to USC Medical Center, like Koon told them to.

I figure the cops book people every day. They ought to know how to do it.

The next witness was Don Farrell, a sergeant with the LAPD. He was an instructor at the police academy, and taught report writing. He said they emphasize writing a report that is brief, accurate and complete. He said the daily field report that Wind did was really for Wind's use only.

To me, Wind's report was the most complete. He was the probationary officer. He left out that they went back to Foothill Station, and that he was in the car. Nobody brought that up.

Only Powell went into the station. I was upset that the other guys talking about reports never mentioned that Wind didn't go inside.

MONDAY, MARCH 15, 1993

The next witness was Martha Esparza, a registered nurse at USC. She described King's facial injuries, said he had no road rash, no signs of PCP and his vital signs were normal.

I guess the prosecution was countering the defense's claim that the only reason the police took King to the hospital was because they thought he was on PCP. It wasn't for his head injuries, because Dr. Mancia had told them he wasn't hurt.

Next up was James Miller, a sergeant with internal affairs, and he went over the reports. Koon's daily sergeant's report said there was a torrent of blows. The use of force report has to be done by someone who wasn't involved in the use of force. Since Koon used the Taser himself, he had to assign someone else to write the report. Wind did a cover sheet, but no use of force report was ever written. Miller's whole point seemed to be that all the reports were wrong or done wrong.

My fellow jurors Anne and Maria were amazed at how badly the reports had been done. Some were wrong, and some just were never written at all.

"Can you imagine? At my work, if I didn't fill out the reports, I'd get fired," Anne said.

It was sloppy work. None of them seemed to be able to do good reports. Their attention was focused on other parts of their jobs. Most of their reports were reviewed and kicked back. Obviously, they were just allowed to do bad reports. It seems to be a systemwide problem.

The next witness was John Amott, a motor sergeant with the LAPD. He was a really big man. He explained the definition of felony evading and misdemeanor failure to stop. If you know that you are being followed and you don't stop, it can be felony evading, even if you weren't guilty of a felony to start with.

Rodney King might not have known that he was being followed, since he never responded to the guy in the backseat who was screaming at him to pull over. Bryant Allen later testified that he was screaming at him, and it made no impression on him. And Melanie Singer testified that he put his hands in the air, so he obviously wanted the police to see that he was surrendering.

Amott said that before the police can arrest someone for a traffic violation, the traffic division has to give approval. They have to present the arrest report and be given approval. He also said that the LAPD has a policy of arresting the person first for the most important thing they did. If they thought he was on PCP, that would have been the most serious charge, so they would have written that down.

If they thought he was on PCP, how come they never tested him for it? If they were serious that he was on PCP, surely they would have tested. Instead, they arrested him for felony evading.

This guy John Amott didn't tell anyone to start with that the report was incomplete, but when he saw the video, he called his boss and said that it was a flaky report. He called his supervisor and said he messed up by letting that report go through.

The report said that the defendant was hostile at the hospital, but the people at the hospital said he wasn't.

None of the reports filed that night mentioned that King had hit

Powell. They didn't charge him with battery on a police officer. They said that he was combative and resisting, but they never mentioned that he hit anyone. How combative could he be, if he didn't hit them?

The next witness was Patrick Conmay, an LAPD lieutenant. He was the watch commander and the one that Koon sent the message to saying that there had been a big time use of force. He gave Conmay a verbal report, too, about the use of force.

Conmay said that another officer had been assigned to do the use of force report and that they had agreed to book King at USC and not at the Foothill station. Conmay said he had never signed Koon's sergeant's daily report. Just another weakness in the report-writing system, it sounded like to me.

Koon's report said there had been a torrent of blows, but Conmay didn't sign it. He may have been trying to distance himself from the whole thing.

That was the end of the government's witnesses. I was a little surprised. I thought they were ending on a weak note. I thought they must be building up to something, but this guy was weak. It wasn't like he was trying to cover anything up, but I guess he got to be lieutenant by not getting involved.

But that was it. Wow. We must be about halfway finished, I thought. The prosecution had put on thirty-five witnesses in thirteen days. Conta and Koon and Harry Smith had all been on the stand for more than a day each, but the others went by much more quickly. Of course, even though it was the prosecution's case, we had been hearing from the defense quite a bit. About half the time was the cross-examination by the defense. They spent a lot of time questioning the prosecution's witnesses.

I don't know if the defense attorneys were just better lawyers than the prosecutors, but it seemed like the prosecution didn't get as much information out of them as the defense did. It was like the defense lawyers were better prepared.

# Chapter Twenty-Nine: The Force Fights Back

The first witness for the defense was Los Angeles City Councilman Hal Bernson. He testified that the Los Angeles City Council makes the laws for the city. He said that the City Council banned the use of the chokehold in 1982 even though there was evidence that barring it might cause more baton injuries.

Kowalski asked him on cross-examination if it was true that they stopped using the chokehold because so many black suspects were dying from being choked, and Bernson said that was one of the reasons.

Next was Mike Yamaki, one of five Los Angeles Police Commissioners. He explained that the Police Commission makes the policies that the Los Angeles Police Department has to follow.

The defense's objective in presenting these witnesses apparently was to make the point that it was the Police Commission that eliminated the chokehold from the officers' repertoire, that they are the guys responsible for that. The defense tried to make us believe that the officers had no other choice than to beat King because they couldn't use the chokehold. If they were going to arrest him, they were going to have to use their batons.

When they had the chokehold, an officer could hit a guy in the shoulder, spin him around and choke him to cut off the oxygen to the brain, and then he could cuff him. This procedure apparently worked like a charm in the days when all of the cops were huge. They got the suspect in the crook of their arm and brought them under control. Then with Affirmative Action, the guidelines were changed to allow women, among others, to get on the police force. They started accepting much shorter and smaller people, and when a smaller officer applied the chokehold on a bigger suspect, the angle was different. Also, the smaller officer may have been more afraid of the suspect, and applied the chokeholds for several seconds longer than officers had in the old days. In any event, some suspects died after they had been choked, and the Police Commission banned the technique.

With the baton, they don't have to get as close to the suspect.

The police want to be sure they don't get into a wrestling match with the suspect where they can get their weapons taken away from them.

If the police officer tells the guy, let me see your hands, and the guy doesn't comply, what are the officer's options? That's where the procedures break down. The officer has a real problem.

Apparently the defense had called the entire Los Angeles City Council and every member of the Police Commission, and they were all waiting in the hall to appear, but Judge Davies put on the brakes. He said, no, you've made your point with one city councilman and one police commissioner.

So the defense called Edward W. Oglesby, a police science teacher who wrote the book on PCP. He was the author of *Angel Dust: What Everyone Should Know About PCP*. He went over the symptoms, which included eyes bouncing, high blood pressure, problems with muscle coordination, a blank stare, agitation, cyclic behavior, animal noises, muscle rigidity, high temperature, memory loss, hallucinations and abnormal strength.

Oglesby said that King had the classic symptoms of being on PCP, so an officer would have to assume that he was. King did not test positive for PCP, but Oglesby said that PCP sometimes failed to show up in urine and blood samples, and the tests would have to be repeated several times over a number of hours to be sure.

Koon thought that Rodney King was sweating, and everyone made a big deal about how it was too cold for anybody to be sweating. They asked George Holliday if it was hot, and he said he needed to go back in to get a jacket.

But to me, whether or not King was on PCP or not doesn't add or subtract from my thoughts about whether the officers were guilty. Because they thought he might be on PCP, they had to use tactics for someone on PCP. But they still could have stopped hitting him sooner.

The PCP stuff was kind of interesting to hear, anyway.

Oglesby presented the LAPD training bulletin on PCP. It said that when an officer is confronted with a suspect on PCP he should use no loud noises or bright lights, because you don't want the suspect to go off. The officers did just the opposite, so it calls into question their insistence that they thought that King was on PCP. It makes you wonder who the defense is working for. Not too bright.

The next witness was Officer Susan J. Clemmer, Tim Blake's partner. The defense asked her if she had swarm training and she said she never had. When she got to the scene, Blake told her to direct traffic, and he went over to where the commotion was. She didn't think she ought to be separated from her partner, but she did as she was told.

She said Powell came up to her and told her that Rodney King was sweating and was out of control. She said Powell said that he was scared and that he thought he was going to have to shoot him.

I was sort of surprised that she could quote what someone else said to her. I thought that was hearsay, or something.

Koon told her to ride in the ambulance along with Wind and she did. She described how King was hog-tied, face down in the ambulance, and the left side of his face was down. The right side probably hurt him. She was sitting to his right. The whole ride, King was spitting blood onto her legs. There was major damage to his face, and he was probably just trying to breathe.

Whatever the case, they were making King out to be a bad guy who was rudely spitting blood on a police woman's leg. I felt sympathy for the guy. His face is all caved in, he's got blood in his mouth and nose, and he's hog-tied down in an ambulance. I doubt he had much control over whether there was blood coming out his mouth. It was just unfortunate for her that she happened to be sitting next to him.

I thought maybe Koon actually displayed an act of kindness in sending Clemmer along in the ambulance. She was a woman who wasn't involved in the beating, and he told her to ride along in the ambulance with King, and maybe it was to protect him.

She testified that when they got to the hospital, Koon came up, and King whispered, "I love you," to him. She said they were within about six feet of each other when King said that.

No one thought that King really loved him. Maybe it was a smart aleck thing. It was bizarre, but that's okay.

She said that Blake later came back and told her what he saw, but no one asked her to tell us what he told her. I was surprised. There was some information here. Why didn't we find out about it? What was it that Blake told her? There were lots of times that I had questions that didn't get answered. That's the way the system works.

The jurors only hear what the lawyers want us to hear, and it can be frustrating, because other questions occur to you, and they don't get answered.

Blake must have told her that the other officers had beat the hell out of this guy for no apparent reason, and the defense didn't want us to know that.

The next witness was Paul Beauregard, a Los Angeles Unified School District police officer. He and his partner were driving along when they heard the radio call and joined the chase. He testified that when the Hyundai pulled up at the park entrance, the other passengers, Bryant Allen and Freddie Helms, got out of the car one at a time and did as they were told. The driver was still in the car, and it took him more than a minute to get out.

Beauregard said the driver didn't comply with orders. He said that King walked around for about two minutes, and that he rose up again after he had been knocked down by the Taser shot. Beauregard heard Koon say, "Get to the ground or I'll shoot." King didn't respond. Koon said, "This isn't working. We'll have to try something else."

Under cross-examination from Prosecutor Alan Tieger, Beauregard said that Powell struck King nine times with the baton, but he was still standing; the blows seemed to have no effect.

He never heard the officers saying, "What's up, killer."

Beauregard said he searched the car and found forty-ounce malt liquor bottles. He said he thought King and his passengers were drunk.

He said he told the grand jury that Powell hit King nine times, and that he used mostly one-handed blows.

Now, I've seen the tape, and I've watched every blow. I do not believe I ever saw a single one-handed blow the whole time. So I don't know what Beauregard was remembering seeing.

Beauregard testified that he is a friend of Powell's family, and he went over to talk to Powell. He said Powell was on the radio, and that he laughed. He said he was making jokes about the school police being there. He said Powell told King he was truant.

Beauregard said that King laughed and asked, "Do I have to do detention?"

Tieger also got Beauregard to admit that King had stopped at all the traffic lights and had never gone faster than forty-five miles per hour on the surface streets during the supposed high-speed chase.

The next witness was Joseph Napolitano, another LAPD officer, who was Ingrid Larson's partner. Napolitano was one of the officers visible in the video. He said he observed six or seven blows, and he thought that King was on PCP and that he kept getting back up. Napolitano said he was about twelve feet away from King, and he didn't see Wind kick him. He saw Rodney King on his hands and knees. He said that King was very aggressive and combative. He implied that King was never on the ground when he was being hit.

He talked about what he called the Folsom roll, where a defendant rolls around to protect himself and then tries to use his body weight to knock the officer off balance and get the baton away from him. He said the prisoners at Folsom Prison teach each other to do that.

So when King was rolling around on the ground, Napolitano thought it was the Folsom roll. I thought that was a lot of baloney. It's got to be a natural reaction when someone is beating on you and you feel pain, to move and to react. This guy had a broken leg. He had to be in pain. It had to hurt. The cops expected him to lie perfectly still, but the natural reaction is to move.

WEDNESDAY, MARCH 17, 1993

Napolitano testified that he saw Tim Wind at a coffee shop the morning after the beating, and Wind said, "I didn't enjoy it."

Napolitano told Wind, "There are going to be times when you have to use force. But don't ever get to the point where you enjoy it."

On cross-examination, Clymer asked Napolitano how he could have missed seeing six kicks Wind delivered. Napolitano didn't report any kicks to Internal Affairs investigators, but he admitted that the tape shows him standing right there while Wind was kicking King.

The next witness, Jerry Mulford, a retired police expert on the use of force, talked about team takedown. They showed the Taser training bulletin and the expended Taser cassette, and he took us through the video on Taser training.

Mulford lived in Washington or Idaho, I forget which, and was an instructor on the use of force. He explained about team takedown, the swarm, the sergeant's daily report, and a lot of those police procedures, from the defendants' point of view.

On arrest reports, he said that some things are "accurate enough." When an officer reads it, he knows what it means. His point was that it didn't matter much if the arrest report was crystal clear to a layman. If the officers understood it, that was good enough.

The next witness was Paul Gebhardt, a Foothill Division training officer. He said he drove over to the scene after he had heard the Code 6 and the Code 4, because he had a trainee along with him and he wanted him to see a little action.

When they got there, Gebhardt said that Rodney King had Taser wires in him and that Wind and Powell were using their batons. Koon ordered King to put his hands behind his back, and ordered the men to hit him in the knees because he was trying to get away, Gebhardt said.

He said he never heard any racial taunts. He also said he thought King acted like he was on PCP. He said, "Any LAPD officer with three weeks on the street would know the man would have to be dusted acting like that."

He said he heard Powell shout, "Watch out. This guy's dusted."

Kowalski implied that Gebhardt was lying to protect Powell.

I really didn't believe anything this guy said. It seemed like somebody had written his script for him. He just seemed cockeyed to me, like he was lying.

THURSDAY, MARCH 18, 1993

Robert Troutt, a motorcycle sergeant who was the watch commander, testified that he approved the booking by phone. This is the guy that Sergeant Amott took over for at the end of his shift. Powell called him and he gave approval, but Powell went back and talked to Amott. When Amott saw the video, he called his superior and said the report was erroneous.

The next witness was Agnes Gordon, a black female LAPD sergeant currently attached to the Rampart Division who had been working at Foothill the night of the incident. She was in the sergeants' room and was told there was a pursuit and to get her gear and get over there. But Koon intervened and said he would take the call.

She didn't seem to want to tell us anything. She didn't look like she was happy to be there. She didn't look like she wanted to be a defense witness.

I couldn't help wondering how things might have been different if a black woman sergeant had arrived on that scene instead of Koon. Would she have done exactly the same thing that Koon did, or would she have shot King? Or would King have cooperated with a black woman cop?

Next was Robert Ontiveros, testifying for the second time. He was the assistant watch commander who had filed a daily field action report. There is a notebook divider that tells how to fill out the daily field report. He was asked about Wind's errors on his daily field report. This guy really blew it on the stand. The report said King had no injuries. His face was caved in but the doctor said no problem.

He was asked how long it takes to drive from Pacifica to Foothill. He said sixteen to twenty minutes. It's a short distance, two signals, but Ontiveros says, well, we're taught to look around, so it takes a little longer.

He was lying. It doesn't take twenty minutes, and he got caught.

I always thought there were penalties for flat-out lying in court. I don't know where I've been all my life. I thought you got prosecuted for lying, but nothing appears to happen.

Why would this guy lie? He's an officer. He's backing his guys up. They're in trouble if they tell the truth.

The next witness was Richard DiStefano, an assistant watch commander who was assigned to write the use of force and pursuit reports. He was going to write them the next day, but he had a flat tire and didn't go to work. He missed the whole day because of it, and by that time, Internal Affairs had taken over the investigation, so he never wrote the report at all. He skipped work because he had a flat tire and then he just didn't write the report. Your tax dollars at work. I worked for the city, too.

On cross-examination, DiStefano said Koon told him Powell's baton strokes were weak. Koon said he thought Powell was tired. DiStefano said he had given a class on baton hitting during roll call that same night and Powell didn't do very well. He said he wasn't using a power stroke. He said an overhead stroke is called a chop and the underhand stroke is called a pool cue jab.

Funny, I didn't follow the Simi Valley trial. The only thing that made much impression on me from that trial was hearing that Powell didn't hit very effectively. I remember thinking that if Powell hit him, he probably didn't really hurt him, because he wasn't very good at hitting with the baton.

DiStefano said that Wind had just gotten out of the police academy and hadn't lost his technique from when he was trained. So Wind was perfect, but Powell was really bad. He didn't hit with enough power. He didn't put enough of his body into it. The baton is designed to break bones. You aren't supposed to use it on your friends, DiStefano said.

On cross-examination, Prosecutor Lawrence Middleton asked him if Powell had complained that the suspect didn't seem to feel the blows. DiStefano said Powell hadn't said that.

The next witness, Robert Faris from the LAPD Harbor Division, taught the team takedown technique at the academy. He said it was not intended to be used on unsearched or jailed suspects. So they couldn't have used the team takedown because Rodney King had never been searched.

The next witness, Ken Klein, another LAPD officer who taught at the police academy between 1983 and 1989, testified that in his lesson plan, he taught that the team takedown was useful on suspects who weren't wearing any clothing.

The defense case was going much faster than the prosecution's case had, because when the prosecution presented a witness, each of the four defense lawyers had to cross-examine. When there was a defense witness, only one prosecutor did the cross-examining.

# Chapter Thirty: Duke, The Defense Force Expert

The next witness, the fiftieth during the trial, was Sergeant Charles L. Duke, a highly decorated LAPD veteran who was in charge of the LAPD SWAT team. Duke looked like a Marine Corps drill sergeant, like a fighting machine. He probably chews nails for breakfast.

He was the defense's use of force expert, their answer to Mark Conta. Duke thought that everything they did was just fine. There was no problem at all with beating the guy into submission. That's perfectly kosher, according to Duke.

Duke talked about how they stopped using the chokehold in 1982 and started using the baton more instead. The defense introduced a letter into evidence from his superior officer telling him not to use the chokehold. He said that in order to arrest a suspect, since they can't use the chokehold, they just have to jump in there and hit them with the baton.

I was a little confused. I was wide awake and feeling good and listening carefully, but this was a little confusing. As far as I was concerned, the excessive use of force in the Rodney King situation had nothing to do with whether or not the police had been crippled in their ability to control suspects by being deprived of their god-given right to the chokehold.

Rodney King was aggressive and combative, and they hit him several times, and I have no problems with that. The trouble is, he gave up, and they kept hitting him. That was the problem. All this talk about how terrible it is not to be able to use the chokehold is just a smoke screen. We weren't deciding if chokeholds are good or bad or batons are good or bad, but whether these people used excessive force. They kept giving us all this information about how great it is to use the chokehold and now we can't use it, so we have to break bones, and in my mind, I keep asking, "Why are they telling me all this?"

I'm listening day after day to all this stuff about team takedown and the swarm, and it is all just background information. The real issue is did they use too much force? They were trying to show that they were forced to use too much force. They had a grab bag of tools and they ran out of tools, but boy, if they just had that good old chokehold, they would have been okay.

I think they should have stepped back and let Rodney King surrender.

Duke had looked at the video, and he had interviewed Koon and reviewed his testimony from the first trial. He had talked to the other defendants in the case too. He said that you can't judge from the video alone, because you don't know what is in the officers' minds, or what they are perceiving.

This is well and good, but I didn't get to interview the officers. I didn't get to hear from all of them. The idea made sense to me, but the defense didn't do what Duke said was important. I would have liked to have heard Wind say that the reason he hit King was because King was trying to escape.

Duke went through the tape frame by frame, just like Conta did for the prosecution, telling us what we were supposed to think about what was happening. Now the prosecution was making all the same objections to what Duke said that the defense had made to Conta.

"Look he's telling them what to look for, he's evaluating the tape."

Duke said everything was in accordance with LAPD policy.

He went through the whole tape. He pointed out the Folsom roll, and said King wasn't properly performing the felony prone position.

Wind's kick looked like it was more violent than a baton blow, but Duke said if he wanted to hurt him he would have kicked him with his toe instead of with the flat side of his foot.

In fact, those kicks might have been the most humane thing that happened out there that night. The kicks might have caused Rodney King some pain, but Wind actually seemed to be pushing him down, rather than kicking him.

These people didn't know that they were being taped.

The only thing that Duke didn't like was Briseno, the turncoat. Everything was in policy except for what he did. He liked the way Koon handled things.

Duke liked himself. He had a major ego problem.

Duke testified that the Sam Browne belt police officers wear weighs a good ten pounds, and that officers are at a disadvantage when they start wrestling with a suspect, because they have so much equipment, and they have to protect it from being taken away.

Duke also said that the officers couldn't have swarmed King because "these police officers on the streets on March 3, 1991 didn't know what the swarm was."

He said that some officers have tunnel vision under stress, but that some are very aware of what is going on when they are in a fight.

He said the person in charge should be in an inactive role, directing the use of force, but stepping back to assess what is going on. Koon was doing that, but he was the one who fired the Taser. Duke said that was different from the way it normally happens.

He insisted all day long that every blow and kick was perfectly proper because King kept trying to get up. "An officer does not have to wait for a suspect to rise to his feet and attack them before they can use force."

Clymer asked him if the LAPD had any written policy that said that officers can beat suspects into submission.

Duke said there wasn't any document that said that.

"You, in your mind as an expert, equate overcoming resistance with beating into submission," Clymer asked sarcastically.

"If it takes a thousand baton blows to overcome resistance, then that's what it takes," Duke said.

TUESDAY, MARCH 23, 1993

Still on the stand, Duke said what caused King's facial injuries was his face smacking the ground when he fell.

I believe that.

The guy was being aggressive and combative, so deadly use of force could have been warranted. The policy is to go up the continuum of your tools, and when you hit someone in the head it is like shooting them; you have to be at the level of need for lethal force. Your life or someone else's has to be in danger to shoot them or to hit them in the head. You can shoot them or hit them in the head, but not until you get to that point.

I have no problem with him being hit in the head, because a reasonable police officer could assume that he was being attacked, so okay, hit him in the head.

So where do these facial injuries come from? I honestly believe the head blow was on the top of the head, the Taser hit King and he went down, and that's when his face hit the ground.

The only officer that Duke didn't have much to say about was Briseno. Briseno's lawyer, Harland Braun, didn't even cross-examine him.

When Stone did his redirect, he used a real loud voice and emphasized things. That was kind of his style. He was easy to listen to. He seemed to have just the right personality and the right speaking voice, the right vocabulary. He was very organized. But sometimes when he raised his voice, it seemed out of character, like he was being directed to do it. Like, there's a juror going to sleep, better raise the volume.

The defense had a jury expert there, and I believe she told them to talk faster or slower or louder, based on how we seemed to be receiving them. She was never introduced as part of the team, but she was always there. She never looked at any of the witnesses. She looked at the jury the whole time, to see how we were reacting.

Witness Number 51 was Ed Nowicki, a police training officer from Wisconsin who just happened to be in town and was an expert in baton training. He works for the Monadnock company that makes the batons, is a certified Monadnock trainer, and is also a police chief in some small town near Milwaukee. He had interviewed Powell to find out about his training in the baton, and he had looked at the video on television when it first was shown.

He thought Powell's training had been substandard. He said there was no way he could have used it properly because he never had the right training. He said Monadnock stresses dynamic training. You can't just hit a post, because the post isn't moving. You have to train by hitting something that tries to duck or tries to move. They had this Red Man Suit, a bunch of padding that a guy can wear, along with a helmet, and wrestle while you try to hit him with your club. The use of force people for the LAPD said they didn't believe in using the Red Man Suit kind of training.

Nowicki was Powell's witness. He said at first when he saw the tape, he thought it was police brutality, but he changed his mind. He thought what the police officers did was proper, but he criticized the LAPD training procedures.

He brought up another obvious issue. He said that you lose a lot of power after the first time you hit someone. The second time is only eighty percent or so, and you keep going down until you have no power at all. He thought Powell's strokes didn't have much power, due to poor training.

The fact that King lived after Powell hit him so much pretty much substantiates for me what Nowicki said about the blows becoming successively less powerful as the officer becomes more fatigued from hitting. Powell must have been pretty tired if those blows didn't kill King.

The prosecutors were objecting every other minute during Nowicki's testimony. On cross-examination they implied he hadn't fully reviewed the facts of the case. Nowicki conceded that he never looked at the medical records about King's injuries.

The fifty-second witness was William Arnado, the chief of police in some little city in Southern Oregon. He used to be a sergeant with the LAPD and moved to Oregon, but he adopted all of the LAPD policies because the LAPD is the best, he said. In 1988 he had gone back to the LAPD to train officers in the use of the baton, team takedown, the swarm and tangle team. Those are all basically different words for the same thing. Everybody grabs a leg and they take the guy down.

Conta had said they ought to have swarmed him. They just should have all gone in and jumped him. The defense is saying, that's easy to say, but none of our guys had any training in the swarm technique. In the testimony they brought out that you can only do the swarm when you are sure that the suspect doesn't have a weapon. King was dressed and had not been searched, so they couldn't very well swarm him, because he might have been armed.

# Chapter Thirty-One: Sergeant Stacey Koon

The next witness was Stacey Cornell Koon. He said he started with the LAPD on August 30, 1976 and used to work at the jail. He said he had used the Taser a hundred times there because it was the only weapon you were allowed to use in jail. When something happens, you pull out the Taser and take care of business. So he was probably as familiar with the Taser as anyone they could have brought in.

He had his master's degree from California State University, Los Angeles, in police science and one in public administration from the University of Southern California. He had two master's degrees and a bachelor's degree, and his intelligence and education showed when he talked. He had a lot of self-confidence. He acted like a guy who knew what he was talking about; a real believable type guy.

He was wearing a navy blue suit and a red tie, and he spoke softly most of the time. He's sure he's right about everything. He never says "I think." It's always, "That's the way it was."

He heard the call for the pursuit while he was still at the station at about 12:30 a.m. on March 3, 1991. He was the one who requested the helicopter.

He got on the radio and said he was on his way. "I wanted to catch up with the pursuit and involve myself in it and take control. I had a duty and a responsibility, according to the policy, to manage and control the situation."

King was on his knees facing east when Koon arrived on the scene. There were CHP and LAPD officers barricaded behind their cars, with their guns drawn, shouting orders at King.

Now, I made maps for a living, and at no time, in any of the sketches the lawyers put up, was I real familiar with what they were showing us. Koon was the only witness when he got up there who talked about directions. The others all said, "facing the front of the Hyundai" or "left" or "right." And everybody had his own perspective, so that's not a very meaningful description.

But Koon talked about east and west, and I still had no idea what he was talking about. I should have been able to understand him best, but nobody ever pointed out which way was east.

Koon described King as big and wet with sweat and tapping on the ground. He thought he was on PCP. "I could see the beads of sweat on his face. The only drug I know that raises the body temperature to cause sweating is PCP."

He explained how dangerous it is for the suspect to choose the place to stop. He'd been in all kinds of pursuits, and the most dangerous is when a suspect chooses his own stopping place, because then there is a chance he will have more places to hide. This place had a chain across the entrance, which is the only reason King couldn't have driven right into the bushes, in which case they might have had to shoot him or something else terrible.

"He's waving at the helicopter and he's kind of doing a little dance, if you will. He grabbed both his buttocks and kind of did a little gyration in the direction of the CHP officer."

Koon said he told the men to swarm him, but King threw the officers off. "When I saw that, it was one hundred percent confirmation that he was on PCP," Koon said. "He had thrown approximately eight hundred pounds of officers off his back."

Koon said he ran to his car and got a Taser gun. "I ordered him to get down, lay down. The look he gave me was, he looked at you but he looked through you. It's kind of a bizarre look. On the street, I've seen that look before many times with drug suspects."

Koon told him to stay down, and King got up, so Koon shot him in the back with the Taser. Koon said he was sure the Taser worked. He left it on for two or three seconds and turned it off. King got up again, so Koon tased him again. He left it on for three to five seconds, and King went down again.

He said that King howled when he was hit with the Taser and he mimicked the sound. "He talked to me in gibberish. He started talking to me, but it's no language I ever heard," he said.

"What I wanted to do was use the lowest level of force necessary to take Mr. King into custody," he said. "The safest thing for Mr. King, the safest thing for the officers, the safest thing for the citizens, is to have Mr. King on the ground."

At one point, Koon said, "That's my responsibility. I'm accountable for that."

We quit for the day right in the middle of all the action. We're into all this heavy stuff and everybody is really concentrating, and then we have to quit and go home. It gives them a chance to reorganize and when they start again it always seems to be at a different pace and a little more organized. In the morning they move right along. In the afternoon it seems to drag. I think at night the psychologist coaches them on whether to talk louder or softer. The lawyers have more energy in the morning; in the afternoon they are dragging and so are we.

Stacey Koon testified that nothing happened to Rodney King before the video camera was turned on, but I have big questions about that. Rodney King said that when he was on the ground and Melanie Singer was drag-stepping toward him that he felt pain in the side of his head. The LAPD was still behind their cars, so I'm wondering what happened to hurt Rodney's head? Did Tim Singer come over and kick him in the head? Where is Tim Singer during all this, anyway? Maybe King just made up that part about his head. He doesn't really know when he got hit. I don't think it happened the way King said.

Koon says Powell hit Rodney on the clavicle and King did a one-point landing. Duke had said that blow hit King in the head, and it looked like that's what happened on the video. I think we must have seen the video a thousand times. Duke testified to that, and I believe that is what happened.

The expert witness for the prosecution said the blow hit him under the nose. How could the baton hit his face if he aimed for the clavicle? I disagree with Koon on that. Duke got that right. It was on the top of his head. He had to think about the damage to his head. I think the blow hit him in the head, and the ground hit him in the cheekbone.

I think there is a good chance that Koon turned on the Taser again. Stone told us that if we listened to the audio we would hear the Taser. We listened but we never heard it. Okay, so what? It doesn't matter to me. I think Powell hit him in the head and there's a good chance Koon turned on the Taser and I don't see any problem with either one of them. It was justified. The man was running right at a police officer. It caused a lot of damage to the side of his face. I don't think police officers should be convicted of anything because of that. They were doing their job. Like Conta said, the man was combative and they were doing their job. I agree with both sides. Everybody said that was within policy.

"My intent was to cripple Rodney King," Koon said. "That is a better option than having to use deadly force, having to choke or having to shoot Rodney King."

Koon said that right after the incident, he talked to Tim and Melanie Singer and they confirmed that King was felony evading.

We took a break, and when we came back, Stone said he had a witness we had to hear out of order because the guy had to get to work, and he had to ride the bus, or something. It seemed kind of bizarre. I mean, they brought experts in from Wisconsin. Why couldn't they just give this guy a lift to work?

The witness was Stanley DeLeon. He refused to be sworn in. I guess he had some religious compunction about swearing. He said he would tell the truth but he wouldn't be sworn in. So there was a commotion and they had to have a sidebar at the bench about it, and finally the court clerk had to say something different that he usually did.

DeLeon turned out to be the operator at the hospital who received the communication that King had lacerations and was on PCP, so that was what they were expecting at the hospital when he was brought in.

He was only on the witness stand for about ten minutes. I believed every word he said, but it seemed like a big mistake to interrupt their most important witness for one who added nothing.

Koon was back on the stand after him.

Right in the middle of a question, Stone would stop and get a drink of water. The witnesses and lawyers all had a glass of water in front of them.

The jurors would like water too. We asked Jim Holmes, the court clerk, if the jurors could have water too, and he said, "No, we've tried that."

Stone drank quite a bit. The defense all had imported bottled water. The prosecution had tap water.

Koon said that just before Powell requested the ambulance, he looked really tired. When you request an ambulance, you have to say where it is, and what happened to the person. Koon said Powell paused, and Koon said, "beating," and Powell repeated, "beating."

That's what I wrote down, that they said, "beating."

We listened to the tape of Powell calling the ambulance. It was unbelievable. The guy was laughing out loud. Somebody testified that it was nervous laughter.

Koon said Powell didn't laugh at all. But what I heard was Powell laughing. And laughing very hard. He was cracking up. It was like this was one of the funniest things he had ever said. He laughed for ten or fifteen seconds. This was no nervous hee-hee-hee. This was a full blown belly laugh.

This guy thought it was funny. He thought the whole thing was funny.

Koon testified about the computer messages he sent from the police car, the one that said, *You had a big time use of force*, and the other that said, *You need another Taser*. I didn't think either one of those messages was out of line. I don't know if they thought that it showed callousness, or what, but to me it was a perfectly logical message to send to your superior officer.

In his report for that day, Koon wrote that there was a torrent of baton blows. He said there ought to be some roll call training for the younger officers so they wouldn't lose control in this kind of situation. He said they should have some game playing or training on how to use the baton when the guy is moving.

He said some of the younger officers were too nervous, too uptight.

Koon went back to the office afterwards and mentioned to DiStefano that Powell was deficient in his use of the baton. He got a new Taser and he went to the hospital.

Koon said that at the hospital, King told him, "I love you."

He talked to Dr. Mancia, who said that King had minor cuts, and since he might be on PCP they were going to take him to USC Hospital to be looked at. Koon said he told Powell to call Valley Traffic Division for booking permission.

I'm wondering, Powell's been around a while. How come Koon had to tell him everything? He told Powell to take the backseat out of the car and tie King to the floor. He tells Powell to do all of these things. I had a zillion questions to ask. You think, "Now why didn't he ask that?" You never get any satisfaction for those questions.

Koon told Powell to go to directly to USC, and he thought it was okay for them to go in a squad car because King had no serious injuries. When Koon left Pacifica, he went back to the station. Powell was there, and Koon said, "I thought you were going directly to USC."

Powell said he had to get the probation hold, some paperwork, and Koon said, "Oh, okay."

If I had somebody working for me and I told him to do something one way and found him doing it another way, I'd ask, "Don't you like working here?"

The officers don't seem to know about booking procedures. They must do this everyday, but they keep having to have twenty people tell us how to book someone. We listened to all this discussion about the proper way to book someone. Some officers think you ought to take him right to USC and some think you have to take him to the station first.

What's wrong with Koon, how come he doesn't know how to arrest somebody?

Koon testified that he got a call at 7 a.m. on March 5 from Sergeant Pollard, who told him about the videotape they were showing on television. At 8:30, an hour and a half later, Koon called Mutz and said there was no problem.

Koon wasn't concerned that there was a videotape. He didn't think anything was going to happen. He figured he was there, and everything was okay.

He didn't feel guilty about anything.

THURSDAY, MARCH 25, 1993

Koon was still on the stand. They presented his in-service training record. He spent a lot of time getting trained. There were some exhibits about the training bulletin, escalation and de-escalation, the video, we went through all those things again.

They discussed the radio calls. The Code 4 was at 00:50:29 and the call for the ambulance was at 00:54:20, so the whole thing took four minutes from beginning to end.

If you took eighty-one seconds off the back of that, you can tell the distance from the Code 4.

How could Koon get there so fast? He must have been going 120 miles an hour. He got there one minute later, and it was two miles away. That was a question in my mind as this was all going on. How did he get there so fast? He must have started before they called a Code 4, when he heard about the pursuit, but that only started two minutes earlier than that.

When he got out of the car, he saw Rodney King, and he was sweating. It was colder than hell that night. Holliday had to go back in his apartment and get a sweater, it was so cold. So they are trying to tell us again that the guy must be on PCP to be sweating on a cold night.

At this point, I'm not sure that is important. It is important only because it detracts from intent. They're trying to convince us that they had to act the way they did because King was a superhuman guy on PCP. Well, Rodney King was holding still. I don't care if he was on PCP, he wasn't moving, and Powell was still hitting him.

The fact is, he was lying there passively and he got hit. So what difference does it make that he was on PCP? All the stuff about his eyes bouncing and the sweating; I don't care about any of that because he was on the ground not moving and he still got hit.

Koon said every time King moved he was worrying about the Taser wires. The man acted through the whole situation as though those wires were important. I was kind of wondering about the Taser and did it really have any effect. The people at the hospital said there weren't any in his skin and the police said it didn't matter whether they were in the skin, it would have worked anyway. So that's always a question; did it work or didn't it?

Koon was asked about the log. Why wasn't the report more accurate? Why didn't you mention the kicks? Apparently in the state trial he had testified that he didn't see Wind apply his foot to King. Well, there were no kicks, but there were stomps. A kick is a more violent thing. You are trying to hurt the person. When Wind stomped him, he was just trying to get him back on the ground. It was more like he pushed him with his foot, than kicked him.

They brought up this point that King was hostile for more than an hour at the hospital. Some people said he was, and some said he wasn't. The paramedics acted like spitting blood was hostile. I think the guy was trying to breathe.

We looked at the tape again. It is amazing how fast things

happened in eighty-one seconds. In slow motion, it takes forever. In regular speed it is over pretty fast. It is amazing how different it looks at the real speed.

Clymer asked Koon, "So this wily convict on PCP puts his hands up and made you believe it was now safe to send in one 150-pound officer to handcuff him?"

"I gave Rodney King the benefit of the doubt," Koon said. "I believed the baton and the pain had gone through his drugged state of mind."

"So you believed that King had been beaten into submission?" Clymer asked.

"That's absolutely correct. He had been beaten into submission," Koon replied.

Clymer also got Koon to admit that the officers didn't follow the procedures for dealing with PCP suspects. If they really thought he was on PCP, they should have moved cautiously and not agitated King.

Clymer showed the tape again and had Koon interpret it.

At a point where King is up on one knee, with his arm up to ward off blows, Clymer asked, "It was your perception that evening that what you saw by Mr. King was a martial arts tactic designed to take an officer's baton and use it against him?"

Koon said it was.

"I take it that what you saw that night you did not interpret as a drunken man trying to protect himself?"

"No, sir, I did not," Koon said.

# Chapter Thirty-Two: Officer Melanie Singer

FRIDAY, MARCH 26, 1993

The fifty-fourth witness was California Highway Patrol Officer Melanie Singer. She was a prosecution witness in the Simi Valley trial, but the defense called her in the federal case we were hearing.

Michael Stone had re-enacted the entire chase on video, with a camera mounted in his Mercedes-Benz, and he played the tape and had Melanie point out what was happening. Now this was not a police car, and most of the time he was in the fourth lane, and Melanie was testifying that she had been in the third lane. It looked on the tape like it was dark, but actually the sun was half up.

She testified they were going eighty miles per hour, and she claimed that the Highway Patrol car stopped twenty-five feet to the left of Rodney King when he finally stopped.

At about this point, they interrupted her testimony to put on another witness, a Dr. David Giannetto, a physician at Los Angeles County-USC Medical Center. They had to interrupt to get him on because he had to leave to go to work, or something.

Dr. Giannetto testified that he talked to Dr. Mancia on the telephone. He said he never would have agreed to having King moved over to USC if he realized he had as many internal injuries as he had. The relevance appeared to be that there was some intent to hurt King by not getting him to the doctor fast enough. That's baloney because they took him to Pacifica, and a medical doctor sewed him up and said he was okay. The LAPD guys aren't doctors. If Mancia said he was okay, they went with that. It didn't take any major intelligence to see that his face was caved in, and Mancia ought to have been able to see that.

Powell had said he had multiple head wounds, but then Mancia looked at him and said, no harm, no foul, take him to USC. Mancia told them it was okay to transport him to the other hospital in the police car.

Giannetto said he examined King between 6 and 6:15 in the morning, started an IV, requested some X-rays and went home. He said Dr. Henderson took over after that.

It was like, *I'm off the clock, I'm out of here.* I got a big kick out of that. It was, *Take over, dude, I'm out of here.*

He said he thought that King had facial fractures and leg fractures. I'm sure that King was in pain. Broken bones hurt.

Giannetto wasn't on the stand long, and then Melanie Singer came back. She testified that it took King two minutes to get out of the car. She testified that he wasn't wearing his seatbelt.

She said that Tim Singer told King to raise his arms and he did what she called a pitter-patter dance, with his left hand on the car, and one hand waving at the helicopter. She said she felt there was a danger from King. He grabbed his right buttock and shook it at her. She told him they weren't playing games, and got out her gun. He got down on all fours, like a dog, she said. Somebody from the LAPD was shouting, "Get to the ground, get to the ground." She told King to prone himself.

I am thinking to myself, he might not have known what she meant by that. She was in the full-blown felony-stop mode. She was using all of the CHP's procedures for handing a super dangerous criminal. She had her gun out.

Then Koon told her to get back, the LAPD officers did the swarm, and Powell came from the left and Briseno from the right, and King broke loose and stood up. She said there were six or eight LAPD guys on King, but the only ones she recognized were Powell and Briseno. That's one of the signs that she was losing it, because she testified that she saw six or eight guys, and really there were only four.

She testified that King got shot with the Taser, staggered and his face was vibrating. She said that Powell hit King and there was blood all over King's cheek. She testified that King yelled and Powell struck him again. I don't think that it actually happened that way. She testified that King's face was split open from ear to chin. Now there might have been blood, but there was no split, no big long cut, on King's face. She said Powell hit King right in the face, but King's hands were over his face, so he hit his hands. One or two people testified that King had his hands over his face. We never heard any evidence that there were serious injuries to his hands, and hands break easy.

But Melanie Singer said he got hit in the head and there was blood all over his face, and then he got hit again, and had his hands over his face. I don't think she was lying. I think that is really what she thinks she saw.

She said the first blow was to the right side of the head, the second to the face, and three, four, five and six were to the left side of the head. Then she testified that the sergeant said, Stop, that's enough, and that's when Briseno grabbed the baton. She never saw King's face hit the ground or heard the clicking of a Taser. I think she testified she had never even seen a Taser before.

She was asked if she was aware that according to the video, Powell never hit King's left side. She said she saw him hit on the left side.

The first blow occurred while King was standing, and then he got knocked to the ground, and that's where the tape gets blurry. So maybe he did get hit in the face during that part. But the blows I saw in the video tape were definitely to his back, not his face.

In the blurry section, I saw Powell swing four times and then King started moving and they hit him some more.

Melanie lost it when she was describing the beatings, and started to cry. She buried her face in her hands. "As soon as he fell and caught himself, Officer Powell came up to the right side of the driver, with his baton out, and struck the right side of the driver's face. I saw blood come out of the side of his cheek; I heard the driver scream. The driver then clasped both hands over his face as Officer Powell then stepped forward and delivered another power swing."

She said the blood was squirting out of King's face.

Stone showed her a big picture of King's face, and said there was no ear-to-chin slash on his face.

"What I remember that evening is what I remember," she insisted.

"You were shocked by what you saw, weren't you?" Stone asked, apparently meaning that maybe she was remembering it wrong.

"I still am," she replied, sniffling.

"That's why you broke down and cried here?"

"Yes, sir, I'm human," Singer answered.

Briseno was holding his face in his hands while Stone was questioning Singer.

She testified that she was afraid to help King after it was over, for fear the other officers would laugh at her. My impression was that she thought it was the right thing to do to help the guy out, but because she was a woman in this macho world, she was afraid they would all laugh at her.

Melanie testified that she thought that Powell was the only one who ever hit King. She never saw Wind hit him at all. She also testified that she was in the emergency room and King still had the darts in him. Actually, he never had the darts in him at all. They were in his shirt.

Melanie Singer was just too much. I believed what she said about the chase, about how they followed him and he didn't stop, and all of that. But I could not believe that a policewoman would cry about blood and violence. I mean, she must see blood and gore every day. How could she possibly do her job as a California Highway Patrol officer if she couldn't tolerate seeing a little blood and guts? She must be at the scenes of accidents. She must see pathetic scenes of injured people, hurt children, dead animals. If she cries at the sight of blood, she's in the wrong business. I was in Vietnam, and I saw some blood. I cannot imagine crying seeing Rodney King. There wasn't even that much blood.

As far as I was concerned, she was completely unbelievable after she cried. The woman was all emotion.

MONDAY MARCH 29, 1993

Melanie Singer resumed testifying. She said that King wasn't sweating, had no vacant stare, and wasn't speaking gibberish. She didn't smell anything on his breath either, and he definitely was not superhuman, because he felt pain.

She also said she didn't hear anyone taunt King or say, "What's up, killer," or any of the things that King testified they said to him.

Tieger briefly cross-examined her. She said King "just appeared to be a very drunk man" who was giving officers a hard time. When he asked her to describe the blows, she broke down again.

Tieger asked why she didn't administer first aid and she said she started to, but stopped because, "I didn't want them to start heckling me."

She said that while they were calling the ambulance she talked to King and he told her his name was Glen. The other officers were standing around shooting the bull. "It appeared to me that they were joking around. I couldn't understand why they were just standing around, while this guy's laying there."

She was very emotional. She cried. It was like reliving a bad dream for her. "I will never forget it until the day I die."

Throughout her testimony, she referred to Tim Singer as "my partner-husband," or "my partner, Tim Singer." She never said, "my husband." Just "my husband-partner." It was kind of strange. I kept wondering where Tim Singer was. When was he going to come on? When were we going to hear from him?

One of the female jurors, Cathy, told me she thought that Melanie Singer looked just like her. She said looking at Melanie Singer was like looking in a mirror. I suppose there is some resemblance, but Cathy was better looking.

# Chapter Thirty-Three: The Defense Rests

Next came the fifty-sixth witness, Kathleen Bosak, the fire department paramedic at Station 81 at Nordhoff and Woodman. She said her partner that night, Victor Cruz, was dead now. She didn't say what happened to him.

She said they left at 1 a.m., with her driving and Victor in the back, and it took five or six minutes to get to the scene.

She said King wasn't really bleeding that much. She said there were approximately two spoonfuls of blood on the ground. Melanie Singer had told us that Rodney King was lying in a pool of blood. Now, if it were my blood, two spoonfuls would seem like a lot.

Bosak said she didn't use any lights or sirens on the way to Pacifica Hospital.

She said that King was combative and swearing and wouldn't let them take his blood pressure. She said he was spitting blood at the paramedics and Victor asked him to stop.

She said there was no sign that King had any pain in his right leg, and that she didn't hear any joking or laughing in the ambulance.

I thought this paramedic was kind of cute. She was petite, with straight dark hair, which she had in some kind of a bun. I guess she looked like she could be a paramedic. But then, everybody appeals to me. It's a sign of growing old that all younger women are appealing.

My pen ran out of ink as the next witness began. That was my government-issued official juror's pen. I had to reach for my own pen.

The next witness was Charles Grongna, who said he had worked for the sheriff's department for twenty-five years, and was now retired. He transported Rodney King on the sheriff's bus more than twenty-four hours later, and said that King had a cast on his right leg and his face was swollen, but he was still being aggressive. He said he put King up front in the bus where he could watch him, and wrote a memo about how aggressive King was being.

He said King admitted to him that he was resisting arrest when he was beaten.

The fifty-eighth witness was Lindsay Brummel, a lieutenant for the LAPD for twenty years. He was doing day duty at the jail. He was Sergeant Schadel's supervisor. Schadel was Witness Number 30, the guy who testified about how to arrest people.

Brummel was really boring. He testified that he was acting commander of the jail division and had ordered an audit of their procedures to check into the booking process. He said that King left Pacifica Hospital at 3:31 a.m., was booked at 4:17 a.m., and arrived at USC at 5:35 a.m. The point was that the way Rodney King was booked was okay, as opposed to what Schadel told us.

He said the stop at the station was "absolutely the best way of doing business."

Next up was Charles Higbee, who retired in 1987 after thirty years as a cop. He taught use of force at California State University, Fullerton. He had investigated the use of force in 1,700 LAPD cases. He talked about how people under stress suffer from tunnel vision, time distortion, sequence distortion and lag time. He said he found in the cases he investigated, that even though people mean to tell the truth, that what they think they saw is not necessarily what actually happened. He said that people who are involved in the use of force are the least likely to get the facts straight, so they always have someone else investigate the situation.

On cross-examination, Barry Kowalski suggested that the LAPD is negligent in investigating the use of force, and Higbee said that in the 1,700 use of force cases he investigated, only nine ended up with the officers being accused of criminal charges.

The next witness was George Davis, the man who taught Powell how to use the baton. He said that Powell could use the baton effectively, but said he had never taught him the team takedown or the swarm.

There was a jar of coffee beans in the Hilton Hotel restaurant, and some of us took to carrying a few coffee beans in our pockets to suck on when the testimony got boring. It tasted awful, but it kept us awake.

TUESDAY, MARCH 30, 1993

Davis came back on the stand and said he had a meeting last week with the government attorneys and the FBI and he now believed that Powell might have actually gotten some training in how to perform the swarm technique, but that he was never tested on it.

I was bored this morning, right off the bat. I was doodling and doing mathematical formulas in the margins of my notebook.

Dr. Dallas Long III testified next. He was a dental surgeon, graduated from the University of Southern California in 1966, and became a doctor in 1972. He had been a resident in surgery in Arizona and was board certified as an emergency room medic.

I was really getting tired.

Long said that five months after the incident, King had to go back and have more surgery to get a small rock or a piece of sand out of the scar, which had been causing him pain.

They showed us a video about the damage to King's head. It was a real nice video, in color. It had a 3-D graphic of a plastic skull that rotated, and showed where the damage was. He said the fractures were probably caused by hitting ground or a flat surface. He said there was no way it could have been from a baton blow.

"Is there anything in the medical evidence that suggests a baton blow like this?" Stone asked, demonstrating with a baton on DePasquale, Wind's lawyer, who was kneeling in the courtroom acting the part of the suspect.

"There is not," Long said.

Still demonstrating on DePasquale, Stone imitated the blows that Melanie Singer described, and Long said that King's injuries weren't consistent with that version, either.

He said there was no injury to King's hands, no hand fractures. Some test they performed showed an enzyme emitted from the muscles that showed there was a lot of injury to the muscles, which is caused by overuse of electricity or other major blows to the muscles. It was obvious that King had major blows to the right biceps, so I don't know what that test proved.

The video showed King talking, but there was no sound. We couldn't hear what he said. It showed the dynamics of how his face worked when he talked. It didn't look like he was in that much pain.

The doctor thought that the injuries were from falling and twisting his head. I think so too. The other test showed he had injuries that could have been caused by the Taser, and we know that this guy got tased.

Clymer tried to undermine Long by questioning his credentials. He pointed out that he never completed a residency in surgery and wasn't an expert in biomechanics.

Long said it was "something of a hobby."

The next witness was Dr. Carly Ward, who was a bona fide biomechanical engineer. She said the body is an "articulated structure." She was an expert in brain injuries, and had been retained to evaluate Rodney King's injuries. She talked about experiments to see what kind of injuries occur from various accidents. She tested dead bodies, dropping weights on them to see how much force it takes to fracture different bones.

We were instructed not to discuss the evidence, but there was some humor in the van on the way back to the hotel about "What do you do for a living, Carly?"

"Oh, I torture dead bodies."

WEDNESDAY, MARCH 31, 1993

Carly was back. She talked about how much force it takes to break the zygomatic arch in the face. She had her daughter and Powell hit some force plates to see if Powell could have caused the fractures with his baton. She said her daughter could hit harder than Powell, but that Powell could still hit with two thousand pounds of pressure. She said the injuries to Rodney King could have been caused by less than five hundred pounds of pressure, but that if Powell had hit him full tilt with two thousand pounds of pressure, it would have pulverized his whole head.

We knew how hard Powell was capable of hitting, but there was no way of telling how hard he actually hit him.

She showed us a video of a Taser experiment where a guy is sitting in his office, and they tase him, and he falls over and hits his head on a stack of books. It didn't look very scientific to me. They should have made some arrangements for the guy's safety.

She talked about a computer program called Dynamo that is used to simulate a body falling. I think she had something to do with programming it. She went though the whole thing and a lot of numbers. She said King was going 11.2 miles per hour when he fell.

She said there was more than enough pressure to cause the facial fractures, and in fact, if Powell hit King in the head with the baton, he ought to be dead. "All of the facial fractures were caused by the fall."

When Tieger cross-examined her, he challenged her qualifications as an expert, introducing evidence that a California appeals court once reversed a conviction in which she testified in a case about little kids' broken bones. The court said they found "flagrant loopholes" in her procedures, Tieger said.

She had this big grin on her face. I felt like she was saying, "What are you going to do about it? I already made my money." She said the court misunderstood what she was trying to do.

I personally was not impressed with the woman. For most scientific experiments you need a big sample. A true scientist wouldn't use her own daughter. She ought to have gone out and gotten policemen who were trained in the baton.

After Ward stepped down, Laurence Powell's lawyer, Michael Stone, rested his case without calling Powell to testify. He walked over to Powell and talked to him for a few minutes, his hand resting on his shoulder, and then he said that Powell rested.

After that, Paul DePasquale started presenting the case on behalf of his client, Timothy Wind. His first witness was Bryant Allen, the backseat man. He said he and King and Freddie Helms had been drinking forty-ounce bottles of Olde English malt liquor in the park, and that he thought King was acting strange. He said when the CHP was chasing them, he kept telling King to pull over.

"I got louder each time I told him. I said, 'Rodney, why don't you pull over?' " Allen said.

His story was a little different from King's. He claimed he didn't hear any racial taunting, but he also answered a lot of questions by saying he wasn't sure or he couldn't remember.

He mentioned in passing that Freddie Helms had died since then, and I thought it was kind of strange that King never mentioned that during his testimony. Nobody ever told us what he died of.

I'm sitting here in the jury box wondering what happened to Freddie Helms? The way the system works, the lawyers ask the questions for the information they want to have come out, but there is a lot of information they don't care about that we just never hear anything about. One of the other jurors said he had heard that Helms had been killed in an alcohol-related traffic accident.

April Fool's Day.

I'd had it up to my eyeballs with having to wait out in the hall every morning for Gary to be the last juror out of his room. Jason, the federal marshal in charge of babysitting us, would race up and down the halls shouting for us to come on out, and Gary would still be asleep. His attitude was that he refused to come out one minute before time to get on the elevator, and he didn't care if the rest of us had to all stand there and wait by the elevator for him.

I'm the kind of guy, if I have to be in the hallway by 7:15, I'd be out there at 6:40, so I'd had it with Gary's attitude.

Since it was April Fool's Day, I got up at 5 a.m., put on my pants without taking a shower and went out and alerted the marshals to my plan so they wouldn't shoot me. At 5:30, I pounded about ten times as hard as I could on Gary's door. I thought there was a chance Gary might come out and hit me, so I just moseyed on down toward my room.

Gary stuck his head out. "What?"

"April Fool," I called out from about fifty feet down the hall.

"Oh, thanks," Gary said vaguely, retreating back inside.

You'd think a guy who valued his sleep enough to wait to get up till the last minute, and who was rude enough to keep everyone else waiting day after day, would have been cranky about my waking him up. But apparently Gary could take a joke. He really wasn't mad.

Court was pretty boring. I was listening, but I wasn't getting a lot out of it this morning. It pretty much seemed to me like the exciting part was over.

DePasquale read aloud some interviews with King in jail in which he said he had been handcuffed and hog-tied before they started beating him. Later he changed his story, which obviously does not jibe at all with the videotape.

The prosecution agreed to stipulate that King had said those things in the interviews.

Then DePasquale stood up and said that Wind rested.

The judge asked if he had anything more and he said, we're outta here.

Clymer looked upset.

Harland Braun got up and put Briseno's left boot into evidence.

In his opening statement, Braun had said that Briseno's boot was light as a ballet slipper. That was an exaggeration, but it was a lightweight boot with a rubber sole, not some kind of combat boot.

Then Braun announced that Briseno rested.

Then Clymer looked really upset. He didn't have his rebuttal witnesses ready to testify, so we got the rest of the day and Friday off. That just meant spending the time at the hotel, watching television and bouncing off the walls, so it was no treat.

The end of the defense case seemed to take everyone by surprise.

# Chapter Thirty-Four: Winding Up

Basically we didn't do anything at all today. They kept us waiting around in the jury room all day. We didn't even get into court until four o'clock in the afternoon, and then we just were sent home.

Judge Davies told us that the federal marshals would make arrangements for us to meet our "religious obligations" on Easter Sunday, which was coming up the next weekend.

TUESDAY, APRIL 6, 1993

We heard from a new prosecution witness, LAPD Deputy Chief Matthew V. Hunt. He was the boss of all training in 1983, and he wrote a letter to Duke telling him to stop using the chokehold. He was forcing Duke to do something Duke didn't think was right, Duke had testified. Duke had said that Hunt told him to train officers to use the batons to break bones, and Hunt said he never gave that order.

There were a lot of exhibits about the baton, and about the use of blankets and nets. I was really bored.

We saw the video of Briseno's testimony in the first trial. I don't really like watching television unless it is real exciting. It puts me to sleep. I was bored watching the videotape of Briseno. He was sitting right there. I kept wondering why they didn't just bring him up, put him on the witness stand, and ask him.

On the tape, Briseno claims he thought Powell's blow was a glancing blow, and that he thought it was just accidental. He said he yelled at Powell to get off. He said many of his actions were intended to "stop Officer Powell."

We could never hear any discussion between the officers the whole time. Gebhardt testified that Powell told him the guy was on PCP and he should get back. We didn't hear that they were discussing anything at all.

Briseno said on the tape that he was angry, upset and frustrated, that he thought that King was non-combative and he saw misconduct on the part of the other officers, which he did not report. He said he thought King was turning to the left when he stepped on him. He says that King never tried to get up.

I thought, oh boy, we're going to get to find out what Briseno said in the first trial. I knew he was the turncoat. "Benedict" Briseno. But I couldn't see the point of this. I didn't know why they were showing this tape.

I was just really tired. A lot of it was emotional. I was separated from my wife and my kid and I was more and more exhausted every day. It was just building up. The pressure was building on me.

All of the jurors were trying to listen and pay attention, but it was just too dry. Even the judge nodded off from time to time, and one of the attorneys, Braun, fell asleep.

So what I got out of this tape was that Briseno had said he was shocked by the other officers' behavior, but apparently not enough to report any misconduct. There was nothing there that affected me one way or another.

After we saw the tape, the prosecution rested and the defense recalled Koon to the stand.

Koon said that Briseno's version didn't square with what he told us, but he accounted for that by saying that they saw it from different angles. "Oftentimes what happens is, different officers are in different positions, different officers have different information. That is why I, as a supervisor, stand back," Koon said.

Clymer pointed out that in the book Koon had written about the Simi Valley trial, he said that Briseno testified that he stopped Powell because Powell was "out of control."

"That's what he said," Koon replied calmly.

Clymer said that Koon had called Briseno a liar in his book.

"I've taken the position he's taken a different perspective," Koon said. "That doesn't make him a liar. That just means he didn't see what I saw."

My notes were going downhill. I was tired of listening.

As Koon stepped down, Judge Davies smiled. "That's it, ladies and gentlemen. You've heard all the evidence."

Judge Davies told us that we had Wednesday off, then would hear closing arguments on Thursday. He said we would probably begin deliberations on Friday and continue through the Easter weekend. The end of another day. We were all tired.

# Chapter Thirty-Five: Fifty-Two Days

On Saturdays, we went on outings that were within an hour's drive of the hotel in downtown Los Angeles. The vans they used to transport us had the windows covered so other motorists couldn't see us, which meant we also couldn't see out, and it would have been unpleasant to ride much farther under those conditions.

The first Saturday we went to the Rose Bowl, and the next weekend we went to Griffith Park. A few of us charged up the hill, with a marshal right behind us. We got up to the top and stood there and enjoyed the view for a while. Meanwhile some of the others decided to walk up, too. They came to a flood control dam with gravel, and when Jim was chivalrously trying to help one of the women, he fell and rolled down an embankment. He got scraped up, but his toupee didn't fall off, which was circumstantial evidence, I guess, that he didn't wear one.

It was an ongoing gag with those of us who sat right behind him in the back row of the van that Jim's hair was just too perfect. Jim never had a bad hair day. Never a hair out of place. We whispered that it had to be a rug, and I threatened to put a strip of Velcro on the ceiling of the van. Then, I said, when we hit a bump, Jim would hit his head on the roof and his hair would stay there. We asked Ruth to run her fingers through his hair and let us know. She reported back that she knew for a fact that his hair was all his. How she knew, we didn't ask.

We went to Griffith Park three times during the trial. Usually we took along sandwiches the Hilton kitchen staff had prepared for us, but on George's birthday, we celebrated by barbecuing hamburgers. On one of our hikes, we saw a baby rattlesnake on the path, and our marshal, Jason, drew his gun. Somebody threw a rock in the bushes, and Jason nearly jumped out of his skin.

On another Saturday, we went on the tour at Universal Studios. First, we had lunch at Victoria Station. We went in a back door and through a side gate and ate in our own little private area. Fred saw some people he knew in the restaurant and they came over to us, but the marshals shooed them away.

After lunch we got onto our own private tram. A public relations guy took us around. There was plenty of room for the fifteen of us.

I had been to Universal Studios when they first opened, but I'm not impressed with Hollywood, so I'd never been back. I didn't mind going when the government was paying for it, though, not to mention paying me forty dollars a day for my time.

I was sitting next to Mark, the exceedingly macho leader of all the Yew-nited States marshals, when we went through the earthquake simulation. When the tram rocked, he grabbed my knee.

"Please," I protested, "I'm already spoken for."

We got to go in first to the bird shows, and the animal show and the western show. We walked right in and sat in reserved seats in the front row. The other people waiting in line gave us dirty looks. I was so spoiled I'll never go there again. I can't imagine standing in line.

On another occasion we went to the Universal Cineplex theater complex and saw the film *Groundhog Day*, which is about a guy who does the same thing over and over every day. We really identified with that guy.

One Saturday we drove down to Newport Beach and went deep-sea fishing. California has a state law that you have to have a fishing license. I was told the marshals got fishing licenses for us, but we never had to sign for them. Usually you have to sign your name to get a license, and of course, we were anonymous.

I asked Mark several times how they were going to get us licenses if we couldn't sign our names and most of us didn't have any IDs with us. Mark kept saying, "Don't worry, Bob, we're going to take care of all that."

I thought it would be pretty funny if the Rodney King jury got arrested for fishing without a license.

It was a real luxury to go deep-sea fishing courtesy of the taxpayers. Everybody went but Daryl. Some of the women were worried that they might get seasick, but the marshal who did our shopping bought those anti-seasick patches for us.

The federal government chartered a whole fishing boat just for the jury. It usually holds fifty people, with a crew in the galley, and we could order all the food we wanted all day long. There was a lot of crew, because they were prepared for fifty people, and they helped the women bait the hooks. I caught my hook on the bottom of the boat and they cut it off and taught me how to tie a hook.

Everybody caught fish. I caught ten, mostly mackerel, but one fairly good size calico bass.

We all put five dollars in a jackpot for whomever caught the biggest fish. Gary got a big fish, and Eric had a big one. Some of the guys were real fishermen. Jim wound up winning the money with a big halibut, about twenty pounds. The crew cleaned the fish and some of the jurors took them back to the hotel with them.

Since it was all free, everybody was going to the galley all day ordering hamburgers and burritos. We bought thirty dollars' worth of candy among the fourteen of us. I brought four candy bars back to the hotel in my pocket. Normally I stay away from candy bars, but I was saying, "I'll have one of those, and one of those."

The only restriction was that we weren't allowed to drink on the boat. And the only misfortune to befall any of us was that Anne, who apparently didn't comprehend the simplistic nature of a bird's digestive system, stood out on the deck looking up while the seagulls were feeding, and wound up with brown globs all over her slacks and shirt, her hair and her face. I helped her mop up with paper towels.

A bad thing about being sequestered was that I missed being outside. I like being able to get up and go out if I want to. Locked up in a courtroom all day and in a hotel room at night was very claustrophobic.

Being outside only once a week wasn't enough, so Mark made arrangements for us to go out on a patio at the Hilton after work. We had to go through the marketing department, and we had to go in groups, accompanied by a marshal. It was April, so it was cold out there by the pool, but at least it was some fresh air.

Sundays were rough. There wasn't much to amuse us besides the weekly hour-long visits with family and friends, which were under the vigilant eye of the marshals, whose further duty it was to confiscate any contraband or illegal substances some friends may have attempted to smuggle in. There was a rumor that some visitors tried to smuggle in marijuana to one of the younger jurors. I don't know if it was true or not, but that's what everyone said. Supposedly the marshals found it when they searched them.

There was a sign-up sheet and you put down which hour you wanted your visitors to come. I tried to sign up for an early hour so it wouldn't ruin my wife's whole day. She came every Sunday but one, when she had a ticket to go to the Music Center.

It was against the rules, but I would write my wife a note and hand it to her during visitations. I didn't write about the trial.

George would have his wife walk over to the window so he could whisper to her.

We never had any privacy at all.

Sex was a hot topic around the campfire, mostly because we weren't having any. Toward the end of the trial, George told me if he started to make a move on one of the women I should shoot him. He said she was starting to look good to him.

I said, "You're a sick man."

The marshals rented three videos for us nearly every day, from a gargantuan list the Hilton provided. There were restrictions, however. We couldn't see anything that had to do with the judicial system, or anything the marshals deemed to be too violent or to have racial overtones. I requested *12 Angry Men* but they nixed it.

Mostly, we had no problems agreeing on what we were going to watch, except for Sunday mornings, when George liked to watch golf matches on television. Now, I am a golfer, but I have to say there are few things more boring than watching golf on television. So sometimes that caused some dissension.

A marshal sat right there with us, with the remote control in his hand, and he snapped it off if anything came on he thought was inappropriate. Some of the marshals turned off the news if it involved Nelson Mandela. Others seemed to think there was a remote possibility that Mandela's situation was going to affect the Rodney King trial in Los Angeles, or vice versa.

There were no television sets in our hotel rooms, or telephones, for that matter. We were allowed to make monitored calls to our families, but when the allotted time for telephoning was over, the marshals snatched those phones up and locked them up in their office.

We got the Sunday papers with holes cut out where any stories appeared involving racial conflict, violence, or, of course, our trial. The result was that you might be reading a perfectly innocent story that jumped to another page, only to find the end missing because the marshals had cut out the story on the other side of the page. One day the entire sports section was missing. Boy, did that make me mad. Later I found out that Rodney King had attended a Dodgers game and there was a photo of him with Darryl Strawberry on the front page of the sports section.

At our meals, we usually ate at one big table. The marshals said we were one of the most congenial juries they had ever seen. They had seen a lot of juries, but never one that got along as well as we did, especially considering how long we were sequestered.

Gary must have been surviving on the snacks, because he didn't eat breakfast and seldom came to dinner. There were cookies, crackers, popcorn, fruit and nuts in the TV room all the time, so it was possible to get by just on the snacks.

Gary had temper tantrums. He wore Levi's with holes in the knees most of the time, and the people who did the laundry at the hotel put creases in them. When you're in your twenties, creases in your Levi's is a major faux pas. Gary yelled at the marshals for allowing his tattered jeans to get creased. He ranted and raved and told the marshals they better not let it happen again. Everybody laughed when the marshal said, "Don't have your pants washed then, man."

Twice a week, the marshals took us to a restaurant for dinner. Liberated from the need to pick up the check, a lot of us were ordering a lot more than we would if we were paying for it ourselves. If a couple of entrees looked good, we just ordered both of them.

The marshals weren't allowed to order food when we went to restaurants. They would have had to pay for theirs. So I would order appetizers for them. I'd tell the waiter to take three or four orders of shrimp over to my dad over there. As long as I ordered it, the government would pay for it. The waiters knew that no one would ever complain. I could order anything I wanted. The marshals appreciated having the food sent over to them. They were having to sit there and watch us eat like pigs.

Fifty-two days of enforced intimacy had made us like kids at camp, acting juvenile at times, but developing real bonds. Interestingly enough, we seemed to develop the closest bonds with the jurors in the closest proximity. Those of us who sat in the back row of the jury box, placed there entirely at random by the drawing of numbers out of a hat, became the closest of friends. We chose to sit near each other at the jury table, and in the vans, and at dinner. We didn't really gravitate toward others of the same age range, or ethnicity, or gender, but towards the people that fate had seated us next to in the back row of that jury box.

When it came time to deliberate, the friendship bonds still held true. We listened to, and were swayed by, the jurors with whom we had developed the closest relationships.

# Chapter Thirty-Six: The Closing Arguments

Whatever the lawyers say during closing arguments is not evidence, and you can't use that in making your decision.

I had been interested in the opening statements, but when they got to the closing, and started telling me what they thought they had proved, I thought, Excuse me, but I'll tell you what you've proved. It's up to me to make that determination. I'll decide if you've proved it or not. I listened, but the closing arguments didn't mean much to me.

Steve Clymer gripped the lectern at first and looked at his notes. Eventually he started pacing back and forth. "Something went very, very wrong at the intersection of Foothill and Osborne that night. In response to that, the defense has presented to you a series of exaggerations and deceptions. They have sought to convince by exaggeration that Rodney King is the most dangerous person on the Planet Earth. That Rodney King is the biggest danger any police officer anywhere has ever faced. They've sought to convince you that the defendants had no choice that night but to continue to beat and beat and beat and kick and stomp Rodney King as he lay on the ground."

Clymer said that King was "beaten into submission" because he didn't follow the officers' orders fast enough.

He scoffed at the notion that the police thought he was on PCP. "He's being drunk, he's being disrespectful, he's being a wiseacre, and they're going to teach Rodney King a lesson. They're going to beat him until he complies."

It didn't stop until King begged for mercy, "which is what they wanted all along." Clymer conceded that King initially resisted arrest after leading police on a high-speed chase and he deserved to be arrested.

"Rodney King should have been arrested that night and Rodney King should have gone to jail. And if police officers didn't beat him, there would have been a trial like this one for Rodney King. Instead, the defendants tried Rodney King at Foothill and Osborne. With Stacey Koon as judge, and Powell, Wind and Briseno as executioners, they found him guilty," Clymer said.

If Rodney King really was so dangerous, and if the officers knew they handled the situation correctly, why was it that they didn't mention in their reports that they had hit him in the head, and why didn't they mention that they had taken him back to the Foothill Station that night? Why did they lie if they didn't do anything wrong?

"Ask yourselves," Clymer said, "why the deception? Why the exaggeration? Why the concealment?"

Clymer said, "We are asking you as members of the community to apply the constitutional rights that have kept us from being a police state, rights that we have fought for in wars. You have to decide what police officers ought to do in a free country. You have to decide whether police officers can beat disrespectful suspects into submission."

After Clymer spoke for more than three hours, Salzman, representing Koon, called the government's case "preposterous baloney" and "rubbish nonsense."

He said that King's testimony that officers called him "nigger" and "killer" was "a figment of his imagination or a civil lawyer's connivance. That phrase was laid as a bombshell in this case to try and inflame," Salzman said. "This case has never been about race."

Salzman said Koon did everything right, making split-second decisions in a life or death situation. "Koon couldn't allow a man who took police on a high-speed chase to escape into the night in a residential neighborhood. Koon was doing what we want him to do. Sergeant Koon couldn't push a stop button. He didn't know how this was going to end up. He couldn't reverse it."

Salzman called the officers "sacrificial lambs foisted on the public altar of justice" and berated Sergeant Mark Conta as "a classroom police officer" and a "PR person." He said the defense's expert, Duke, had arranged security for the visit of the Pope.

Salzman also claimed that Koon never tried to cover up the incident or to deny that force was used to arrest King. "No one can seriously deny the integrity and moral courage that Sergeant Koon brought to his testimony."

Salzman blamed King for the riots after the first trial. "People lost their homes because someone wanted to go to Hansen Dam without interruption. Because of that, people died."

Michael Stone summed up for Laurence Powell for nearly four hours. Sometimes he roared. He asked all four defendants to stand up. "Look at these men. They're not robocops. They have fear. They hurt. They feel pain. They bleed and they die just like the rest of us. We leave it to them to face the mean streets."

Powell could have "preserved his own safety. He didn't do that. He chose to stand his ground. He chose to do his duty," Stone said. "Duty did not require Officer Powell to be wheeled into an emergency room himself on a hospital gurney. Duty did not require Officer Powell to end up toes up on a slab in the morgue. These officers do not get paid to lose street fights . . . They're expected to win. They don't get paid to roll around in the dirt with the likes of Rodney Glen King. They are, after all, the thin blue line that protects law-abiding citizenry in the community from criminal elements."

He scoffed at the prosecution's argument that the police acted the way they did because King shook his buttocks at them and failed the attitude test. "There is no evidence, ladies and gentlemen, of anyone's intent to summarily punish Rodney King because he was disrespectful. He was assaultive, he was combative, he was actively resisting arrest."

Stone said the whole thing was King's fault. He got drunk, he sped, he failed to stop, he staggered back to his feet after being felled by a Taser gun, and he refused to get in the infamous felony prone position.

"From start to finish, it was Rodney Glen King who controlled his own destiny." Stone said King lied when he gave his account of that night because "he did not want to go back to the slammer, prison. And you know what? It worked . . . a great example for the youth of our community.

"The evidence may convince you it could have been done differently and force was unreasonable at some point," Stone said. "The difficult burden the government has to manage here is to prove beyond a reasonable doubt that these officers knew at the time that it was wrong and continued to do it, and that's where the case fails.

"It was Officer Powell who stood between Rodney King and his escape into the woods of Hansen Dam Park." Powell was "faithful to his charge on March 2, 1991. He was faithful to his duty. He deserves to be acquitted. It is right. It is just. He is innocent."

Stone asked us not to use Powell as the scapegoat if we felt we had to convict at least one of them. "Forgive me if I am direct, or perhaps blunt. Don't make Laurence Powell a throwaway, please. Don't make Larry Powell a compromise. He was involuntarily cast into the role, ladies and gentlemen, of the obstacle to Rodney King's escape. He deserves to walk away from this nightmare acquitted."

DePasquale was the last to speak that day. He said that his client, Wind, the rookie cop, was just following orders. DePasquale played the videotape yet another time, stopping to point out Wind. He said that Wind properly stopped and evaluated the situation before he used more force.

"Tim Wind checked that swing," he pointed out. "Tim Wind appears to be checking that swing, rather than swing into the head of Rodney King. Wind is in no frenzy. He's not out of control. He's a policeman following his sergeant."

He pointed out that we didn't have to convict all of them.

"You must consider and decide the case of each defendant separately," he said. "This is not a team sport."

SATURDAY, APRIL 10, 1993

It was Harland Braun's turn to make his closing argument, and maybe because it was the day before Easter, he brought up the Bible and Pilate. He said that Jesus Christ was found guilty because the crowds wanted to crucify him.

"No man should be condemned in this case because of the fear of a riot. My client is on trial. But you are also on trial. Your courage is on trial," he warned us.

He was telling us not to find someone guilty just because the crowds wanted it that way. I never thought that anyone wanted these people found guilty. The President of the United States wanted a new trial, and that's why we were there. But I don't think the President was telling us what we had to decide. Obviously a lot of people were interested in this trial, since there were fifty photographers outside

*Moral Uncertainty*

the courthouse all the time.

I thought the country was divided. The majority of people would say that the officers were innocent, and a small minority of people wanted them found guilty. Basically, the rednecks wanted to let them go free, and the liberals wanted to convict. It was almost like I wasn't involved.

Braun talked for two hours, using a lot of Biblical and historical references and attacking the government for having the gall to indict his client and accuse him of lying.

"You call an American citizen—a police officer—a perjurer?" Braun asked. "Prove it."

Braun also implied that Briseno was prosecuted for tactical reasons, to help get the other guys. "The indictment of Ted Briseno is so immoral, so terrible, that it should undermine your confidence in the government. Don't be fooled. Don't use him to convict someone else."

Braun said it was a good thing that Steve Clymer wasn't around during Christ's time, because "he would have indicted the apostles."

Clymer didn't react to that remark, but just about everyone else in the courtroom laughed.

I am not a church-goer myself, but I thought that for this guy to tell me there was a connection between this case and Jesus Christ was far-fetched. The Christians were incensed because they felt like he was pulling their strings.

When it came down to thinking about Briseno, I wanted to be sure that I wasn't swayed by this lawyer. And the Christians were saying, "We'd better look a little more closely at this guy." So it worked to his detriment.

He kept saying, "What evil has this man done?" and turning and pointing to Briseno.

Kowalski spoke last, for the prosecution. He didn't respond directly to what Braun said, just, "it is easier to attack the government than it is to attack the defendants."

He said that the defendants and their lawyers had distorted the testimony and the facts. "You can expect defendant Koon to say whatever is in defendant Koon's interests," Kowalski said. "The truth doesn't change."

The officers used unreasonable force, he said, and they knew they were using unreasonable force when they did it.

Kowalski played the videotape for us one last time. He told us to "watch the videotape. Use your common sense. It's wrong to beat a man who's lying on the ground. You know that in the schoolyard when you're a kid. You don't kick a man when he's down . . . The law demands that we follow that schoolyard rule."

He emphasized again that the officers had lied. He pointed out that none of the reports filed by Wind, Koon or Powell mentioned that the officers hit King while he was on the ground. They left the information out of their reports because they knew what they did was wrong, and they didn't know they were going to get caught, because they didn't know that George Holliday was videotaping them. "The world learned what happened at Foothill and Osborne for one reason. That's because George Holliday had a videotape," Kowalski said.

"There's one thing that everybody from Paris to Tokyo saw. There was one thing that causes horror and outrage throughout the world. The thing that everybody saw, that everybody was so outraged about, was that the defendants were beating a man who was on the ground.

"Let's tell it like it is, ladies and gentlemen. They were bullies with badges."

Kowalski accused the defense expert, Sergeant Duke, of lying on the stand. Duke told us that officers are supposed to break bones "if that's what it takes." He said that Deputy Chief Matthew V. Hunt had ordered that kind of training. But Hunt testified that he never said that.

"Sergeant Duke, as accomplished and as brave as he is, lied to you," Kowalski said. The prosecution's expert, Mark Conta, was "an honest man," he said. "He doesn't deserve the name-calling he got."

After the lawyers were finished, Judge Davies read us thirty-nine instructions.

When people who watch Court TV think they know more than the jury does, because they've listened to the testimony, they forget about the jury instructions. Juries can't just listen to the facts and use their own values and guidelines to decide what's right and what's wrong. Juries are supposed to follow the instructions given to them by the judge, which have been agreed to in advance by both the prosecution and the defense.

He told us to view the incident from the standpoint of a reasonable police officer under similar circumstances, and to remember that police officers often have to make quick decisions under difficult circumstances.

He told us to set aside any information we had learned about the case outside of the courtroom. "Your verdict must be based solely and exclusively on evidence presented in court. You should not be influenced by any external consequences of your verdict," he said.

"You are now in the hands of the marshals," Davies said at 3:07 p.m. "You may retire to the jury room."

# Chapter Thirty-Seven: Deliberations, Revelations and Rehabilitation

It was just after three o'clock in the afternoon when we got the case. We worked for about two hours, but we didn't get much accomplished.

As soon as we got into the jury room, everyone started talking at once. We had been under orders not to discuss the case for so long that it was like opening a spigot. Everybody just babbled. We realized that after forty-five days of being spectators—and spectators with gags in our mouths, at that—finally we were the ones running the show, and we could say whatever we wanted.

"Man, did he get beat up! Did you see how they hit that guy?" someone exclaimed.

"I think that guy was lying," somebody else said.

Maria, Gary and Anne were talking down at one end of the table; Ruth, Norman and Cathy were in another discussion; and Fred and George were talking to me. Eric was probably involved in one of those conversations. Marty is pretty reserved; he was just listening.

I asked everyone to be quiet.

The first order of business was to elect a foreman, and of course, I had been politicking for this for weeks. I had been conducting myself with that goal in mind. On the very first day after we were sworn in, I sat down at the head of the jury table, and I deliberately kept that seat for the whole trial.

I had assumed a leadership role in other ways too, acting as go-between with the federal marshals who were our guards and social directors for the various outings and field trips. Because I was the only one on the jury who had spent much time working in downtown Los Angeles, I was familiar with area restaurants, and I made suggestions about where we might go for Wednesday and Saturday night dinners.

I had confided to both George and to Fred that I hoped to be elected foreman. When I told Fred, he said he thought George ought to do it. I said George wouldn't want to do it, so he said, well then, what about Anne? I said that Anne was too bossy and would alienate people. What you need in a foreman, I told Fred, was somebody soft, who will let other people have their say, who just functions as the team leader. If the leader tries to be too rigid, it will just take longer, I told him. If the leader tries to run it with an iron fist, the others are going to revolt. I told him I thought we all ought to vote on what to discuss, and the foreman ought to be sort of a moderator. Fred repeated that he thought George would do a good job.

So I got everyone's attention, announced that it was time we elected a foreman, and asked if anybody wanted to serve. At first, nobody said a word. There was a little discussion down at the other end of the table. I probably waited too long before I said, well, I'd like to be the foreman. I didn't get it out of my mouth before Anne piped up that she wanted to be foreman too.

Then George said, "I was thinking Cathy would make a good foreman."

"Oh, no, not me," Cathy said. "I'm no good at making big decisions."

Cathy was a housewife with three children who worked part-time at a family business in Central California. As it turned out, she did a fine job of making decisions during the deliberations, but she thought being foreman would be too much for her. And as I discovered, it is a pressure cooker job.

Without blinking an eye, I said, "Well, how do you want to do it, by show of hands or by secret ballot?"

Somebody said, "Secret ballot." The previous night, I had torn a piece of paper into twelve pieces, so I was ready and I passed them out.

"Write 'Anne' or 'Bob' and put the ballot in this Styrofoam cup," I instructed. I asked Eric and Marty to count the ballots. They probably weren't the most trustworthy ones I could have asked, but Eric most likely would vote for me, and Marty probably would vote for Anne, and they could keep each other honest. They went over by the sink on the other side of the room to count the ballots.

I hadn't written anything on my slip. I just left it blank and folded it in half.

I didn't turn around to watch them count. After a couple of minutes, Eric said, "Bob won."

Somebody asked, "Was it close?"

Eric said it was seven-five.

"How is that possible?" I asked. "I didn't vote."

Eric looked embarrassed. He admitted there was one vote uncast, but said he gave the benefit of the doubt to the loser so it wouldn't seem so lopsided.

Somebody said maybe we should vote again.

"Why?" I asked. "Are you going to change your vote? Because if you're not, there's no reason to vote again."

Nobody said anything, so I said, "Well, I guess I'm the foreman then."

I had given some thought to how to handle the deliberations. I knew if I took the floor and said I thought we ought to talk about the issue of PCP first, some of the stronger-willed jurors would have gone through the ceiling and they would have got themselves a new foreman. So I said I thought we ought to get a game plan, that we ought to open up the discussion about the format we were going to follow.

"Does anyone have any ideas?"

Maria said she thought we ought to talk about Sergeant Koon first.

"You think we ought to talk about individuals rather than the evidence as a whole?"

"No, the evidence as a whole."

"Should we go witness by witness, or fact by fact about each individual defendant?" I asked.

Norman interrupted to point out that the judge had instructed us to consider all the evidence. The judge had a habit of talking with his hands. When he said, "This is not to concern you," he would put both hands up in the air and flap them up and down for emphasis. Norman tried to imitate the judge's gestures, flapping his hands up and down as he said, "consider all the evidence."

Somebody offered as an aside that he didn't understand the bit about the PCP. Somebody else said he didn't understand why the prosecutor made such a big deal about how long it took to get Rodney King to the hospital or why the defense seemed to minimize it.

"Why don't we just start at the beginning?" someone suggested.

George said we ought to consider the evidence chronologically. Others said, no, we ought to go witness by witness. Of the twelve of us, there seemed to be six opinions, each with two proponents.

I said maybe we ought to take turns talking. I suggested that they raise their hands like school children, and I would call on them. Then everyone seemed to be exaggeratedly polite, trying not to interrupt each other or talk over each other. But one person would say they wanted to do one thing, and the next person would say just the opposite.

We really needed a leader.

Throughout the whole procedure, George didn't say much, but when he did speak, everyone listened. George thought we should start at the beginning of the incident, and just go through it.

I said, "How about if we take one of the officers, and start at the beginning and go through it chronologically with what happened with that defendant?"

That led to a discussion about which defendant to discuss first.

Maria said she wanted to talk about Koon, and Anne said she agreed with her. Anne and Maria agreed on everything. They were a surprising duo, a young black postal worker and an older, upper middle class white insurance executive, but they sat next to each other every day and had been fast friends from the beginning.

Gary agreed with Maria and Anne that we ought to talk about Koon first.

The three of them, plus Marty, had pretty much already made up their minds that all four defendants were guilty. I think that Maria, Eric and Gary started out on jury duty thinking that the police officers were guilty as hell. They wanted to start with Koon because they considered him the most convictable. He had accepted responsibility on the witness stand. Basically, he said he didn't do anything wrong, that this was just the way the police work.

"Well, we have one problem," I said. "The judge just read us the instructions, and we have to go by his guidelines. Koon is accused of allowing his officers to violate Rodney King's rights. How can we convict him of allowing them to do something, unless we convict them of doing it? If we don't convict anyone else, how can we convict him? How can we talk about whether or not he allowed somebody to do something before we talk about whether or not they did it?"

Norman and Fred backed me up.

We decided to start with Powell instead. We didn't actually vote, we just agreed that was how we'd do it. We'd start at the beginning with the pursuit, and we'd talk about the evidence against Powell in a chronological fashion.

Next we tried to set the hours that we would work. We decided that we would work from noon to four on Sunday and work normal working hours Monday through Friday. Some people expressed annoyance that we were working on the weekend at all. We had always had Saturday and Sunday off. How come we had to work on Saturday, and especially on Easter Sunday? Gary, in particular, was incensed that we wouldn't get Easter Sunday off. Gary was younger than most of us, and he seemed to think we were all a bunch of old fogies. He hadn't taken part in field trips, or eaten dinner with the rest of us most of the time, and he had certainly never attended church on previous Sundays. But he was irritated that we were going to have to work on Sunday because it meant his girlfriend couldn't come visit him.

I felt exhausted already. We had only been "deliberating," if you could call it that, for two hours. The stress was already affecting me. By this time it was five o'clock. All we had gotten done was to elect me foreman and to set up the ground rules for how we were going to work. Two hours seemed like a long time, but some of it was taken up with the marshals bringing in the exhibits, which they piled up in the room where we had to work. That made it too crowded, so we carted them into the little anteroom where the marshals had been sitting up until the time the deliberations started.

Before we could really get started, we also needed some supplies. We wanted notebook dividers, so I wrote a note to the marshal listing the things we needed. Also the VCR was not yet working. They had it all set up but it wasn't working yet. They told us it would be ready by Sunday.

We got in the vans and went back to the Hilton. The three alternates, Jim, Daryl and Mike, had already been taken back to the hotel. From now on, they would be kept separate from us. It really seemed strange not to have them there. From the beginning, neither Daryl nor Mike had eaten many meals, but Jim, who was a big guy, never missed dinner. Starting that night, he sat alone with a marshal guarding him at a table about a hundred feet away from us in the Gazebo restaurant at the Hilton, where we had dinner every night.

When he got up to leave, they paraded him by us, and we called out, "Hey, Jim, how's it going," and stuff like that.

Most of the time on Saturday nights people stayed up late and talked about religion or sex. Those were the two favorite topics. But this Saturday night was like a work night, because we were going to have to get up and work the next day. I was very tired and I went to bed early, so I don't know what any of the rest of them talked about.

EASTER SUNDAY, APRIL 11, 1993

They brought breakfast up to us at 8:30 on Sunday morning. This was the first Sunday that families couldn't come visit us, and Gary continued to fume. My wife had been planning to come see me for Easter, so she was unhappy, too.

Because it was a religious holiday, five jurors asked to go along to a Lutheran church in Pasadena—more than had been going on previous Sundays. They weren't all Lutherans, but that was the church the Christian jurors had compromised on attending. The pastor there had been forewarned by the marshals not to sermonize about current events. Once we began deliberating, the twelve of us weren't supposed to be separated, but the five of them did leave the rest of us to go to church.

We all had a lunch of cold cuts at 11 a.m. at the hotel. We couldn't eat at the courthouse, as we usually did, because the food services were closed on Sundays. We got to the courthouse and began deliberations at about 1 p.m.

We had decided on Saturday that we would try to discuss the evidence chronologically, about each defendant, starting with Officer Powell. It seemed logical to talk about each of the three officers, and then Sergeant Koon.

So we started talking about the pursuit and what each witness who had talked about the pursuit had to say about Officer Powell.

We needed to talk about what Melanie Singer said, as well as Officer Beauregard, the Los Angeles Unified School District cop who got in on the chase.

"Why are we starting on the freeway?" George asked. "Powell wasn't even on the freeway."

"You wanted to start at the beginning," somebody said. "Rodney

King is the main actor, so we have to set this up."

We talked a little about why King didn't stop for the highway patrol, why he didn't pull over to start with. We got to the part where Powell, who was coming from a traffic stop, joined the chase and Wind called in on his radio that they were in pursuit.

Cathy and Norman and Ruth all had really good notes, but they were having a hard time jumping back and forth from what Beauregard said to what Melanie Singer said. Cathy said she needed some time to review her notes, and she'd like to be able to take them back to the hotel at night to review them.

Fred hadn't taken any notes, but he had an unusually good memory and didn't seem to have any difficulty recalling testimony.

We were getting bogged down because it was hard to try to recreate the sequence of events in the pursuit. It was confusing, and at this rate, we'd never get through all of the evidence against each officer.

We had our first altercation when Eric insisted that Rodney King had not committed any felony, so he couldn't be accused of felony evading. If the officers were arresting him for a felony, they were allowed to do certain things that they would not be allowed to do if he were only being stopped for a misdemeanor, or for a traffic infraction. Eric insisted that King was speeding, and was just being stopped on a traffic violation.

He pointed out that California Highway Patrol Officer Melanie Singer had testified that as the LAPD cars pulled alongside the CHP car, her husband, Officer Tim Singer, had shouted to them that King was being stopped for speeding and for failure to stop.

According to the testimony, King was driving very erratically. Even though he was being pursued, he stopped at some traffic signals and went right through others. Sometimes he stopped at green lights. It was very bizarre driving. Melanie Singer testified that she almost ran into the back of King's car when he finally stopped, and that another car slid right past her on the right side. This whole scene was like the Keystone Kops. These people were out of control. When a police officer skids up beside a pursued car and then has to back up, that's not a safe procedure. Both cars had to back up.

Melanie testified that her husband yelled out, "All we want him for is speed and failure to stop," which would be misdemeanors.

So Eric said this was not felony evading.

I said, "Well, we really don't have anything in our jury instructions about the definition of felony evading and failure to stop, so we're talking about stuff we're not sure about. All through the testimony, the lawyers never went into the technicalities of these laws."

It made a difference, because we needed to know whether when they started beating on Rodney King they had a reason to do that because he was a felony suspect. They kept telling him to assume the felony prone position. If he wasn't a felony suspect, they could have had him down on his knees with his hands behind his head, instead of insisting that the guy eat dirt.

Eric said we were trying to push him into something he disagreed with, because he didn't think King was felony evading. Eric tends to see things in black and white.

There was so much we had to discuss, and we were bogging down on this one point, which really didn't seem like it was very important.

Some jurors thought they would like to hear Melanie Singer's testimony again, so I wrote a note to the judge asking if we could have that portion of her testimony re-read to us.

The judge said no. He didn't really offer any explanation. I read later that judges sometimes refuse to allow testimony to be re-read because they are afraid that taking something out of context will blow it out of all proportion. I thought perhaps the judge didn't want the whole world to see that the jury was focusing in on such an insignificant detail.

I asked Norman to read the judge's instructions aloud. We had heard the judge himself read them the previous day, but we wanted to be clear on what we were being told to do. I asked Norman to do the reading because he had a strong voice. Norman is used to standing up and reading aloud from the Bible at church. He reads aloud really well.

We were bogging down. We realized the way we were doing it was not going to get the job done, and that we were going to have to give everybody some time to review their notes.

Eric and Norman began bickering. Eric felt that all four officers were clearly guilty, and that we should just vote and get out of there. Norman, who is an engineer and likes to be methodical, asked him,

"What's the hurry? We need to do this right."

Eric accused Norman of having a hidden agenda. He insinuated that perhaps some of the jurors were enjoying living high on the hog at the Hilton Hotel and eating in posh restaurants every night at the expense of the federal government.

"You people are stalling," Eric said.

"What do you mean, stalling?" Norman demanded.

Both men called each other names.

Cathy said she was eager to get home because she missed her husband and her three children, but she needed more time to review her notes before she could reach any decisions about anything.

Norman said that everybody agreed that King was felony evading except Eric, and that Eric was trying to push us into guilty verdicts.

Eric said Norman was just slowing us down and we wouldn't be finished until Christmas.

Fred, who really didn't have any reason to care whether we went fast or slow, since his wife had left him while we were sequestered, and he had nobody to go home to, suddenly turned on Norman. "What are you? Some kind of a girl? You don't act like a man."

Norman turned beet red. Norman was an engineer, like me. We may have been nerds, but that doesn't mean we were homosexuals. Fred was a rugged biker type, and perhaps he wasn't used to being around us sensitive engineers, but Norman had never had his masculinity questioned before.

Norman said, "I don't care. I'm going to review my notes."

We decided to take the last hour for review. Cathy and Norman went into the adjacent room to study their notebooks, and Fred looked over the evidence book.

Gary kept arguing about how unnecessary all of this was. He made so much commotion, nobody was able to concentrate very well. There was no way Norman and Cathy could review their notes while Gary was screaming and yelling and making snide comments about them from nearby.

I told him if he kept talking they wouldn't be able to review their notes, and he said, "But Bob, there is no reason for this."

Gary had not taken many notes himself. He remembered the testimony, and he sincerely couldn't understand why other people needed to consult their notebooks. I couldn't understand how

*Moral Uncertainty*

anybody could be so insensitive.

"How can you discuss something with someone who isn't ready to discuss?" I asked him.

Finally, I'd had as much stress as I could take. "We're going home now, guys," I said, pounding on the door for the marshals to get us out of there.

We were all exhausted. On Saturday when we were setting up the schedule, some of the jurors had been pushing for working into the evenings as late as we needed to get done. Maria, who worked at the post office, likened it to working overtime, and scoffed at those of us who wanted to work 8:30 to 4:30.

Anne and Eric were also pushing for working late and finishing as quickly as possible. They implied that the rest of us were wimps. But I was in charge, and I knew that if I was too tired to work nights, the others had to be emotionally wrung out too.

Maybe it was selfish of me, but I needed to regroup my mind to figure out how to bring this unruly band into a discussion, something they weren't showing any talent about doing, acting like a bunch of spoiled children. I had wanted to be foreman, and I wanted to do a good job of it.

Part of what you promise when you raise your right hand to be sworn in as a juror is that you will discuss the evidence with your fellow jurors, that you won't be a rock. Here I was the foreman, and I couldn't get these guys who swore to do it to discuss the evidence. I knew I had to pull in the reins and assert myself more. I didn't want to be a heavy-handed boss. I was feeling stress because of it. The others had a right to their opinion, and to think what they wanted and to say what they thought in the jury room. I wondered where I had gone wrong.

At this rate, Gary and Eric complained, we'd still be here for Christmas. Early in the trial, I had bet Marty five dollars that we wouldn't still be sequestered on May 5 for Cinco de Mayo, a Mexican holiday, which is celebrated in Los Angeles. Marty had already paid me off, and I was beginning to think I was going to have to repay him the ten dollars. If I did, I'd have to get some cash from my wife, because I was down to nine dollars, and with no visitors' hours, my wife couldn't replenish my funds.

It was obvious that the jurors who favored hurrying up had

made up their minds, and the ones who hadn't made up their minds wanted to take their time, look over the evidence and think about the whole process. These were people's lives at stake. I was determined to give the slow people all the time they needed, because they were entitled to it. So were the defendants. And so was the United States of America, when you stop and think about it.

MONDAY, APRIL 12, 1993

We started out by letting everyone have some time to review their notes. I told anybody who didn't want to review their notes, they should just sit and be quiet. Read a book or something.

Fred wanted to look at the evidence book.

Anne had taken the most notes, twice as many as anyone else. She had eight to ten notebooks. Norman probably had five. I only had one, but I had written on both sides of the pages.

It's probably a personality defect of mine, but I'm the son of a printer. When your dad is a printer, you get used to throwing paper around, because about the only thing he brings home from work is dirty hands and a lot of nice scratch paper. We always had wonderful notepads. But as I get older, I think about trees, and now I write on both sides of the pages of the notebook.

After giving everyone a chance to look over their notes, we watched the whole video and looked at each blow, discussing whether or not it was a head shot.

We had a hard time getting started with Powell. We talked about King getting out of the car and Powell wrestling with him for a few seconds. We talked about whether King knocked the officers off of him or whether they fell off of him. It looked like the Taser worked the second time, and then King turned around and Powell was still hitting him. It was hard to figure out what Powell was doing during the period from the end of the tasing.

We decided it was going to be too complicated to try to just go through the evidence chronologically, so we changed strategies, and started discussing the witnesses one by one, with what they had to say about Powell.

I basically read my notes aloud. If somebody else had written down something interesting that I had missed, or if someone else

*Moral Uncertainty*

had something to say, then they would contribute it. I asked the others not to read their notes to the rest of us if they were merely repetitious of what I had just read. I wanted everyone to have a chance to say whatever they had to say, but I didn't want to repeat everything twelve times. What we were doing was getting the evidence straight in our minds.

We would make side comments and sometimes somebody wanted to add something. It had taken us six weeks to hear this testimony and now we were going over it at lightning speed.

We got two-thirds of the way through reviewing all of the testimony on Monday.

By the end of the afternoon, all of us were very tired. We had been sitting in the jury room the same number of hours that we had worked every day of the trial, but somehow it was much more exhausting in deliberations than it was while we were listening to the testimony. Going from being a spectator to being a participant made a huge difference.

During one of our breaks, Anne told Maria that Norman had made a racist comment the night before. She said that Norman had referred to blacks as "those people."

Norman denied it. I was sitting there amazed. I hadn't heard anything about this before, and it seemed out of character for Norman, who was so mild-mannered. I was surprised that anyone could be mad about what he said, because it seemed like a very innocent remark, but Maria was obviously very annoyed.

I thought we should get it all out in the open, so we tried to talk about it. Norman started reeling off all the things he had done in support of integration, various committees he had served on, and volunteer work he had done in the past. He said he had been on the Affirmative Action Council at his work.

Maria was not appeased.

However, after dinner on Monday evening, the two of them sat and talked and resolved the issue. Maria seemed satisfied that either Norman had never made the remark, or if he had made the remark, he didn't really mean it.

It was amazing, but almost every fight or unpleasant incident during the deliberations included Norman as one of the combatants. Despite being a very quiet and unassuming man, he was a central figure in almost every dispute. Norman is very quiet, but he was unwilling to be bullied into anything before he thought it through in a methodical fashion.

Poor old Norman didn't have to say anything for them to be mad at him. I didn't think it was my responsibility to protect him. He's an adult and perfectly capable of taking care of himself.

### TUESDAY, APRIL 13, 1993

We continued going over the testimony, witness by witness. I would read my notes aloud, and ask if anybody had anything else to add.

Suspects are innocent until they are proven guilty, supposedly. No one was saying Powell was innocent, but we just couldn't prove him guilty. We reviewed the tapes again and watched each of the blows.

We hadn't taken any votes on Powell yet. We had a pretty vocal crowd and you could tell who was for what. We were voting with our mouths. Why take a formal vote when it was obvious how everyone would have voted? We would just say, okay, what makes you think he is guilty?

Gary got us off on the subject of the police saying they were afraid of King because he was on PCP and supposedly had superhuman strength. Gary seemed to have some expertise about drugs and flashbacks and how people act on PCP, and he had also been a security guard, so he knew how hard it was to get somebody into handcuffs. Gary actually had the experience of using a baton on a suspect.

He said that the wrist lock that they put on King should have hurt him a lot. I tried to discourage Gary from using his personal experience, because it wasn't really relevant to what happened to King.

Gary pointed out that if King actually had been on PCP, then they didn't follow the police procedures because the policy says if the guy is on PCP you don't put the bright lights on him, and you try to calm him down. They did just the opposite of what they should have done if they thought that he was on PCP.

It was a point I didn't care about. Even if he was on PCP, the first blows were okay with me. He was a suspect trying to escape, and as far as I was concerned, they had a right to try to subdue him. If he tried to escape and they had shot him, I would have thought they were within their rights to do it.

Maria and Anne reiterated that we ought to work until six or eight o'clock and not stop in the late afternoon. They thought we were being lazy by going back to the hotel at 4:30.

Hey, I was forty-seven years old. I got tired. I was not ready to work until eight o'clock. I guess I was getting old. "You want to eat, don't you?" I asked.

Eric was one of the ones who wanted to work late, but if we worked late, we would miss a meal. Eric wouldn't want to miss dinner. Then Gary and Norm got into it.

Norman said he couldn't absorb any more. "I'm not going to discuss anymore today. I can't do it."

Norm and Cathy said they thought we were going to have to take a day off. They said it didn't look like we could keep this up day after day. We were exhausted and emotionally drained.

Since some of us were feeling so tired, while others thought we should work even longer hours, one of the compromises we agreed on was that we would have breakfast at 7:30, so everyone could sleep a little later, and then leave at eight o'clock for the courthouse.

I was feeling a lot of stress. This was likely the most important thing we had ever done in our lives, and half of us wanted to barrel right through it and get home, and the rest of us wanted to step cautiously through the land mines. I felt like I was trying to put my finger in the dike to hold back the flood of people who wanted to work and the ones who wanted to go home.

WEDNESDAY, APRIL 14, 1993

The best laid plans of mice and men. We were supposed to get to sleep a little later, but on Wednesday, breakfast showed up at 6:30. When the cart was trundled down the corridor, its wheels squeaked and its wobbly wheel wobbled, so everyone could hear.

Since I'm always an early riser, I was already up. At 6:30, I was already coming out of my room. I hadn't read the paper yet, but I headed on into the breakfast suite and sat down with Stanley. Stanley served in the Marines, starting in 1947. He was a pretty healthy old guy, rode his bike every day, a real athlete. Stanley and I were in the habit of eating breakfast together. We were usually the first two people to arrive in the breakfast room.

On Wednesday morning, Anne and Eric were at one table and Stanley and I at the other table. It was a full hour earlier than we had expected breakfast to be served, and we were having a bleary conversation about how did you sleep, etc.

From the other table, Anne called out, "Bob, you know, if those people think they can get away with taking a day off, I'm going to write the judge a letter. We're not going to do that."

I paused to think about how I wanted to respond. I certainly didn't want any of the jurors writing to the judge, making it look as if I wasn't doing my job as the foreman.

"Don't write to the judge. I'll take care of it." I tried to say it nicely, but it was early in the morning.

She thought it sounded like I was giving her an order.

"Don't tell me what to do," she said. "I'll write a letter if I want to."

"You're an asshole," I said.

She said no one had ever called her a name like that before. I said that she had interrupted me before I could finish. I hadn't finished my sentence. She said, well, now she had another reason to write the judge a letter.

I had ordered a special breakfast. Usually I had toast, yogurt and cappuccino. This morning I was having eggs with corned beef hash and cappuccino. But I lost my appetite.

I went back to my room and lay down on the bed.

We were having a lot of conflict. People were not showing respect for other people's opinions. Anne and Maria were not respecting Norman and Cathy's need to be slow and methodical, and their need to have a day off. It seemed to me that they were behaving like bullies.

I didn't think that it was unreasonable for people to take it slow and to have time to rest. I needed to explain to Gary that if he would just be quiet for an hour they could review their notes.

No one was being respectful of the others' rights and the rules.

I thought to myself, I've really blown it now. This is real important to these four policemen and I'm losing control. I just called some lady an asshole.

My style—or my lack of style—is that if I can't get my way, then I'm childish. I'm not a violent person, but I can be childish. I wouldn't have hit her, but that childish retort was not uncharacteristic.

I lay on my bed in my room and thought about it. Anne and I have problems. We need to talk it out. Anne won't listen to me, so how can we talk it over? Anne is not as smart as she thinks. I can out-think her. I should be able to solve this problem.

I was lying there thinking and someone knocked at my door.

It was Ruth, but I didn't know that, because I didn't answer. Two minutes later there was another knock at the door.

Then another knock. This time I answered, and it was Anne.

"I know we have our problems, but George is really sick," she said. "I think you should come."

I rushed back over to the breakfast room.

George usually came to breakfast, but he hadn't shown up while I was there. Now he was sitting surrounded by Cathy, Ruth, Norman and Stanley—all the back row people, except me.

"Hey, George," I said. "What's wrong?"

"I don't know," he said.

He was shaking.

George had been complaining about not being able to sleep. He had brought along a bottle of Jack Daniel's for medicinal purposes, which he kept stashed in his room to help lull him to sleep at night. But the marshals had confiscated it the week before, and George had been having trouble sleeping ever since. He said he had hardly slept at all since we began deliberations. He had high blood pressure and he was shaking. I mean his whole body was shaking violently. He was also breaking out in a rash. He was feeling really bad.

I thought there was a possibility that George could die.

George's room was right next to the breakfast room, so he probably had heard me call Anne an asshole. I knew it was going to be a very stressful morning. I didn't think we should go to work, with him in this condition. George said he wanted to go ahead and deliberate.

"Hey, this is your life we're talking about," I said.

I had to figure out a way to get George to a doctor. Somebody had already talked to the marshals. They were planning to take him to his own doctor and then to a dermatologist in the afternoon. I thought we should just sit around until it was time for George to go to the doctor. In my mind, George was dying.

George said, "No, I've got to go to work."

If George was too sick to work, or if he died, the judge might put one of the alternates on. George didn't want to be removed from the jury. He felt like he had a job to do and let's just do it. I didn't feel that it was my job to push him or to stop him. I didn't see how he could listen without getting stressed, but he made the decision to go, so we got in the vans and went to the courthouse.

Not everybody knew everything that had happened.

I tried to explain what happened at breakfast when Anne interrupted me and I called her an asshole. I didn't want anyone to get the impression that I was apologizing. I refused to apologize. I just recited what had happened. I thought she was rude because she had interrupted me and yelled at me. I wasn't about to apologize.

George was sitting to my left, still shaking.

Anne told her version. She said no one had ever spoken to her in that manner in her whole life.

I said that the only two people who were in the habit of interrupting were Anne and Bob and that she and I should agree not to interrupt. She agreed, but she wanted me to know that she thought my behavior was childish. I agreed that it was.

Eric said what bothered him was that the same people who kept complaining about being tired were the same people who rushed back to the hotel and did aerobics for three hours. He couldn't fathom how people who said they were so tired could go home and exercise. He seemed to have no comprehension of the difference between emotional exhaustion and physical exhaustion, or that when you were emotionally exhausted it could be a relief to engage in physical activity. That seemed to be beyond Eric.

He had no concept of mental fatigue. He kept saying, "If you're so darned tired, how can you run a mile?"

Cathy, Maria, Ruth, and sometimes Norman and I did aerobics at the hotel. Norm and Cathy and Maria had done aerobics on Tuesday night. Eric's room was across the hall from Cathy's. Eric, who kept claiming he wasn't tired at all and we should work late, was trying to take a nap, and Cathy and Norm, who claimed to be exhausted, were doing aerobics and keeping Eric awake with the loud rock and roll music.

At this point, Fred took his shoe off and beat it on the desk, shouting, "Nyet, nyet." I think he was trying to be funny.

There was a lot of noise in the room.

Marty jumped up and shouted, "Who wants to fight? I'll fight everyone in the room."

Everyone was quarreling. Gary and Maria were talking loudly.

"I'm willing to fight any one of you," Marty said.

I heard later that we could be overheard shouting. But the marshals weren't allowed to come in unless I summoned them, even if they thought we were killing each other. The agreement was that if they wanted to talk to us, they had to knock and I would open the door.

After Anne said she wouldn't interrupt me anymore, she said I owed her an apology. Fred spoke up and said he thought Anne and I should talk over our differences.

I said that if I had to talk to Anne at all, I would knock her lights out. Boom!

I was still being childish, but my point was that I had no intention of apologizing.

It was break time. We'd been fighting for two solid hours without getting anything accomplished at all. I said I was going to get a soft drink from the refrigerator and asked if anyone else wanted one. I gulped it down fast and got up to walk around the room.

Anne came up and said, "Do you really hate me, Bob?"

I gave her a big hug, which she accepted as an apology. I wanted her to start calming down. "No, I don't hate you," I said. "Everybody is stressed out. A day off is really not the worst idea. We're all stressed."

Anne realized that I was right.

Ruth, in the meantime, was sitting at the table, and she suddenly burst into a fit of sobbing. Everyone stopped what they were doing and looked at her.

In a hysterical pitch, Ruth began pouring out some personal family problems that she somehow imagined had some bearing on the case. She had taken me aside the previous evening and made the same confession. She was afraid the fact that she hadn't mentioned this family secret when she was being questioned during jury selection might mean that she had perjured herself, or that they wouldn't want her on the jury.

I had told her that her worries were foolish; none of her personal problems had anything to do with the Rodney King case, and as long as she could set aside her own problems and listen to the evidence impartially, that's all the lawyers expected of us.

She was weeping and screaming now, unburdening herself of her concerns to the whole jury. She kept saying how embarrassed she was to be telling us all of these sordid details. We were embarrassed too, and wished she would stop. She begged us all not to reveal her family secrets if there were books or movies written about the trial.

"Man this is like a rehab meeting," Fred exclaimed.

He was right. Everyone needed to ventilate his or her tense feelings.

We were all still bickering. George said we were acting like a bunch of little kids. He clearly wasn't feeling good.

Then he started sobbing.

"Bob, get me out of here."

I knocked on the door and told the marshal that George was sick and he had to get out of this room now.

"I've got to clear the courtroom first," the marshal said, in some surprise.

George went into the adjoining anteroom. He was embarrassed to be bawling in front of everyone.

The marshal cleared the courtroom in record speed. In two minutes, everyone was out of there.

The marshal knocked, George went outside and disappeared.

The rest of us were left sitting there. We couldn't deliberate because George was gone. It was almost lunchtime and people were starting to calm down. A few people talked about evidence among themselves. Fred went through the evidence book. Maria and Anne looked over the judge's instructions again.

At 11:50 a.m. lunch came. They knocked on the door. I opened it. They wheeled in the cart and I pushed it the rest of the way into the room and started passing out the sandwiches. We were a bunch of congenial, friendly people again. The marshals brought George back in and he ate his lunch too, then we went back to the hotel, at about one o'clock.

*Moral Uncertainty*

George was taken to a doctor. The office had been cleared out, so that he wouldn't come into contact with anyone else. There was no receptionist, no patients. George went right in. The doctor gave him a vitamin shot and sleeping pills. He came back to the hotel and slept through dinner, twelve or fifteen hours straight, and by morning, he was feeling better.

The rest of us just spent that afternoon hanging out at the hotel.

Zero had been accomplished, but we had cleared the air. There was hardly any fighting after that.

# Chapter Thirty-Eight: Agreeing Beyond a Doubt

After Wednesday's histrionics, we got right down to business. Up until now, whenever anyone wanted to speak, they raised their hand and I called on them. By Thursday, everyone had something they wanted to say on every issue. I had to start writing names down in my notebook, and calling on people according to the list. I always had six or seven more jurors waiting in line for their chance to talk.

Even Stanley wanted to talk. Stanley was a quiet guy. He was awake and paying attention; he just usually didn't participate in the discussion. Now even Stanley had his two cents' worth.

The question was whether or not Powell violated Rodney King's civil rights by using excessive force. We were having trouble deciding. We went around the room and everybody said if they thought he was guilty or if they hadn't made up their mind. Most people thought that they had seen some head blows.

We looked at the videotape again.

I finally made up my mind when we were watching the tape for the umpteenth time.

There! That's it. That is the blow right there. When Powell hit him in the chest while King was lying on his back, that to me was excessive force. Up to that point, he was an officer trying to subdue a suspect. With that pounding blow to the chest, he crossed the line.

"Okay, I see it." I pointed out the blow I thought was the one.

The jurors who had already made up their minds that Powell was guilty weren't concerned about why I thought he was guilty. They were already sure of themselves. It was the ones who were still uncertain who were interested in seeing what I perceived.

To my mind, it didn't matter whether or not we all agreed on the exact blow that made Powell guilty. If we all thought he was guilty, who cares whether we agreed why? If I think he is guilty beyond a reasonable doubt and someone else thinks he's guilty beyond a reasonable doubt, that's all we need, as far as I am concerned.

So I tried to explain to the ones who were still wavering what I thought. King had given up three times. He had done his best to cooperate, but the beating continued.

Gary was hung up on the blurry part of the tape. He thought that what Powell was doing during that portion was excessive. Not all of us agreed on that. I would never convict a person on a blurry tape—you cannot really see enough to convict. There would always be a doubt.

Some of the others thought the first head blow was acceptable, but subsequent ones were excessive. Others thought the very first one was too much. On the first blow to his head, King was running right at Powell. There is definitely a doubt in my mind about that blow. I would give Powell the benefit of the doubt on that one. I am sure the police had every right to hit him, so I couldn't convict anyone on that first head blow. Powell was fighting for his life, and he hit the guy in the head. I'll give Powell that one. I think one head blow was justified, and the one head blow and hitting the ground could have caused all of his injuries.

But later, they were like sharks in a feeding frenzy. They were too emotional. They just couldn't stop. There was nothing I heard in any testimony about why Powell was so mad at Rodney King. He ran right at him, and he hit him for that. He hit him four times, two horizontally and two vertically during the blurry portion of the tape, and King still tried to get away, so okay, he hit him again. Then he was rolling on the ground, and the police say that was the Folsom roll, and the sergeant says, "Hit him on the bony parts of the legs," so they did. Then Rodney King finally stops rolling and it should have been all over with then.

Anne and Maria and Gary and Eric convicted Powell in their minds on those shots. They saw what they were convinced beyond a reasonable doubt was King being hit when he wasn't being aggressive, when he was down.

They say that first head shot is what they convicted him on. I voted only for the chest blow at the end of the video. But we agreed there was enough excessive force to violate his civil rights. We just didn't agree on which blow it was.

I thought we were all going to get right down to, oh, look, right there. I thought we would all agree on which particular blow and one time when they were breaking the law, but it turned out it wasn't like that.

We all agreed there was excessive force. I think we were allowed to do that within the jury instructions. Was there excessive force, did he get harmed, were they in California, and were they acting under the color of law? I said yes, I voted guilty.

If you ask the others, they say yes, but they have different points of view on when he did it.

Besides deciding whether or not Powell used excessive force, we also had to consider what his intent was. Gary felt that Powell showed his intent to violate King's civil rights through his lack of concern for his well-being, the fact that it took him over two hours to get the man to the hospital, when he was in pain with broken bones.

There had been testimony, of course, that the doctors at Pacifica Hospital told Powell that King was basically okay. So some people thought that gave Powell an acceptable excuse to dawdle on his way to the second hospital.

Apparently you can't book a traffic suspect without getting the traffic division's approval, so Powell called this guy and got his permission to book King. He was using his computer to do his report at the station, instead of having to use a typewriter at the hospital. But this doesn't make any sense if he really thought that King was on PCP and he needed to take him to USC for observation.

On the other hand, Powell himself had phoned in describing King as having "multiple head wounds." So no matter what the doctors told him, Powell knew all along that King had head injuries. He knew that he was hurt and he still waited two hours to get him to the hospital. It didn't really matter what the doctors said. Powell knew. That was callous.

Then there was the way he laughed when he called the ambulance. There was some testimony that it was nervous laughter, but it didn't sound like nervous laughter to me. The man was cracking up. It is cold to laugh just after you've beaten a guy up.

Koon, on the other hand, was very businesslike. He wasn't laughing. He wasn't nervous. He was a police officer doing the job he was trained to do.

That laugh did a lot to convict Powell.

That and the joking computer messages to his ex-girlfriend. She testified that they weren't still seeing each other and that they were just close friends. I assumed that meant that she had been his girlfriend.

The judge had instructed us that in the absence of a single piece of evidence, where you can find only circumstantial evidence, that it must be overpowering circumstantial evidence.

Put altogether—the laughter, the computer messages, the delay in getting to the hospital, stopping at the station to brag about the beating—to me and to the other jurors, this spelled a lack of concern. We thought this was overpowering circumstantial evidence that the guy just didn't give a damn about the well-being of Rodney King. He didn't care one little bit about him.

We covered a lot of ground on Thursday morning. We just voted once. Everyone went around the room and stated his or her position again, and then we were ready to vote.

I told the rest of them that I wanted to be sure that everyone had an opportunity to say what they had to say, and that no one felt that they had been bullied into making the decision. "You people need to vote what you believe. Don't come back here and say something else," I told them.

I asked those who believed that Powell was guilty of violating Rodney King's civil rights to raise their right hand. All twelve jurors voted to find him guilty.

We had wasted three whole days, but on Thursday we got down to work. We had needed Monday and Tuesday to go over the evidence, but Wednesday had been completely wasted.

After lunch we took up the case against Officer Timothy Wind. Wind was much easier to talk about than Powell had been. We simply looked at the tape again, this time watching it from the perspective of what Wind was doing at each juncture, and then we talked about Wind's intent.

Then we took a vote.

Eight voted not guilty, and four—Maria, Gary, Anne and Eric— voted guilty.

So we looked at the video again.

I asked, "Can anyone point out any real evidence about what Wind's intent was?"

It was clear that Wind hit King a lot of times, but a lot of the blows—most of them, in fact—weren't improper. We discussed the fact that Wind was clearly striking King and then stepping back and evaluating. We had heard testimony that a prudent officer would stop and assess the situation before hitting again. So it appeared that Wind was doing a textbook job of using his baton on King. Wind jumped back about three feet and stopped to see if King was rolling in pain or from being aggressive. Wind hit him a couple of whacks after that when the sergeant was yelling, but there was not a lot of aggression in the way that Wind did it.

The question was, did Wind intend to deprive him of his civil rights?

We talked about Wind's behavior when he was riding with King in the police car, and at the police station. He just rode along. He never made any disparaging comments or jokes.

When I think back, hey, does anybody know if Wind laughed? He's the guy who stayed an hour and a half sitting with King in the car at the station. He stopped the other cops from shining a light in his face. He never seemed happy. Nobody ever said anything bad about Wind.

We didn't get the feeling that Wind was a bad guy. He was a good cop, the only one who tried to protect Rodney King. When some cops came out to the car and were looking King over, Wind was the one who said, "Hey, leave the guy alone."

I said it seemed to me that Wind was intent on doing his job, on following orders, on doing what was right at all times.

"Can anybody find anything that shows any other intent?" I asked. "Can anybody help me out on that?"

I reminded everyone of the five things the government had to prove in order for us to find Wind guilty. We had to be convinced that Wind was, number one, in the state of California; number two, acting under the color of law; number three, using excessive force to violate Rodney King's civil rights; four, that he had an intent to violate his civil rights; and five, that he had harmed him when he did it.

We didn't have any problems with the first and second points. Nobody had ever denied that they were in California, or that they were acting as police officers at the time.

According to the judge's instructions, if King felt pain, then he had been harmed. So it was pretty obvious that he had been harmed.

The problem was the matter of intent. Nobody could come up

with anything to prove that Wind had an intent to violate King's rights. "We can't convict Wind if we can't come up with intent," I said.

The prosecution had shown us how Powell demonstrated a lack of concern for King's well-being, but we never heard anything about Wind's intent to violate King's civil rights. I thought maybe it was a game plan on the part of the prosecution. I thought maybe they just prosecuted the four of them so that we could acquit two and find two guilty.

Maria, Eric and Gary had all pretty much come into jury duty figuring that all four officers were guilty as hell. Maria, having grown up in a black community, knew better than I did that the LAPD beat on black people. But when I said, "Okay, Maria, if Wind is guilty, show me the witnesses," she was reasonable enough to think about it. She was on my side immediately.

"What evidence do you have to show his intent?" I asked.

Nobody could point to anything in the evidence, so we moved along rapidly, voting to find Wind not guilty in the early part of the afternoon.

Next, we took up the case against Officer Briseno. We went around the table and each juror said what his position was on Briseno. Initially, there were two who thought he was guilty and ten who said not guilty.

The only issue of excessive force raised against Briseno was the one stomp.

We played the video about twenty times.

Then Eric said, "Wait, let me show you something else."

There's a point where King falls, and Powell hits him twice. Briseno runs over. King is up on his hands and knees, and Powell has his baton raised. Briseno tries to stop the blow and holds Wind back.

No one had ever mentioned Briseno stopping Wind. We had heard about him blocking Powell's baton when Rodney King was starting to get up, but nothing about him stopping Wind. We were all very excited that we had seen something that the lawyers had never even mentioned to us, that showed that Briseno was trying to stop the violence.

King was starting to get up, and Powell was still hitting him.

Powell was out of control.

To the question of whether or not Ted Briseno had the intent of hurting Rodney King, the answer was: just the opposite.

"What did he do later?" I asked. "Do we have any testimony on what he did there and what he did later?"

We watched the stomp again, and we watched how Briseno put the handcuffs on King. After all this violence, the smallest officer on the scene—Briseno is a little guy—was the one who put the cuffs on King. Of course, King was being cooperative at that point. He had surrendered and the littlest guy there had no trouble putting handcuffs on him.

We looked at the stomp again in slow motion and nobody could say beyond a reasonable doubt whether Briseno was using excessive force or just trying to hold King down to subdue him.

I went around the room asking each juror where they stood and everyone said not guilty on Briseno. It had taken us a total of a couple of hours to get through the three of them.

I believe that either the government lawyers didn't have enough evidence or didn't present enough evidence to show intent on the part of Wind and Briseno. My own feeling was that Tim Wind did use excessive force against Rodney King, but I don't think that he meant to hurt him.

By the end of Thursday afternoon, we had voted on all three officers and we were ready to start on Sergeant Koon. Things were going so well, I could hardly believe it. We couldn't have done it on Monday or Tuesday, and I think we needed Wednesday to clear the air.

We had spent four days coming to three major decisions.

On Thursday night, I lay on my bed and wondered, how much longer is this going to take? I thought that it would probably take us another day and a half or two days to talk over the evidence against Koon. I reviewed the law, and had thought about Koon a lot. My guess was that we would deliberate on Koon on Friday, Saturday, Sunday, Monday and Tuesday, and that we would be out of there sometime on Tuesday.

That night, there were some discussions between Fred and Eric. Even Gary was getting along pretty good with everyone now. The whole jury was feeling pretty friendly toward each other, but the six of us from the back row, we were bonded.

On Friday morning, we started in on Koon. The four people who had been surest that Powell was guilty also thought that Koon was guilty. Everyone else had their doubts.

Eric, Gary and Maria were the strongest in favor of finding Koon guilty.

We started off on Friday morning talking about the different laws and what Koon was accused of compared to what the others were charged with. The question for Koon was whether or not the sergeant allowed Rodney King's civil rights to be violated. Under the law, he is required to protect the civil rights of suspects who are in custody. So it was an issue whether or not King was in custody. We had heard some testimony that a suspect is in custody when a reasonable person would realize that he was not free to leave.

King was clearly in custody because he obviously was not free to leave.

We watched the tape some more, this time from Sergeant Koon's standpoint, focusing in on Rodney King and Koon.

Maria and Gary thought Koon should have stopped all action immediately, as soon as King was hit in the head the first time. They believed that Koon was allowing King's civil rights to be violated from that moment on.

I thought that King was trying to escape, and that up to the time that Powell hit him in the chest, everything that they were doing was an appropriate use of police force. But after that chest blow, Rodney King was immobile. It was so obvious at that point that King had given up, and the sergeant looked away, as if he was wondering what was going on with the passengers, Bryant Allen and Freddie Helms. That was the first time that he allowed himself to look away at anything else, so he must have thought that the situation was beginning to be under control.

Rodney King was moving his hands and legs at that point, and Wind and Powell continued to hit him. The sergeant was yelling at them to hit him in the bony parts.

Powell and Wind were doing that. Rodney King was rolling

back and forth and he was clearly trying again to surrender. His hands were under his body; he had surrendered. This is the point where Briseno is trying to stop them, and King got hit eight times after that.

Finally he is in a sitting position and Wind stomps on him, and Rodney King says, "Please stop."

The guy tried to surrender three times, but the first time he was vocal about it was when he said, "Please stop." Then, finally, the sergeant did stop it.

When Koon turned away, Rodney King was still. So maybe he didn't see the chest shot. But after the guy was in the felony prone position, it's not until eight blows later that he verbalizes that he wants them to stop. The sergeant's duty was to protect Rodney King, and he didn't do it. When he saw Rodney King lying still, he should have known that King was giving up. That is probably why he allowed himself to look away.

Before lunch on Friday we took a straw poll on what everybody thought.

By this time all of us thought that Koon was guilty, but we all had different reasons. Norman, Cathy and Ruth were the only ones who weren't absolutely sure by this point.

I thought that Koon should have stopped everything after the chest blow. A lot of the others thought that it was the first head blow where things got out of hand. What difference did it make whether we agreed on which blow it was that made him guilty if we all thought that he was guilty? I figured that it was not worth our time and energy to try to come to agreement on which precise blow it was that went over the line.

If you think he's guilty and I think he's guilty, what difference does it make when he became guilty? All of us agreed that Sergeant Koon was guilty of allowing his officers to violate King's civil rights.

We still had three more counts to consider. There were charges of aiding and abetting against each of the officers. I reread those charges.

There was some question as to what that meant. We considered asking the judge to explain the charges of aiding and abetting, but I said, no, the judge and the lawyers spent a lot of time to make these instructions as plain and simple as they could. We are just going to

*Moral Uncertainty*

interpret the instructions and make the decision the best we can.

The only person who disagreed with me was Marty. He was one of the quietest and least active of the jurors, but this was the issue he chose to take a stand on.

On these counts we still had to prove the same five things—did it happen in California, was it under the color of law, did they violate his rights, did they have intent, did they harm him—but we also had to prove that they were working together. So we had to consider whether they were beating him on purpose, and were they working together to do it.

We talked about whether or not the officers were communicating with each other. The only real communication was the sergeant's orders. When Briseno was blocking the blows, he and Powell were looking at each other.

Wind works with Powell, so it would be normal for him to take the lead from Powell. Was Powell telling Wind what to do, or were they working independently? They all worked for Koon.

Marty thought we ought to ask for a more precise definition.

I thought that we had enough to go on.

Did Powell aid and abet anybody? He could have aided Koon. He didn't egg any of the others on, or help them or get them to help him. He was doing his job and they were doing theirs.

We voted slowly and cautiously on each of the three aiding and abetting counts and everybody voted not guilty.

By 3:30 we had finished. It had taken us since we finished lunch at 12:30 to get through the aiding and abetting issues.

I was simply amazed that we were finished. We felt like our team had just won the Super Bowl, or like we had just seen our newborn baby for the first time. What we felt was joy.

It wasn't that we were happy or proud that we had convicted two officers, or relieved that we had acquitted two others. We were just glad that we were going to get to go home and see our families. We were proud and happy that we had completed our job and we were going to be able to go home. We wanted to eat something other than Hilton food, see our families and to walk around outside. We wanted to be free of the mental pressure.

The only thing left to do was figure out how to fill out the forms. I started filling them out, and I made everyone look at them to make sure they agreed with everything.

I had never heard of the concept of polling a jury. I had no idea that there was any possibility that they might make each juror speak up and say that they agree with the verdict. I thought it was all my own original idea that I wanted to make sure that every single juror was comfortable with the decision and was able to say that they were certain beyond a reasonable doubt, with an abiding conviction, to a moral certainty. I didn't want anyone to say that they were pressured, or that the verdict wasn't what they really thought.

I filled out the forms and I signed them, "Juror Number 483" as I had been instructed to do.

We had all been dressing pretty casually during deliberations. Fred was wearing a tank top and Maria had on pants. We felt underdressed to appear in court. Some of the jurors expressed a desire to get freshened up and put on clean clothes before we went into the courtroom to announce the verdict. So I sent a note to the judge saying that we had made our decisions and that we requested that we be allowed to go back to the hotel and change our clothes before we came into the courtroom.

The marshal came back and told me that the judge wanted me to seal the verdicts in an envelope and give them to the marshal, and that we would be taken back to the hotel. We wouldn't appear in the courtroom to announce the verdict until seven o'clock the next morning.

The marshals seemed to have a plan for how they were going to get us all out of the courthouse after that, but they didn't give us any of the specifics.

They drove us back to the hotel, where we had dinner in the dining room at 6:30 p.m. We were told to get our stuff packed up and put it out in the hall before we left for court in the morning, sort of like a group on a European bus tour.

I was just exhausted. In the mail that day, I had gotten a packet of pictures of me in Vietnam. Some of the jurors had asked to see my Army pictures, so I had asked a co-worker to get the photos out of a desk drawer at my office and mail them to me. I had gone to some trouble during the trial not to reveal my last name to any of the jurors. I had received only one other letter with my name typed on it. I did have some shirts that had been laundered in the past and had my name stamped on the shirt tail, but I usually wear my shirts tucked in, so the other jurors wouldn't have seen my laundry mark.

On Friday night, I showed the other jurors my photographs and some of them noticed my last name, written on my name tag on my military uniform.

There was really a party atmosphere at the hotel that night. Some of the others stayed up nearly all night talking, and exchanging numbers. I was feeling like I had a lot of work to do to get all of my things packed up and organized. I packed until dinnertime, and then packed some more. The marshals had instructed us to put our big bags out in the hall that night so they could collect them.

The two-drink maximum rule still applied that evening, much to the chagrin of some of my fellow jurors, who felt that now that our work was over, we should be free to relax. The stress level was still really high.

We were all really glad to be going home to our families.

# Chapter Thirty-Nine: Delivering the Verdict

SATURDAY, APRIL 17, 1993

If we weren't feeling stressed already, one look at the federal marshals would have sent our blood pressures skyrocketing. There were at least twice as many marshals as usual, and they were wearing bulletproof vests. They had stern expressions on their faces, like they thought it was going to be their last day on earth. They looked like soldiers ready to go to war.

The fact that the marshals looked worried made me worried.

Up until this point, the only real repercussions I had thought about as a result of sitting on this jury was that if our names were revealed to the public, my nice secure life with my family might not be so nice and secure. I thought I might have to sell my house and move somewhere nobody knew me if there were anger about the verdict. I knew that the first jury had been harassed, and I realized that the same thing could happen to us.

The thing was, it really didn't matter what the verdict was. Somebody was going to be mad. If we acquitted the officers, it was going to enrage the black community, and there could be riots, like last time.

On the other hand, if we convicted the officers, the police might be after me. During the trial, there were times I thought the LAPD was intentionally trying to intimidate us. Sometimes an unusually large number of LAPD officers lined our route to the courthouse, and there was one morning when two undercover LAPD officers blocked our path as we approached the vans. The federal marshals, who usually cleared the way for us, seemed to be surprised that they were there. It made me uncomfortable.

Inciting civil insurrection or antagonizing the police. I wasn't sure which was worse.

Since we had reached a half-and-half verdict, I wasn't sure who was going to be after me. There never was any discussion during deliberations about compromising, or about deciding half one way and half the other to avert riots. That's just the way we decided. If there was anyone who was individually thinking that acquitting two and convicting two would appease the masses, nobody voiced that.

Now, marshals dressed for battle gave me the distinct impression that they thought that we were about to make somebody mad. Of course, the marshals had no way of knowing what we had decided.

I lay on my bed for fifteen minutes before it was time to get in the vans and go to the courthouse and thought about what might be going on outside. Some of my co-workers had expressed the opinion that getting myself on this jury was an incredibly dumb thing for me to do. They said I was risking my life and my wife's and daughter's, and for what?

I said, well, I went to Vietnam, and that was dangerous too. I didn't not want to serve on the jury nearly so much as I didn't want to go to Vietnam. But I went. Both seemed like jobs that somebody had to do, and if I was called to do them, then maybe it was my duty to do them.

We went out and got in the vans.

During Rodney King's testimony, he was asked why he didn't stop for the Highway Patrol when they were pursuing him. What did he think was going to happen if he kept driving? He answered that he thought maybe they would just go away.

We were all incredulous at that testimony. Who in the world who has ever been pursued by a traffic cop could possibly believe that there was any hope that he would just go away? We weren't supposed to talk about the trial before deliberations began, but we used to make jokes about how maybe the cops would just go away.

As the van drove through the empty early morning streets of downtown Los Angeles that Saturday morning, the tension inside the van was palpable. Nobody spoke. We couldn't see out the opaque windows of the van, but we could always tell when the news photographers were snapping pictures of the vehicles, from the flashes of light.

As we neared the courthouse, there were those flashes again.

In mock surprise, I exclaimed, "The television crews are all still here!"

My fellow jurors gaped at me as though I had taken leave of my senses.

"Did you think they wouldn't be here this morning for the verdict, Bob?" somebody asked.

"I thought they would just go away," I said.

Everybody burst out laughing. I thought it helped relieve the tension.

Inside the jury room, the marshal returned the sealed envelope to me and asked me to unseal it and make certain the verdicts were all there, the way I had left them. He told me to carry them into the courtroom. He said I wouldn't have to say anything.

I thought that Jim Holmes, the court clerk, was probably the best court clerk in the whole federal system. He was a very nice human being, very efficient. When the jury wanted notebook dividers with tabs, and fresh pencils, Jim was the one who got them for us.

The marshal handed the verdict to Jim Holmes, and he read it aloud. His perfectly modulated voice cracked, and his hands were shaking. I was amazed that a guy like that, who does this for a living, and must have read hundreds of verdicts aloud, would be shaking.

I was watching Koon. From my seat in the back row, I couldn't see Briseno or Powell because the lawyers' podium was in my way, but I could see Koon and Wind.

Koon was like a rock. He showed no emotion whatsoever. He never changed expression; not a muscle moved. Koon was a pretty arrogant man, forceful, used to being right. He was probably a good police officer. And now he was listening to himself being found guilty of a major crime. I was impressed at his emotional stability. Almost like he expected it.

Then Holmes read the verdict on Powell. I couldn't see him.

Two guys guilty.

Wind didn't smile when Holmes read his not guilty verdict, although it had to be the best news Wind ever heard. He sagged, and let air out of his chest.

Then Holmes read the not guilty verdict on Briseno.

The judge asked the lawyers if they wanted to poll the jury, and then basically went down the rows and asked each juror if they agreed with the verdict.

It was kind of dramatic. I had asked each juror to verbalize why they felt the way they did, so I knew they could do that.

Then we all went into the jury room and said, "Allllll right! We can go home."

We could hear helicopters hovering, and some of the jurors looked out through the little peephole at all the people outside the courthouse.

We went into the judge's chambers. We were all standing, and Judge Davies thanked us, and warned us about not talking about each other. He said there would be a strict punishment if anyone published our names. He said he couldn't tell us to stay away from the press, but he recommended it. He told us we had done an excellent job, that we had served our country, and he thanked us.

The marshals told us that we could keep our notebooks, and he said the judge had granted a request that I had passed along the previous Wednesday, that we be given three work days off to unwind. I knew what my stress level was at that point, and I felt like we needed some time off before we had to go back to our regular jobs. I had some vacation time of my own, but I didn't think I should have to use that.

When I came home from Vietnam, my whole family was waiting at the airport, and I could hardly talk like a civilized human being. I was using cuss words every other word. I had the same kind of feeling now. I missed my family, my house, my dog, my car, but I had the same kind of stress that I hadn't felt since Vietnam.

I started coming up to the surface, wondering what was going on outside. I hoped there wouldn't be any riots.

The marshals had a plan to get us home. They were sending one van in each direction. Since I lived in San Pedro, on the south side of Los Angeles, I was going in the van that went to Watts and Inglewood. If there were riots, I figured I was going to see them.

They planned to drop George off, then Daryl and then take me home to San Pedro. Another car followed us and was in radio contact with us during the drive. It would fall back and watch to make sure no one was following us.

We let George off at his house, and then we drove to Inglewood. Daryl's mother was waiting with a camera to get a picture of her hero son coming home from battle.

Daryl had a typical reaction. "Ohhhhhh, mother!"

The marshals were laughing.

I helped the marshals unload Daryl's bags, and then we drove the twenty-five minute trip to my house.

The marshals had orders to take me into my house, and they did.

I kissed my wife and called my boss.

# Chapter Forty: Living With It

Within an hour after I got home, *CBS This Morning* called. A producer said they wanted me on the show. She said I could do it by telephone, go to the studio in Hollywood or go to New York. I said no way and hung up.

She called back later and I said, "Do you really mean I could go to New York?"

She said sure.

I said, "Okay, I'm ready."

That was Saturday and on Sunday night my wife, my daughter and I were on a plane to New York. That was one of the nicest things that happened. I had always wanted to go to New York. Every time that I had gone to a travel agent to buy a ticket to New York, I wound up finding something else I'd rather do instead. In 1971 my wife and I had reservations to go to New York. The round trip tickets were $280 apiece. Then we got a chance to go to London for $200. We went to London for a month instead of New York for a week.

When you become a juror, they tell you not to form any judgments, to wait until after you've heard all the evidence. You're supposed to listen to testimony all day, but when you aren't in court, you aren't supposed to think about it or to discuss it with anyone. So you have to put it out of your mind. All there is left to do at night is watch television and think about your family.

I was home after six weeks of thinking about a subject I hadn't been allowed to talk about, and six weeks of missing my family. Now I was in great demand to talk about the topic that had preoccupied me. The networks, the local stations, the newspapers, were all trying to get in touch with me, and I had an opportunity to say what I thought, and to take my family along for some once-in-a-lifetime experiences and travel.

I had decided in advance that I would give an interview when I got home to the *Oceanside Blade-Citizen* newspaper because my niece worked there. I told my wife to tell my niece I would give them an interview. They called within a couple of hours after I got home. I told them to call back in the afternoon. I needed a little while to get myself acclimated to being back home.

I drove over to Isaac Cafe in Wilmington, my favorite spot to get a burrito for lunch, and talked to the reporter for the *Blade-Citizen* for an hour straight. It was exciting for this small newspaper to scoop the *Los Angeles Times*.

My friend Joe Enzmann, another engineer with the Port of Los Angeles, had been talking with the people at the newsmagazine show *A Current Affair* about my giving an interview, so he and I drove to the Fox Studio in Hollywood. I walked in there in my Levi's and cowboy boots and the producer, a Hollywood-type guy in a denim jacket with the collar sticking straight up, asked the local KTTV reporter who had been in the courtroom to verify that I really was the jury foreman.

After talking to them for half an hour, I decided I didn't like these guys very much and didn't want their money. I didn't want to be interviewed by them. The newsman from Channel 11, the local station, followed us out and said he couldn't offer me any money but he'd love to interview me, but I said not now.

We went out to the car, and Joe called *Inside Edition* on his cell phone. I agreed to tape an interview with them the next day on Sunday afternoon.

I went home and telephoned all my friends and relatives. Clairene and I went to a fast food chicken place, El Pollo Loco, for dinner. It's one of my favorite places. I could eat lunch there every day.

On Sunday afternoon, Clairene, Joe and I drove up to the Bel Air Radisson Hotel off Sunset Boulevard in Brentwood. *Inside Edition* had two camera crews and two sound guys in a hotel room there. Joe talked to the lady from the legal department about the contract, and I talked to the producer about makeup.

Bonnie Strauss did the interview. She's a nice lady, skinny as a rail. I looked fat on television.

They had me go through the George Holliday tape pointing things out to them. Later on, they took us down to the Santa Monica Third Street Promenade so they could take pictures of me walking along like a normal person. That was fun. I walked along, stopped to get a drink of water, watched the street musicians playing drums and instruments. I had to sit on a park bench, and then pick up the newspaper and show them the headline. It was kind of corny, but they had me do it about eight times. An old man in his eighties was sitting there on the same bench with me. I told him the two of us were going to be on television.

Some woman from Florida asked me if I was somebody famous. I said, "No, I'm a civil engineer."

I had to get home by 5:30 because we had to leave for New York at eight and I still had to wash a load of underwear. We flew coach, and leaving at 10 p.m., it was pretty miserable. Even though we had an extra seat, it was hard to get comfortable.

A limo picked us up at the airport and took us to Le Parker Meridien hotel, on the same block as Carnegie Hall. We crashed until noon, and then we went out to see the sights. I asked how to find the Statue of Liberty, and the concierge gave me a map. We took the subway, which was pretty exciting.

When we came out from the subway, the Staten Island Ferry was sitting right there. I had always wanted to ride the Staten Island Ferry. We had missed a boat to the Statue of Liberty, so we had some New York pizza. It was the best pizza I ever had. We stood up and ate it, and then paid three dollars for a Dove Bar. Everything in New York was expensive. My wife and I sat on a bench while our daughter walked up to the top of the statue, then we all got lemonade and hopped on the next boat.

My wife is a real shopper and all she could think about was getting to a big department store. We got off the subway at 50th Street and walked six blocks to Bloomingdale's. Later on, we had dinner at a deli across the street from the hotel. It was only thirty-five dollars for the three of us. CBS was paying for the trip, but I never sent the bills for the food. It was almost my pleasure, really.

The next morning, a limo whisked us to the CBS studios. I could get used to this.

An intern showed us around and took us into the Green Room. An eleven-year-old girl was on the show who had AIDS and they didn't know how she got it. I thought it was pretty amazing how strong this little girl was. I was glad for my eighteen-year-old daughter to meet her. How can you be strong if you don't know what strong looks like?

Paula Zahn was simply gorgeous in person. I was tired from the airplane trip, and I had big bags under my eyes. I thought I looked really nervous. They did a six-minute interview, broke for a commercial, and then did another six minutes that was only seen

*Moral Uncertainty*

in the East. Being on live is worse than being taped, because if you stutter or pause they can't cut it out. They asked me a lot of questions, and I just answered them honestly. I was nervous, but I had a great time.

CBS had offered to put us up for a week, but my wife had to be back at work on Wednesday, so after the interview, we went out to see the town.

We spent three hours at the United Nations, had a hot dog on the street, and went to the Empire State Building. I had dreamed my whole life of going to the top of the Empire State Building, and it was pretty darn impressive. The visibility was poor, but we could see the Statue of Liberty and it looked small from up there. All the buildings just looked like little matchboxes.

We took a cab to the East Village. There were people selling jewelry and incense and peace signs, like Haight-Ashbury in San Francisco during the 1960s. I don't know what I thought Greenwich Village was going to look like. I wanted to see New York University, but we were tired of walking and short on time, so we got in a cab and drove around New York University and then back to Bloomingdale's, where Clairene and Kelly bought more clothes.

The limo was supposed to pick us up at the hotel at 5 p.m., but it didn't get there until 6:10. I kept telephoning, and finally it arrived. We got to the airport all right, but I was pretty shook up.

As soon as we got home from New York, *Nightline* wanted me to fly to Washington, D.C., to be interviewed along with Dorothy Bailey, the foreman of the Simi Valley trial. I called my wife and said, "We're going to Washington tomorrow." Her boss understood that to normal people, free trips to New York and Washington are a good thing, and gave her more time off.

We arrived at Dulles International Airport at 3:15 p.m. on Thursday and got to the ABC studio by 5 p.m. The year before I was on jury duty, I had gone to Weight Watchers and lost thirty-five pounds. I had gained back fifteen, but my suit still fit pretty good. I'd handed that verdict to the court clerk dressed in Levi's and a cotton shirt, but being on *Nightline* called for my suit.

We taped for two hours, and when we got finished, Ted Koppel asked Dorothy, "How long do you think that was?" and she said, "Twenty minutes."

The cameramen were all asking us a lot of questions. They said they learned more about civics and how juries work than they had in school.

Afterwards, in the Green Room, everybody sang happy birthday to Dorothy. Ted Koppel had gone out himself and bought her a chocolate cake, because it was her birthday and she had flown to New York all by herself because her husband didn't like to fly.

I think that being on *Nightline* with Ted Koppel was the highlight of my life.

In the limo, Dorothy asked us if we wanted to go to dinner together and we went to an Italian restaurant the driver recommended. She told us that the first jury had gotten together a few times almost like a support group because they had been so vilified. Stacey Koon attended one of the meetings to thank the jurors for acquitting him.

The NBC network crews in Los Angeles interviewed me so many times during the trial of the men accused in the Reginald Denny beating that they gave me an NBC beeper to carry around so they could reach me when something happened they wanted my reaction to.

During the media frenzy after the arrest of O.J. Simpson for the murder of his wife, Nicole, and waiter Ronald Goldman, there was a quote in the paper from Harland Braun, one of the defense attorneys in our case. He said that any juror in a celebrated trial could make between $25,000 and $50,000 in the first twenty-four hours after the verdict.

Well, I was the foreman in one of the most celebrated trials of the decade, and nobody offered me close to that sum. I got some free travel at the networks' expense, and they put me and my wife up in some nice hotels, and I really enjoyed it, but I also had to take vacation time from my job to do the interviews, and I had to do something in return for the perks; namely I had to go on television and give my so-called expert opinion.

I was paid $150 and flown to Phoenix to appear on a panel for the Arizona Bar Association with Jo-Ellan Dimitrius, the defense's jury expert I had watched scrutinizing the jurors every day in the courtroom.

She confirmed that the defense had really wanted me on the jury. In fact, she said that of the 750 jurors who filled out questionnaires, I was number forty-two on the defense's list. Then, of the seventy-five who were called back for voir dire, I was their number one choice. She said the defense was overjoyed when they found out that I was the foreman.

Dorothy Bailey and I both spoke on a panel at Southern Utah University in Cedar City, Utah, about six months after my trial. There were about seven hundred students and members of the community crowded into an auditorium there, and they asked us questions for an hour and a half. Afterwards, they came up to the stage to talk to us.

Apparently there were a number of retired Los Angeles police officers and firefighters, and we got a lot of questions that started out with the preface, "I lived in Los Angeles for forty years and . . ."

A lot of them wanted to know what we thought about the riots.

I told them that riots aren't caused by juries; they are caused by pent-up frustrations on the part of poor people.

One man asked me what my definition was of civil rights.

I said I thought those were the rights we have under the constitution, as human beings. I said they included the right to go out on the street without having the police beat you up.

My interrogator repeated, "Well, what's your definition of civil rights?"

I said I had just given him my definition.

One student gestured to my wife, and said, "I assume that's your wife there. I'd like to ask her a question."

He asked Clairene what she thought about the verdicts. To my complete surprise, she said that she thought I was wrong. She said that she had thought that Rodney King was combative, that he was never under control, and that he deserved everything he got. She thought the officers all ought to have been acquitted.

She'd been traveling around with me listening to me pontificate on the subject for months, and never once had she mentioned that she disagreed with me. She knew that I had reached the decision as conscientiously as I could, and that I firmly believed in it. She also knew that I had been the one sitting there in the courtroom listening to the evidence.

Dick Bailey had watched most of the Simi Valley trial on television, and he had been stunned by the verdict his wife's jury reached.

Juries see and hear more than the television audience or newspaper readers. And they are bound by the judge's instructions, which the poll of public opinion disregards. The perspective from the jury box is far different from what anybody understands from following news accounts.

Dorothy Bailey and members of the first jury were blamed with starting the worst civil insurrection in American history. They received death threats, censure by the President of the United States, and national hatred. They were labeled racists and bigots. My jury was hailed as having reached a "compromise" verdict which averted rioting, although the idea of compromise was never uttered in that jury room.

Dorothy and her jury looked at the evidence and did the best job they could. And so did we.

# ABOUT THE AUTHORS

© ABC News Nightline—April 27, 1993

BOB ALMOND, a professional engineer for the Port of Los Angeles, was forty-nine when this book was written. He recounted his memories verbally, relying on his courtroom notes, to veteran journalist Kathleen Neumeyer in the weeks immediately after the trial. Born in Glendale, California, Bob Almond lived in the Los Angeles area until 2006 when he moved to Bellingham, Washington. He studied engineering at California State University, Los Angeles, where he met his wife, Clairene, a retired Los Angeles County librarian. Their daughter Kelly and her husband Sean also live in Bellingham. The Almonds have one grandson, Ian.

Bob Almond is a Vietnam veteran who served for eight months with the United States Army attached to the 1st Marine Division in Dong Ha, eight miles south of the DMZ. In retirement, he enjoys traveling, golf and hiking.

Prior to being elected foreman of the federal civil rights trial of four police officers accused of beating Rodney King, Bob Almond's only courtroom experience came about fifteen years earlier when he was on a jury panel that acquitted a defendant accused of grand theft firearms.

DOROTHY BAILEY was sixty-seven years old when she wrote her account of her experience as foreman of the first Rodney King trial, using the comprehensive shorthand notes she had taken during the testimony. She and her husband of twenty-eight years had eight children between them, twenty-seven grandchildren and three great-grandchildren.

© ABC News Nightline—April 27, 1993

Before her retirement two weeks after the verdict in the Rodney King trial, she had held the position of Program Manager for a small, black-owned business engaged primarily in government contracts to supply newly constructed U.S. Navy and foreign military ships with technical manuals for each piece of equipment aboard. After the trial, she and her husband sold their house, which was in a small town near Simi Valley, and returned to their home state of Utah. She never lived in Simi Valley.

The trial of the four officers accused of beating Rodney King was the first trial Bailey ever observed. Prior to being foreman of the jury, her only courtroom experience was when she was a plaintiff in the uneventful dissolution of her first marriage three decades earlier.

Dorothy Bailey died in 2012.

KATHLEEN NEUMEYER, as a reporter for United Press International, covered the murder trials of Sirhan B. Sirhan for the assassination of United States Senator Robert F. Kennedy, and of Charles Manson and the Manson Family, as well as the Daniel Ellsberg Pentagon Papers trial. Later she covered the federal drug trial of John DeLorean for *The Times* of London, and the murder trial of Elisabeth Broderick, a San Diego woman who killed her ex-husband and his new bride, for *Ladies Home Journal*.

She has written extensively about the law for *California Lawyer*, *Lawyers Weekly of Canada*, the *Massachusetts Law Quarterly*, *Los Angeles Lawyer* and the *Western Law Quarterly*. She was a contributing editor of *Los Angeles Magazine* for twenty years and taught journalism for forty-two years.

She served as foreman of a criminal trial in Los Angeles, in which the jury convicted one defendant in a drive-by shooting and was unable to reach a verdict on the other defendant.

Former California Attorney General John Van de Kamp praised Kathleen Neumeyer's writing about allegations of police brutality in the Los Angeles Police Department as "excellent, both informative and balanced. That can't be said for much written about this volatile issue."

Made in the USA
Middletown, DE
12 April 2017